Esoteric Traces in the Formation of Psychoanalysis

John Boyle provides an in-depth account of the neglected contributions made by Western esotericism in the formation of an occluded "psychoanalytic parapsychology" active within psychoanalysis since its inception, the distinguishing features of which he argues have continued to persist within psychoanalysis to this day.

The book provides a conceptual framework for understanding how the debates between Sigmund Freud, Sándor Ferenczi and Carl Gustav Jung on the status of the "occult" in psychoanalysis contributed to the formation of an "Orphic fragmentation" within psychoanalysis. It argues that the consequences of these discussions were covertly transmitted to later generations of psychoanalysts in the form of an "Orphic trajectory" encrypted within the main body of psychoanalytic theory and practice.

This book offers new and original insights into the role played by heterodox forms of spirituality in the development of psychoanalysis. It will interest scholars of psychoanalysis and religion as well as those with a general interest in the role of the spiritual in contemporary psychoanalysis and psychology.

John Boyle is a UKCP-registered integrative psychotherapist, psychoanalytic psychotherapist and clinical supervisor. He has a PhD in psychoanalytic studies from the University of Essex and an M.A. in Western esotericism from the University of Exeter. He lives in Northern Ireland.

Comparative Psychoanalysis Book Series
David Henderson & Jon Mills
Series Editors

Comparative Psychoanalysis studies controversy and dialogue in psychoanalysis. Intellectual, personal, and institutional conflict are endemic to the history of psychoanalysis. Alongside this there are creative efforts to establish understanding and communication among differing perspectives. Comparative methodologies are encouraged among all schools of psychoanalysis regardless of topic, theoretical or clinical orientation, or application to the behavioral sciences and humanities including historical reassessments, conceptual clarification, clinical exploration, reflections on the future of applied psychoanalytic thought, and attempts to articulate the conditions for fruitful dialogue. All subject matters in the arts and humanities, philosophy, anthropology, cultural studies, and the human sciences are ripe for comparative investigation within the frameworks of theoretical, clinical, and applied psychoanalysis. As an inherently interdisciplinary field of study, psychoanalysis requires a robust understanding of comparative methodology. Controversial discussions and criticism are invited. In the spirit of pluralism, Comparative Psychoanalysis is open to any theoretical school in the history of the psychoanalytic movement that offers novel critique, integration, and important insights in comparative scholarship.

Titles in this series:

Carl Jung and the Evolutionary Science
A New Vision for Analytical Psychology
By Gary Clark

The Craft of the Psychodynamic Case Study
A Practical Guide
By Aner Govrin

Esoteric Traces in the Formation of Psychoanalysis
Before and After Science
By John Boyle

Esoteric Traces in the Formation of Psychoanalysis

Before and After Science

John Boyle

Routledge
Taylor & Francis Group

LONDON AND NEW YORK

First published 2026
by Routledge
4 Park Square, Milton Park, Abingdon, Oxon OX14 4RN

and by Routledge
605 Third Avenue, New York, NY 10158

Routledge is an imprint of the Taylor & Francis Group, an informa business

British Library Cataloguing-in-Publication Data
A catalogue record for this book is available from the British Library

ISBN: 978-1-032-76036-0 (hbk)
ISBN: 978-1-032-76034-6 (pbk)
ISBN: 978-1-003-47673-3 (ebk)

DOI: 10.4324/9781003476733

Typeset in Times New Roman
by Apex CoVantage, LLC

Contents

Acknowledgements

I would like to thank Professor Roderick Main from the University of Essex for supervising the doctoral thesis upon which this book is based. His good-humoured wisdom helped me to circumvent more than one scholarly impasse of my own making. I would also like to thank Professor Matt ffytche for his advice on Chapters 2 and 4 of this book.

I would like to express my thanks to Professor Júlia Gyimesi for reviewing Chapter 4 and for sharing some of her more difficult-to-obtain papers with me. I would also like to thank Professor Peter Rudnytsky for sharing his research on Nandor Fodor and for his encouragement more generally. Dr Maria Pierri very kindly shared with me advanced publisher's drafts from her books: *Sigmund Freud and The Forsyth Case: Coincidences and Thought-Transmission in Psychoanalysis* [trans. Adam Elgar] (New York: Routledge, 2022) and *Occultism and the Origins of Psychoanalysis: Freud, Ferenczi and the Challenge of Thought Transference* [trans. Adam Elgar] (New York: Routledge, 2022).

I would like to acknowledge the encouragement I received from Professor Jeffrey Kripal and the late Dr David Henderson, both of whom supported this project from the outset. I would also like to acknowledge the late Professor Nicholas Goodrick-Clarke, who introduced me to the academic study of Western esotericism, and the sadly now defunct EXESESO network, which inspired me to take these initial studies further.

Closer to home, I would like to thank the SHSCT Research and Development Department for agreeing to fund the fees for the doctoral thesis upon which this book is based. I would also like to express my appreciation to the members of the Northern Irish Institute for Human Relations psychoanalytic reading group for their friendship (which now spans many years) and for their very helpful comments on some of the earliest drafts of this book.

Most of all, I wish to thank my wife, Maureen, for her good-humoured patience throughout the lengthy period of time it has taken me to bring this book to completion. It is to Maureen that this book is dedicated.

Chapter 1

Methodological considerations

1.1 General introduction

> No culture is able to achieve the integral fullness of the real, nor can any develop all the potentialities of the human being, for the latter is always in excess of itself. . . . Each culture explores certain sectors of the real, privileges and develops certain dimensions of experience, and, because of this fact, sacrifices other dimensions, other possibilities, which return to haunt it . . . against which the culture protects itself through a number of mechanisms.
>
> Bertrand Méheust, *Le Défi du magnetisme*[1]

It has been observed that "modern theories of human development are heir to much older spiritual and cultural structures and themes" (Kirschner, 1996, p. 5). This imbrication of earlier currents and traditions with more recent theories of mind and personhood can be traced back for millennia and across cultures (Ellenberger, 1994; MacDonald, 2007; Whyte, 1960). From the Enlightenment through to post-modernity and beyond, commentators such as Jason Josephson-Storm (2017, p. 43) have remarked on the extent to which "scientific and magical worlds were often intertwined." This superimposition of paradigms is inscribed into the fabric of our language, as can be seen, for example, in terms such as *psychical*, in which we find the rubric of *psyche* aligned to ideas of the physical, the occult, the fantasy and the mind (Frosh, 2013, p. 167; Kripal, 2017, pp. 248–249). One of the more recent manifestations of this entanglement of "scientific" with "magical" and "religious" modes of discourse can be observed in the cultural and conceptual matrix conjoining psychoanalysis to *fin de siècle* "occultism," including psychical research, telepathy, alternations in consciousness and the Jewish Kabbalah (Frosh, 2013; Luckhurst, 2002; Boyle, 2016; Berke & Schneider, 2008; von Stuckrad, 2015). Moreover, the various challenges encountered by psychoanalytic trainees during the course of their training have been likened to "a succession of stages of initiation into the mysteries of a secret society" (Reghintovschi, 2025, p. 5). Consequently,

---

1 Cited in Kripal (2010), p. 199. Permission to use this epigraph was also received from the author.

DOI: 10.4324/9781003476733-1

the perception that psychoanalysis constitutes an essentially "secular" and "materialistic" endeavour is one that requires substantial revision in the light of the contributions made by Judaic, Christian, occult, esoteric and Kabbalistic sources to its creation (Vitz, 1988; Burdett, 2014, pp. 49–65; Berke, 2015). Furthermore, ideas concerning "secularity" and "materialism" have been problematised and reformulated in the light of evolving conceptualisations of secularity as a derivation of religious modalities of thought, in tandem with the "new materialist" reconstitution of the "body" as something that can be both "physical" and "non-material," in a manner that is intriguingly reminiscent of the idea of the "subtle body" encountered in esoteric discourse (Taylor, 2007; Johnson, 2015, pp. 659–671; Keller & Rubenstein [eds.], 2017).[2] While reports of telepathic and paranormal processes in psychoanalysis have recurrently featured as a liminal theme in the clinical literature, the present book sets out to integrate the findings from these studies into the wider historiographic, conceptual and reflexive framework provided by recent developments in the academic study of Western esotericism.[3] It argues that, despite its purportedly materialist credentials, Freudian psychoanalysis is permeated by esoteric "traces" that remain active within the *corpus* of its theory and practice. The persistence of these traces within contemporary psychoanalysis is attributed to their original *encryption* through a process of *preservative repression* mediated via an occluded "esoteric matrix" active within Freudian metapsychology since its inception.[4]

---

2 Magee (2021) has observed that "physicalism is not a theory *derived from* scientific investigation; it is a theory that scientists *bring to* their research and that guides them, leading them to include or exclude certain questions or avenues of inquiry" (p. 250). Moreover, in the estimation of Mills (2022), "the whole reductionist enterprise" constitutes "an ideological artefact that is scientifically indefensible" (p. 29). Notably, Galen Strawson has extended the idea of "physicalism" so as to incorporate "panexperientialism or panpsychism" into its conceptual framework (Strawson, 2006; see also McGilchrist, 2021, p. 1059).

3 Rabeyron et al. (2021) have posited three major phases in the history of psychoanalytic research into telepathy – the first phase (1920–1953), during the course of which it was considered to be a legitimate topic for professional interest; the second phase (1953–1980), during which time interest in its study diminished considerably; and a third phase (1980 to the present), when a growing interest in the topic began to reappear. For a very helpful overview of the history of the paranormal in psychoanalysis, see Reichbart (2019), chapters 6 and 7.

4 See Farrell (1983) and Calvesi (1983). On the concepts of the *crypt* and *preservative* repression, see the following:

> The concepts of secret, crypt, incorporation, and the phantom enlarge upon or redirect the Freudian definition of personal identity as beset by unconscious conflicts, desires and fantasies. . . . In contrast to this Freudian structure of oppositions, Abraham and Torok explore the mental landscapes of submerged family secrets and traumatic tombs in which . . . actual events are treated as if they had never occurred. Instead of the shifting fortunes of opponents locked in combat (repression verses repressed instinct), what matters is the preservation of a shut-up or excluded reality. . . Preservative repression seals off access to part of one's life in order to shelter from view the traumatic monument of an obliterated event.
>
> (Nicholas T. Rand), "Introduction," in Abraham and Torok (1994, p. 18)

It is generally acknowledged that "For Freud, psychoanalysis is a natural science" (Fulgencio, 2005, p. 99). However, for many of its revisionists, critics and detractors, its collective disciplinary efforts to chart the depths of the unconscious seemed – at times – to constitute something closer to "the dream of a science" – or perhaps even a "pseudoscience" (Shamdasani, 2003; Leahey & Leahey, 1983).[5] As William James (1842–1910) astutely observed,

> When, then, we talk of "psychology as a natural science" we must not assume that means a sort of psychology that stands at last on solid ground. It means just the reverse; it means a psychology particularly fragile and into which the waters of metaphysical criticism leak at every joint. . . . [We have] not a single law in the sense that physics shows us laws. . . . This is no science, it is only the hope of science.[6]

In the estimation of Thomas and Grace Leahey,

> Psychology is an interesting case because it seems to sit astride the line between science and pseudoscience. . . . Psychoanalysis and especially parapsychology, for example, are frequently under attack and seem to occupy the pseudoscience end of the scientific continuum.
>
> (Leahey & Leahey, 1983, p. 4)[7]

However, more recent commentators, such as Elizabeth Mayer, have sought to reverse this evaluation by critiquing the "tired but long-lived debate" surrounding the putative "scientific" status of psychoanalysis, contending that "our work is quintessentially subjective and intersubjective . . . a science based on the capacity to make observations characterised by ideals of objectivity, certainty and precision is a science that is frankly irrelevant to us" (Mayer, 1996b, pp. 711–712). Moreover – and more radically – Mayer has argued for the deployment of parapsychological research to enhance our understanding of "the cognitive and communicative processes entailed by psychoanalytic subjectivity and intersubjectivity" (Mayer, 1996b, p. 710, pp. 717–735).[8] It has often been observed that the techniques of "science" do not extend to the domains of meaning and value, thereby resulting in

---

5 For a more recent critique of the idea of a strict binary opposition separating "science" from "pseudoscience" that draws extensively upon the methods of discourse analysis, see von Stuckrad (2015, pp. 180–181). For a brief but helpful discussion on the historical genealogy of "science," see Josephson-Storm, 2017, pp. 59–60. For a more expansive account of the complex relationships that pertain between "science," "religion" and the "supernatural," see Harrison (2015, 2024).

6 William James (1890), cited in Rowland (2017, p. 15).

7 For an astute sociological analysis of the role played by the paranormal in demarcating "legitimate" from "illegitimate" forms of knowledge, see Northcote (2007).

8 See Mayer (2007, pp. 69–96) for an intriguing "revisionist" account that emphasises the methodological sophistication and rigour of the best parapsychological research.

an ontological "lack" that dialectically stimulates the need for its own compensatory alterity:

> If science is a pragmatic search for puzzle solutions, it does not ask, and cannot answer ultimate questions . . . [Pseudosciences] . . . are not sciences because they try to delve deeper than any science can.
>
>   To say that they are not sciences is not to condemn them, except to the believers in scientism . . . the searcher after Truth ought not to go to science in the first place. Instead the searcher should go to philosophy, art, literature and religion. Not every human question has a scientific answer.
>
>   (Leahey & Leahey, 1983, pp. 241, 245)[9]

The question as to how such tensions have been variously negotiated across the wider scientific and socio-cultural fields is complex, and its systematic investigation lies outside of the immediate purview of this book.[10] However, one particular approach that I would like to draw upon for my current purposes entails the reframing of these binary oppositions by substituting in their place a sense of the "doubleness" of "science" as conceptualised by Carl Gustav Jung (1875–1961), so that the empirical and the metaphysical, and the sacred and the secular, can be reconstituted as complementary aspects of an underlying unity (Main, 2013). In support of this proposal, it is worthwhile observing that both psychoanalytic and parapsychological theories of mind have been conceptualised as sharing a dual-aspect monist ontology.[11] However, it is also important to acknowledge that there are nuances of opinion on this topic and that not all scholars of psychoanalysis necessarily subscribe to the view that Freud was a de facto dual-aspect monist.[12]

---

9   Cf. the following:

> The psychical register can be the *cause* of material events and cannot be reduced to solely its effect. In the final analysis, Bertrand Russell . . . concluded, the psychical appears to be more real than the physical. These findings redefine the boundaries of the rational and the irrational, the natural and the supernatural. In this respect, the highest merit of mechanistic science is that it solidly demonstrated that the explanatory power of mechanistic logic is limited and that the big questions of life seek their answer elsewhere.
>
>   (Desmet, 2019, pp. 12–13)

10 See Asprem (2014b) and Josephson-Storm (2017) for exemplary in-depth exegeses of these questions.

11 See Solms and Turnbull (2011, pp. 4–5), who argue that the psychoanalytic theory of mind is essentially dual-aspect monist in terms of its ontology. On the association between dual-aspect monism and "paranormal" theories of mind, see Kripal (2017, pp. 197–200) and Kripal (2019, pp. 118–122).

12 For example, Auchincloss is of the opinion that most psychoanalysts function as "*property dualists*, meaning that even if we understand that mind emerges from brain, we know that we must separate mind and brain for clinical purposes" (2015, p. 4). In a similar vein, Britton argues, "It is clear that psychoanalysts following Freud are monists who nevertheless accept that mind exists as a function of brain" (2015, p. 9). While such divergences of opinion on this question are to be acknowledged, it nonetheless worth observing that, as the editor of the Revised Standard Edition of Freud's writings, Solms' views on this topic are firmly anchored both in his deep acquaintance with the entirety of the Freudian *corpus* and in his internationally acknowledged expertise in neuropsychoanalysis. For a

The potential vistas opened up by such debates nonetheless support a recognition that "mind or consciousness is the subject and locus of *all* scientific practice and knowledge; that science, at the end of the day, is a function of human subjectivity and consciousness" (Kripal, 2019, p. 15). One theoretical elaboration of this insight is known as decompositional dual-aspect monism, a philosophical position which has been defined as:

> the conviction that the mental and material domains of our ordinary experience are epistemologically dual (with an inside/outside or subjective/objective structure) but, in ontological fact, emerge or "split off" (the decomposition part) from a more fundamental monistic super-reality that is neither exclusively "mental" nor "material," but rather both or neither. Put most simply, while human experience is ordinarily experienced as two, reality itself is one, or One, hence the expression "dual-aspect monism."
>
> (Kripal, 2021, p. 361)[13]

It is from within the matrix of possibilities arising from such speculations that the "before" and "after" of "science" that this book sets out to investigate can be situated. Within the human sciences, there is an increasing acknowledgement "that scientific and non-scientific ideas and practices have strongly influenced and enriched each other" (von Stuckrad, 2022, pp. xvii–xviii). Moreover, within the field of psychoanalysis, there exists a growing awareness of the extent to which "the non-psychoanalytic sources influencing a given theory not only fail to be acknowledged, but undergo a process of conversion and change that conveniently adapts them to the theory and distances them from their roots" (Govrin, 2016, pp. 20–21).

In the light of these prevailing circumstances, discourse analytic approaches possess a certain utility with regard to the mapping out of the various discursive "hybrids," "knots" and "entanglements" conjoining the "scientific" to the "esoteric."[14] Moreover, given that complex terms such as "soul" or "self" can only be comprehended amidst the wider matrix of historical and cultural associations from within which they acquire their meaning, questions of "definition" will need to be tailored accordingly.[15] Kocku von Stuckrad has proposed the existence of three major discursive trajectories within psychology, each of which exemplifies a different strategy for developing a vocabulary of the "soul" (von Stuckrad, 2022, pp. 120–123). According to von Stuckrad's analysis, the first of these trajectories sought to "eliminate" the soul as part of a wider Faustian endeavour to obtain methodological "objectivity." The second worked towards achieving a similar goal by means of adopting a process

---

trenchant critique of the "misuse" of the concept of dual-aspect monism in contemporary neuropsychoanalysis, see Barratt (2022, pp. 51–58).

13 For an illuminating, book-length exposition of this concept, see Atmanspacher and Rickles (2022).

14 See von Stuckrad (2015) for an exemplary book-length exposition of this kind of approach.

15 See von Stuckrad (2022, pp. xv, 244). In the light of these considerations, matters of definition as encountered throughout the course of this book will be addressed primarily in the footnotes.

of "scientification," the enactment of which entailed the "translation" of "soul" into the nomenclature of "science." In marked contrast to these first two approaches, the third of these discourses sought to create a more poetically charged "Orphic science" imbued with the energies of the Dionysiac.[16] While it is evident that the various psychoanalytic "schools" have, at different times, inhabited – to a greater or lesser degree – all three of these discourses, it is with the "Orphic" trajectory that this book is most fully concerned.[17] The diachronic processes of superimposition and divergence that exemplify relations between these three discourses have more recently been conceptually reconfigured within contemporary psychoanalysis in the form of the uneasy relations that pertain between the psychoanalytic communities of the *fascinated* and those of the more *troubled*.[18]

It is these combined frames of reference that provide the wider theoretical context to this book, the arguments of which draw upon a wide range of primary and secondary sources in order to develop a theoretical exposition of how esoteric "traces" came to be "encrypted" within psychoanalysis during the course of its formation, resulting in the development of an *Orphic trajectory* whose effects it argues have persisted within psychoanalysis to this day. The present chapter outlines the theoretical context of this book and introduces the range of historiographical and conceptual perspectives that it draws upon in order to undertake the task of its exposition. Chapter 2 makes the case for identifying the precursors to the Orphic trajectory within psychoanalysis as originating in the Christian theosophical, German philosophical and Romantic traditions, as exemplified in the writings of Jacob Boehme (1575–1624), F.W.J. von Schelling (1775–1854), G.W.F. Hegel (1770–1831) and Arthur Schopenhauer (1788–1860). The imbrication of their respective modes of thinking with the ideas propounded by the various "schools" of esoteric mesmerism and somnambulism that preceded the rise of hypnosis as the prevailing medicalised alternative to its more metaphysically troubling predecessors is subsequently illustrated. Chapter 3 focuses on the role of Sigmund Freud (1856–1939) as an exemplar of the "dark enlightenment," as evidenced by the demonstrable significance of telepathy, psychical research and the Jewish Kabbalah in the formation of a specifically Freudian psychoanalysis.

---

16 von Stuckrad (2022, p. 121). My coinage of the term "Orphic trajectory" in this context was arrived at independently of von Stuckrad's adoption of the "Orphic" rubric to denote a particular "web" of psycho-spiritual discourse, having previously been derived from my reading of Sándor Ferenczi's *Clinical Diary* (1932) as described in Chapter 4. This thematic convergence may conceivably be thought of as providing mutually supportive evidence for the appositeness of this term – see Boyle (2021).

17 I would like to emphasise at this point that my account of an Orphic trajectory within psychoanalysis is not by any means intended to delimit the existence of alternative "pathways" for the transmission of the esoteric within psychoanalysis.

18

throughout its history, psychoanalysis has successfully embraced an amalgam of . . . *fascinated* and *troubled* communities. A *fascinated community* is a group who adopts a psychoanalytic theory . . . as presenting their world-view. A *troubled community* is one that is not satisfied with the state of psychoanalytic knowledge and seeks to generate a fundamental change that does not square with existing traditions.

(Govrin, 2016, p. 2)

Chapter 4 locates the explicit instantiation of the Orphic trajectory within psychoanaly-sis in the collaboration between Sándor Ferenczi (1873–1933) and Elizabeth Severn (1879–1959) and concludes with a brief account of Severn's only "heir," the largely neglected "psychoanalytic parapsychologist," Nandor Fodor (1895–1964) (Rudnyt-sky, 2022, p. 148). Chapter 5 traces the continuation of this Orphic trajectory in the writings of W. R. Bion (1897–1979), as illustrated via his covert adoption of Jungian, parapsychological, Kabbalistic and theurgic perspectives in his later writings. The book concludes with a brief exposition of the esoteric themes adumbrated in James Grotstein's (1925–2015) *Who is the Dreamer Who Dreams the Dream? A Study of Psychic Presences* (2000a), a work which is concomitantly identified as constituting a textual exemplar for the Orphic trajectory in contemporary post-Bionian psychoa-nalysis. It is further proposed that elements of the "oneiric" school of post-Bionian psychoanalysis can be conceptualised as constituting an avatar for the psychoanalytic parapsychological "tradition" translated into a contemporary psychoanalytic idiom.

1.2   A brief outline of the author's "personal equation" in this book[19]

In view of the avowedly "esoteric" themes that are explored throughout this book, it seems a reasonable expectation that its readers be provided with some kind of preliminary account as to how its author came to settle upon this admittedly obscure topic of research. Stripped to its essentials, the origins of this book can be traced to three discrete "encounters" – clinical, textual and artistic in nature – that subse-quently converged to form a kind of "constellation" in the mind of its author.[20] The first of these encounters can briefly be outlined as follows.

Many years ago, when I was training as an integrative psychotherapist, I worked with a female client I shall refer to as "Sophia," whom I saw on a once-weekly basis for a period of about a year. It was during the course of our work together that the following incident occurred. To set the scene, since the therapy room was on the sec-ond floor and the waiting room was on the ground floor, each session began with my collecting Sophia from the waiting room in order to escort her to the therapy room. Over the time that we worked together, I had observed that Sophia often liked to make small talk on the way up to the therapy room. However, I had also noticed that she tended to fall silent whenever there was something that was particularly troubling

---

19
  The "personal equation" was first nominated to designate a calculus of observational error in astronomy. It became the hallmark of the attempt to develop an objective experimental science of psychology, and then conversely, an epistemological abyss that delimited the selfsame project.
  Shamdasani (2003, p. 30)

  See also William James (1950 [1890], v.1, pp. 413–414).

20 My use of the term "constellation" in this context is indebted to Walter Benjamin's conjectures regarding "a clear connection" between his ideas concerning an "occult astrology and his notion of the constellation as a way of revealing hidden correspondences" (Josephson-Storm, 2017, p. 231).

her. On this occasion, Sophia was silent, which alerted me to the possibility that something might be wrong. As I was mulling over what this could possibly be, I was suddenly gripped by an absolute sense of certainty that she was pregnant. I have to emphasise that this awareness came to me not in the form of rumination or speculation but in the form of a "sure and certain" knowledge. Once we entered the room, Sophia sat down, burst into tears and informed me that she was indeed pregnant.

I recall having to hold back a spontaneous urge to respond to this disclosure by saying "I know," as I felt that such a response would make me sound too disturbingly omniscient. Moreover, my ostensible "omniscience" was in fact underpinned by an equally disconcerting ignorance as to how I had actually "known" this, only that I had, and that, consciously at least, I could discern in Sophia's appearance no visible signs of pregnancy. More importantly, from a clinical perspective, my initial response to this exchange was guided by the fact that Sophia was deeply distressed by the implications of her pregnancy, which meant that her need for me to help her address her situation took precedence over any sense of perplexity I had concerning the precise nature of the "communication" that had just transpired between us. As I reviewed this session subsequently, my sense of the "uncanny" nature of this exchange deepened. Although Sophia was in the early stages of a relationship, neither the desire for, nor the fear of, pregnancy had been prominent as content, symbol or metaphor (at least insofar as I could consciously discern) either centrally or tangentially. Moreover, at the time in question, I was unaware that such instances of "anomalous communication" in psychotherapy are a comparatively common occurrence.[21] My subsequent attempts to obtain clarity in supervision regarding the precise nature of what had occurred during this session were largely unsatisfactory, insofar as its more "uncanny" elements tended to be obscured beneath a range of rubrics, such as "unconscious communication," "projective identification" and "communicative countertransference" – or even olfactory cues. As a consequence, I was left with a growing sense that

> [T]he world we ordinarily know is confined by our imaginations, phantasies, perceptions, and conceptions . . . we live in a veritable bell jar of our epistemic limitations, a bell jar that is surrounded by mystery.
>
> (Grotstein, 1996, pp. 48–49)

The second of these encounters was textual in nature and occurred a few years later. It concerned my response to reading James Grotstein's *Who is the Dreamer Who Dreams the Dream? A Study of Psychic Presences*, in preparation for a series of lectures its author was due to deliver on the late writings of W.R. Bion as part of a clinical psychoanalytic training I was undertaking at that time. While I was cognisant that Grotstein had been analysed by Bion and that his work was usually categorised as

---

21 When, in 1997, the late Elizabeth Mayer and a colleague set up a discussion group titled "Intuition, Unconscious Communication, and 'Thought Transference'" under the auspices of the American Psychoanalytic Association, the conveners were promptly "inundated" with enquiries from psychoanalysts keen to join (Mayer, 2007, pp. 13–16).

being "post-Kleinian" in terms of its orientation, I nonetheless found myself intrigued and perplexed in equal measure by the contents of this "elaborated Gnostic gospel of depth psychology," the text of which seemed to me to read as though the contents of a magical *grimoire* had somehow been "downloaded" into the nomenclature of a psychoanalytic treatise (Gordon, 2004, p. 18). My ongoing preoccupation with the clinical and theoretical implications arising from this apparent "superimposition" of genres constitutes the central focus for the concluding chapter of this book.

My final encounter was with the work of the "paraconceptual" artist Susan Hiller (1940–2019). I first came across Hiller's work during the course of a visit to The Freud Museum in London sometime in the 1990s.[22] While I was initially disconcerted by the peculiar sense of the "uncanny" that her art installation *From the Freud Museum* (1991–1996) evoked in me, I found I could make little sense of it at that time and consigned its peculiar resonance to the penumbra of my preconscious, where it lay dormant in a state of suspended animation, as a kind of aesthetically rendered *enigmatic signifier* awaiting its moment of *Nachträglichkeit*.[23] However, I subsequently had an opportunity to attend a major retrospective of Hiller's work held in Tate Britain in 2011, during the course of which I experienced an intense receptivity to her creativity, as exemplified in works such as *Dream Mapping* (1974), *Automatic Writing* (1979–1981), *Psi Girls* (1999) and *Witness* (2000). I became fascinated by Hiller's approach to artistic creativity and was intrigued by the references in her writings to Freud's papers on telepathy, as well as her citation of liminal figures from the field of "psychoanalytic parapsychology," such as Nandor Fodor and Jules Eisenbud (1908–1999) (Hiller, 2008, p. 40). The influence of Hiller's work is pervasive throughout this book, its subtitle being taken from an eponymous essay of Hiller's in which she references her indebtedness to the work of all three of these authors (Hiller, 2008, pp. 239–243).[24] As Adam Phillips has observed:

> If the aim of a system is to create an outside where you can put the things you don't want, then we have to look at what the system disposes of – its rubbish – to understand it, to get a picture of how it sees itself and wants to be seen. The proscribed vocabulary in anybody's theory is as telling as the recommended vocabulary.
>
> (Phillips, 1995, p. 19)

22 Hiller's usage of the prefix "para" in this context is reminiscent of the usage of this term by the vitalist biologist Hans Driesch (1867–1941), who was similarly "convinced of the relevance of occultism and psychology for the emergence of a new understanding of science" – see von Stuckrad (2015, p. 66).

23 *Nachträglichkeit*:

> Term frequently used by Freud in connection with his view of psychical temporality and causality: experiences, impressions and memory traces may be revised at a later date to fit in with fresh experiences or with the attainment of a new stage of development.
>
> (Laplanche & Pontalis, 1988, p. 111)

Laplanche's concept of *enigmatic signification* is discussed later in the present chapter.

24 "Before and After Science" is, of course, also the title of an album by Brian Eno (1977).

Hiller's *From the Freud Museum* engages in an exemplary fashion in "the wilful blurring of archive and debris" as part of its aesthetic *modus operandi*, while the totality of her work as a whole has been described as "populat[ing] the world with 'enigmatic signifiers'" (Kokoli, 2011, pp. 148, 152). In a manner of speaking, one of the central tasks of this book can be thought of as the undertaking of a close examination of the paranormal "debris" that more usually gets expelled (via historiographical strategies derived from psychological "mechanisms, such as denying, forgetting, ignoring, excluding, suppressing, ridiculing . . . rationalizing" [Hanegraaff, 2025, p. 200], alongside phenomena such as "negative hallucinations")[25] to the "outside" of the psychoanalytic "archive," in the hope that, by engaging in such acts of retrieval, we can more readily establish what glimmers of "gold" might conceivably lie therein. In particular, Hiller's notion of the *paraconceptual* has been adopted as a central organising principle throughout this book as a means for conceptualising relations between the esoteric and the psychoanalytic:

> Just to the side of Conceptualism and neighbouring the paranormal . . . the "paraconceptual" opens up a hybrid field of radical ambiguity where neither Conceptualism nor the paranormal are left intact: the prefix "para" allows in a force of contamination through a proximity so great that it threatens the soundness of all boundaries.
>
> (Kokoli, 2011, p. 144)

Having summarised the central themes of this book, we can now move on to provide an outline of its theoretical and conceptual framework.

1.3   Trace, spectrality, trauma and transcendence – the haunting of psychoanalysis by its esoteric *other*

As Jacques Derrida has observed, archives are invariably haunted by that which they attempt to exclude (Derrida, 1998).[26] This "haunting" can at times take on a rather more literal quality than one might expect amidst the various hermeneutic occlusions that are habitually encountered within contemporary cultural theory.[27] In the light of

---

25 *Negative hallucination*:

> [A] phenomenon with the following . . . characteristics: (1) it is the converse of hallucination and constitutes the non-perception of an object or perceptible psychic phenomenon, (2) it involves a wish to reject a distress-inducing perception, (3) it plays an important role in repressing and repudiating aspects of external reality, (4) it is not limited to external objects and can affect internal perceptions.
>
> (Akhtar, 2009, p. 185)

26 Viewed from a slightly different perspective, we could also say that "our conclusions are really a function of our exclusions" (Kripal, 2019, p. 40).

27 For an illustration of what is meant by such processes of "occlusion," see, for example, Roseneil (2009, pp. 411–430). In this paper, we find that the text is itself "haunted" by its own disavowed "spectre." On p. 413, the author, in the course of invoking the "conceptual metaphors" of "ghosts"

such prevailing circumstances, it is worthwhile extending the "conceptual metaphors" of *haunting* and *spectrality* so as to include within their ambit the interrogation and problematisation of a cultural regime in which ongoing attempts to police the disciplinary parameters of the ontologically permissible possible "real" constitute a recurring feature of the academic milieu.[28] While the more immediate origins of *hauntology* are to be found in Derrida's engagement with Marxism and psychoanalysis (with particular reference to the writings of Nicolas Abraham and Maria Torok), its more distant antecedents can be traced to a diverse range of sources, including Romanticism, the Gothic, Spiritualism and fin de siècle psychology, as might be inferred from the confluence of associated metaphors that emerged from the then newly evolving media of telegraphy, photography and cinema.[29] According to Derrida,

> Freud did everything possible to not neglect the experiences of haunting, spectrality, phantoms, ghosts. He tried to account for them. Courageously, in as scientific, critical and positive a fashion as possible. But by doing that, he also tried to conjure them. . . . His scientific positivism was put to the service of his declared hauntedness and of his unavowed fear.
>
> (Derrida, 1998, p. 85)

Derrida's invocation of *hauntology* is avowedly indebted to Abraham and Torok's investigations into the role of the *phantom* as a vehicle for the transgenerational transmission of traumas that have become *encrypted* as "traumatic secrets," leading to a "loss of the self" (Abraham & Torok, 1986, 1994). However, while Abraham and Torok's concept of the *phantom* denotes the covert instantiation of a "lie about the past," Derrida's notion of the *spectre* expresses a more hopeful aspiration

---

and "haunting," asserts that this kind of terminology was not actually employed by any of the research participants. Yet, by the time we get to p. 420, we find that one of these same participants has related verbatim a story about a purported encounter with the ghost of his late father. In the text, the research participant's subjective experience and explanatory frame of reference ("it was a ghost") are intellectually filed away (or *said away,* to use Jeffrey Kripal's evocative term for denoting the strategic deployment of reductive explanatory strategies) under the sociological rubric of "idionecrophany" (i.e. the "relatively common" experience of "contact with the dead as reported by the bereaved"). This observation is not intended to be a criticism of what is an otherwise fine paper. Rather, it suggests that such instances can be viewed as indices of a wider academic milieu in which "anomalous" disclosures are covertly policed by conceptual demarcatory processes, through which the limits of the academic possible "real" are protected from the destabilising effects of a more "spectral" infiltration, as described by Méheust in the epigraph to this chapter.

28
  A conceptual metaphor . . . differs from an ordinary one in evoking, through a dynamic comparative interaction, not just another thing, word or idea and its associations, but a discourse, a system of producing knowledge. Besides fulfilling an aesthetic or semantic function, then, a conceptual metaphor "performs theoretical work."

(Blanco & Peeren [eds], 2013, p. 1)

29 See Davis (2007, pp. 8–9); Blanco and Peeren (eds.) (2013, pp. 2–19). For a helpful account of a specifically "English" current within hauntology (derived from the work of the late Mark Fisher in particular), see Coverley (2020).

"towards a still unformulated future" (Blanco & Peeren [eds.], 2013, pp. 7, 58).[30] Both of these respective distinctions are drawn upon in an ad hoc fashion throughout the course of this book. Hans Loewald (1906–1993) has highlighted the importance of transforming "ghosts" into "ancestors" as constituting an essential clinical feature of the "therapeutic action" of psychoanalysis (Loewald, 1960, p. 29).[31] Moreover, we find, embedded in Loewald's account, a "stunning re-definition of the unconscious as a crowd of ghosts" (Orange, 2017, p. 92). However, as Terry Castle has astutely reminded us,

> The problem with displacing the supernatural "back" into the realm of psychology . . . is that it remains precisely that: only a displacement. The unearthliness, the charisma, the devastating *noumenon* of the supernatural is conserved. One cannot speak in the end . . . of a "decline in magic" in post-Enlightenment Western culture, only perhaps of its relocation within the new empire of subjectivity itself. . . . But the effect was to demonize the world of thought. We have yet to explore very deeply the social, intellectual, and existential implications of the act of demonization.
>
> (Castle, 1995, p. 189)

More recent psychoanalytic theorists such as Adrienne Harris and her colleagues have augmented the "conceptual metaphor" of the "ghost" in order to articulate the associated features of its more disturbing manifestations, to which they ascribe yet darker rubrics such as "demons" and "vampires" (Harris et al. [eds.], 2016, 2017). As the authors remark in the introduction to the first of their two edited volumes, "words like uncanny and haunted are required, the words and language of object relations and internal objects seem too orderly for the experiences the authors in these books are describing" (Harris et al., 2016, p. 7). For my current purposes, the "revenants" thereby conjured have been psychoanalytically reconceptualised as spectral "traces," trans-generationally transmitted via processes of *enigmatic signification*, that possess the potential to "affect institutions and cultures no less than they do individuals" (Gerson, in Harris et al., 2016, p. 202). Hence, a distinction can usefully be made between the "vertical" (intergenerational) and "horizontal" (interpersonal) "communications" brought about by such processes (Frosh, 2013, pp. 5–6, 45–46). Moreover, this act of retrieval has been extended to include neglected figures such as Elizabeth Severn and Nandor Fodor, whose theoretical and clinical contributions have thus far largely been consigned to the peripheries of psychoanalytic historiography.[32] It is in the light of such considerations that a specifically hauntological historiography has been adopted as a resource to assist

---

30 See also Davis (2007, pp. 10–11) for a helpful elucidation of this distinction.

31 Notably, Loewald (1960) references an allusion in chapter 7 of *The Interpretation of Dreams* (1899) in which the "indestructability of unconscious mental acts is compared by Freud to the ghosts of the underworld in the *Odyssey*" (p. 29).

32 See Chapter 4.

in the formation of a spectral cartography of the uncanny and decentred Freudian subject "haunted" by *traces* of its occluded, esoteric *other*.[33]

Theories of trauma and its treatment – often contested – have been central to psychoanalysis since its inception.[34] What has been less frequently remarked upon is the potential for trauma – albeit in comparatively rare and exceptional cases – to act as a gateway for accessing transcendent alterations in consciousness.[35] Young-Bruehl and Schwartz have drawn our attention to the extent to which the history of psychoanalysis has been riven by disavowed processes of trauma, fragmentation and dissociation, which have led to the formation of a series of defensively appropriated narratives, the deconstruction and revision of which necessarily requires a frank "recognition of the inevitable investment we make in any construction of the past, and the interminable process of becoming conscious of the structure and purpose of that investment" (Young-Bruehl & Schwartz, 2012, p. 158).[36] Building on the insights of these two authors, it is argued that in order to more adequately facilitate a corrective to such deleterious processes, it is helpful to adopt a hauntological approach to historiography that explicitly focuses upon matters of recognition and retrieval, through which these occluded processes of trauma – and of transcendence – can more readily be discerned under the aspect of an *Orphic trajectory* active within psychoanalysis since its inception (see Kleinberg, 2017). Rhodri Hayward has drawn our attention to the manner in which the "unconscious self . . . was something constructed in the nineteenth-century struggles over the historical status of the supernatural" (Hayward, 2007, p. 63). In an analogous fashion, the central argument of this book proposes that the various discourse "entanglements" arising from the imbrication of the "occult" with the aspirations of a nascent psychoanalytic "science" acted as the "canvas" upon which the semiotically encrypted *hieroglyphs* of the esoteric came to be both preserved *and* negated (in the Hegelian sense of "sublation") within the substantive fabric of

---

33

I used the term haunting to describe those singular yet repetitive instances when home becomes unfamiliar, when your bearings on the world lose direction, when the over-and-done-with comes alive, when what's been in your blind spot comes into view. Haunting raises specters, and it alters the experience of being in time, the way we separate the past, the present, and the future.

Avery Gordon (1997) cited in Frosh (2013, p. 2)

34 For an in-depth exposition of Freud's theorising on trauma, see Fletcher (2013). See also Rudnytsky (2022) for an illuminating account of the innovative theory of trauma and its treatment, conjointly developed by Sándor Ferenczi and Elizabeth Severn. We will return to this topic in Chapter 4.

35 For notable exceptions to this assertion, see Mayer (2007, p. 101) and Rabeyron et al. (2015, pp. 1–17). See also Kripal (2014, pp. 198–204, 284–286) and Kripal (2024, pp. 225–226) for an intriguing account of the importance of the "traumatic secret" as a catalyst for triggering transcendent alterations in consciousness.

36 See also the following:

the error of ontological realism is that it fails to recognize the limitations of our own historical horizons, the extent to which our personal perspective is determined and directed by our past. The current epistemological understanding of the past is taken to be the ontological reality of the past.

(Kleinberg, 2017, p. 107)

a conceptually "traumatised" psychoanalytic metapsychology, whose instantiation was simultaneously co-opted to act as "an immense defence, a *Reizschutz* against the so-called 'outside'" (Borch-Jacobson, in Dufresne, 2000, p. x).[37]

While the Kabbalistic and Derridean resonances generated by the rubric of "trace" connote the conceptual interpenetration of the mystical with the postmodern, its central inflection is provided by Sigmund Freud's 1925 paper, "A Note Upon The 'Mystic Writing Pad,'" in which the image of a wax palimpsest is set forth as a metaphor for describing how memory is simultaneously made subject to the processes of inscription and erasure (Wolfson, 2002, pp. 475–514; Derrida, 2001, pp. 246–291):

> Thus the Pad provides not only a receptive surface that can be used over and over again, like a slate, but also permanent traces of what has been written, like an ordinary paper pad: it solves the problem of combining the two functions *by dividing them between two separate but interrelated component parts or systems*. . . . The layer which receives the stimuli . . . forms no permanent traces; the foundations of memory come about in other, adjoining, systems.[38]

It is proposed that this composite notion of "trace" characterises the relationship that pertains between the esoteric and the psychoanalytic as set out in this book. This conceptual metaphor is further extended to denote the significance of such "traces" as "vehicles" for the transmission and *enigmatic signification* of the esoteric within the psychoanalytic:

> [Enigmatic signifiers] disrupt psychological life, conveying a sense of signifying something *to* the subject. *What* they signify is an enigma, like finding a hieroglyph in the desert. The story of relationships and culture is the story of our repeated attempts to translate them, to respond to them.
>
> (Hinton, 2009, p. 185; see also Laplanche, 1997)

---

37 It has been observed that "the Freudian uncanny is a function of *enlightenment*" (Castle, 1995, p. 7). For an intriguing account of the origins of Freud's "witch meta-psychology," see Bonomi (2015, pp. 208–232). Freud's use of the term "metapsychology" occurs as early as 10 March 1898 in his correspondence with Fleiss (Masson, 1985, pp. 301–302). However, by the time we get to "Analysis Terminable and Interminable" (1937), Freud has come to liken his metapsychology to a "witch," whose activities inhabit a liminal state of mind located somewhere between the realms of "speculation" and "phantasying." When read in conjunction with Duffy (2020), Prokhoris (1995) and Vitz (1988), the "witch" metaphor begins to acquire the attributes of a subliminal "imaginary," whose longitudinal persistence recurs throughout the corpus of Freud's writings.

38 Freud (1925): in S.E. XIX (1923–1925), pp. 225–232/Freud (1991, pp. 427–434). Notably, Derrida (1998, p. 83, n. 17) construes certain themes in the correspondence between Freud and Wilhelm Fleiss (6 December 1896) as prefiguring specific ideas developed in this later essay – see Masson (1985, pp. 207–215). For a close reading of the significance of this letter for Laplanche's recasting of Freud's original seduction theory, see Fletcher and Ray (2014, pp. 33–37). For a helpful commentary on the historiographical implications of Freud's 1925 essay, see Kleinberg (2017, pp. 65–68).

It lies outside my remit to provide a detailed exposition of Jean Laplanche's (1924–2012) "Copernican" re-reading of Freud's early seduction theory, his substantive revisions to which constitute the theoretical scaffolding for his ideas concerning the enigmatic signifier or "message."[39] For my current purposes, it is sufficient to observe that his account of a "general theory of primal seduction" entails the "implantation" of "an irreducibly 'alien' unconscious" within the neonate, thereby giving rise to a psychoanalytic anthropology in which "the radical heteronomy of the human subject" is emphasised (Fletcher & Ray, 2014, pp. 19, 25–26). It is this primal interpenetration of the intrapsychic with the interpersonal that marks the instantiation of a wider process of cultural transmission through which the "message" of a particular enigmatic signification is encrypted and remains opaque both to "sender" and to "receiver" alike. To summarise, my usage of the term "trace" is intended to denote the *encryption* of an esoteric *hieroglyph* into the semiotic register of the psychoanalytic via a process of *enigmatic signification*.

As we shall see in Chapter 3, there are grounds for supposing that the significance of nineteenth-century psychical research in particular – and of "esoteric" currents more generally – for the development of a specifically psychoanalytic conceptualisation of the decentred human subject has suffered from a tendency to be consigned to the peripheries of psychoanalytic historiography.[40] However, before we can engage with such questions in more detail, it will be helpful to begin with a brief overview of the main developments in the academic study of Western esotericism so as to provide the proper context for evaluating the often-neglected contributions made by the "occult" in the development of psychoanalysis.[41]

---

39 For a general overview of Laplanche's ideas to which I am indebted, see Fletcher and Ray (eds.) (2014, pp. 14–54).

40 The subtle yet pervasive downplaying of the significance of the "occult" in psychoanalytic historiography was amply illustrated by Ernest Jones in his highly influential 1953 biography of Freud. Commenting upon chapter XIV, which deals extensively with the topic of Freud's occultism, Anna Freud wrote to Jones as follows: It gave me the feeling that here you remained as an outside critic instead of seeing it with my father's eyes. . . . I have an idea that you would not have disagreed if you could have felt his feelings about the matter more fully. [24/11/1955] – cited in Pierri (2022a, p. 1) However, this exclusion of the "occult" from the psychoanalytic "system" can also be conceptualised as the manifestation of one of the former's intrinsic attributes. As Kripal has observed, "The paranormal is marginalised because it *is* the marginal. . . . The paranormal is an anomaly that points *beyond* the system" (Kripal, 2014, p. 244). Viewed from this perspective, it is by no means an accident that psychoanalysis, parapsychology and esotericism have all been assigned a liminal role in the contemporary academy.

41 The notion of "occultism" was poorly articulated and heterogeneously misapplied throughout the early history of psychoanalysis and so came to encompass a wide and disparate range of ostensibly "anomalous" phenomena, including telepathy, astrology, theosophy, animal magnetism and clairvoyance. See Gyimesi (2017a, pp. 3–8) for more on this topic. In the estimation of Wouter Hanegraaff, the occult has in more recent years come to be seen "as a significant manifestation *of* modernity" (Hanegraaff, 2013, p. 9). For a scholarly overview of this term, see Hanegraaff (2006b), pp. 884–889.

1.4 A very brief introduction to Western esotericism

Since the study of Western esotericism arose as a sub-specialism whose origins lie within the comparative study of religions, it will be useful at the outset to begin with a very brief synopsis of the ongoing dialogue between psychoanalysis and the academic study of religions. While it lies outside my remit to provide a detailed overview of the various developments in hermeneutical perspectives that have arisen within this field between Freud's time and our own, a very brief overview of this interdisciplinary endeavour can nonetheless be summarised as follows.[42]

It is not surprising to find that commentators – beginning with Ernest Jones – found that "no single topic in the Freudian corpus, excepting that of sexuality, had evoked more interest than that of religion" (Parsons, 1999, p. 3). Indeed, some analysts have gone so far as to speculate that "a religious 'vision' may be the ultimate destination of the road on which psychoanalysis is an important early step" (Black, 2006, p. 8). With regard to the importance of calibrating the historical context of psychology as a distinct discipline, it has been remarked that "psychological language is parasitic on religious and theological traditions" and entails

> a particular type of introspective discourse constructed through empirical and statistical models. . . . These models are always parasitic on the present cultural registers of what it is to be human. . . . The future of the psychology of religion is therefore to be found in its past – by overcoming its disciplinary amnesia.
>
> (Carrette, 2001, pp. 118, 121, 123)

As a consequence of the constraints associated with these cultural parameters, some commentators have sought to critique the Kantian-derived constructivism that has become normative within much of the contemporary academy as part of a wider attempt to develop what has aptly (and perhaps provocatively) been described as a "mystical epistemology" (Parsons, 1999, p. 121). In Chapters 5 and 6, we will see how analogous attempts to develop a "mystical epistemology" within Bionian and post-Bionian psychoanalysis have affected the wider field of psychoanalytic metapsychology.

While Freud was one of the most important instigators of what subsequently came to be known as the *psychology and religion movement*, the centrality of his role in the formation of this interdisciplinary endeavour is one that he shares with C.G. Jung and William James (Parsons, 2021, p. 3). However, while the theories developed by all three of these figures can be captured under the rubric of "depth psychology," their respective views on how the "unconscious" or "subconscious" should be construed places them at significant variance with each other. Yet, despite these explicit theoretical divergences, post-Freudian developments

---

42 See Parsons (1999, 2021), Hewitt (2014) & Black (ed.) (2006) for helpful scholarly overviews of this topic.

in psychoanalysis and religion have nonetheless displayed a tendency to covertly re-instantiate Jungian and Jamesian perspectives, "albeit in psychoanalytically specific ways" (Parsons, 2021, p. 5).

While it is true that Freud's "ideas on religion are an inextricable part of the entire theoretical and conceptual structure of psychoanalysis itself" (Hewitt, 2014, p. 4), it is perhaps in his correspondence with Rolland Romain (1866–1944) concerning the nature of the "oceanic feeling" that we can most clearly discern the ambiguities and tensions inherent within Freud's ideas concerning the location of the "mystical" within psychoanalysis.[43] Indeed, Rolland himself can be understood to be one of the first advocates for pursuing a "mystical psychoanalysis" (Parsons, 1999, p. 38). Moreover, a strong case has been made for viewing their correspondence as constituting a kind of conceptual "holograph," within whose ambit subsequent developments in the psychoanalytic understanding of mysticism (i.e. the "classic," "adaptive" and "transformational" approaches) can be discerned in utero (Parsons, 1999, p. 181). It is this "transformational" approach within psychoanalysis that is most clearly imbued with the attributes of the "esoteric. Hence, it is the historical and conceptual... that constitutes the central focus of this book.[44]

It is impossible within the present context to provide a comprehensive account of the complex historiographical and theoretical disputes that have contributed to the development of Western esotericism as a distinct sub-specialism within the wider academic study of religions. Consequently, a very brief outline of this rapidly evolving – and, at times, controversial – specialism within the history of religions will have to suffice.[45]

---

43 For lucid historical overviews of the term "mysticism," see Parsons (1999, pp. 8–11) and Rousse-Lacordaire (2006). For a helpful account of some of the definitional problems associated with the term "mysticism," see Parsons (2021, pp. 165–168). For an engaging introductory overview, see Critchley (2024).

44 Notably, in this regard, Kripal has sought to develop "the erotic" as a cross-cultural comparative category to describe "a dimension of human experience that is simultaneously related both to the physical and emotional experience of sexuality and to the deepest ontological levels of religious experience" (Kripal, cited in Parsons, 2021, p. 252).

45 For useful historiographical and methodological overviews, see Goodrick-Clarke (2008); Rudbøg (2013); Hanegraaff (2012, 2013); Asprem and Strube (eds.) (2021). For an in-depth account of more recent definitional developments and debates, see Engler and Gardiner (2024a, 2024b). For an exemplary account of contemporary developments within the academic study of Western esotericism, see Hanegraaff (2025). The following brief historiographical outline of the various Western esoteric "traditions," "currents," "discourses" or "topoi" is indebted to these sources. It is outside my remit to enter fully into the debates concerning the comparative value of the various scholarly approaches employed to facilitate the academic study of the esoteric, other than to remark that each of these orientations comes freighted with its own particular matrix of methodological, epistemological, ideological and ontological baggage, whose presence necessarily serves simultaneously to facilitate, circumscribe and define – at least to some degree – the subject of their investigations. These difficulties are further compounded when we consider the complex historical, linguistic and conceptual entanglements of esotericism's proximate analogues, which include terms such as "mysticism," "occultism," "Gnosticism" and "Hermeticism," each of which has attracted a small

It has been proposed that the origins of these various (contested) "traditions," "currents," "discourses" or "*topoi*" can be traced to a series of syncretic developments arising out of a range of ancient "heterodox" spiritualities, such as Gnosticism, Hermeticism and Neoplatonism, that flourished within the Hellenistic world during the first centuries AD and which subsequently developed both within and across a range of cultures, including the Hellenistic, Judaic, Christian and Islamic. During the Renaissance, the rediscovery of the Hermetica and other associated ancient texts led to a renewed interest in ceremonial magic, astrology, alchemy and Kabbalah in scholarly circles. After the Reformation, these developments gave rise to movements such as Rosicrucianism, Christian theosophy and freemasonry, each of which made specific contributions to the rise of the modern occult revival, whose exemplars included nineteenth-century spiritualism, Helena Blavatsky's theosophy and the various European magical orders of the fin de siècle. Significant twentieth-century esotericists include figures such as Rudolf Steiner (1861–1925), George Ivanovič Gurdjieff (1866?–1949) and the founder of analytical psychology, C. G. Jung (1875–1961).[46] Studies in contemporary esotericism have sought to extend these investigations by augmenting traditional historiographical approaches with a range of sociological, psychological and critical methodologies adapted to enhance our understanding of the multifaceted role of the esoteric within historical and contemporary cultures (Asprem & Granholm [eds.], 2014).

Wouter Hanegraaff has argued that the construction of Western esotericism as a distinct domain of academic inquiry can be traced back to attempts made during the Renaissance to establish an "ancient wisdom narrative," which sought to align philosophers such as Plato (427–347 BC) and Plotinus (204–270 AD) with mythological figures such as Hermes Trismegistus. However, during the latter part of the seventeenth century, Protestant German theologians set out to undermine this narrative as part of an agenda to "purify" Christian teaching from the sources of "pagan" contamination. It was this attempted exorcism of "pagan influences" that contributed to the creation of a heterogeneous category of "rejected knowledge," which came in time to constitute the historiographical substrate for the academic sub-specialism known as "Western esotericism."[47] Following the

---

library of exegetical literature. These difficulties have led some scholars to view esotericism as an "umbrella term" encompassing a wide and potentially quite disparate field that embraces a heterogeneous range of concepts, ideas and historical currents (Rudbøg, 2013, pp. 33–34).

46 In the estimation of Hanegraaff (2025, p. 140), Jungian analytic psychology can be described "as a highly sophisticated and innovative form of applied esotericism." Moreover, he deems Jung's *Liber Novus* to "count among the most important primary sources of esotericism in the twentieth century" and considers that "Jungian psychology as a whole was grounded in intense visionary experiences that basically deconstruct the very distinction between mind and matter, consciousness and reality, or internal and external worlds" (Hanegraaff, 2025, p. 164).

47 In the estimation of Hanegraaff,

we do not actually need a definition of *esotericism* to study the historical traditions, currents, ideas or practices that are covered pragmatically by this label. All we need to do is explain why,

Enlightenment, derogatory categorisations of the "heretical" were superseded by those of the "irrational." Despite this shift in nomenclature, the underlying impetus remained that of separating the excluded "other" from normative standards whose existence could thereby be reinforced and promulgated via complex (and often occluded) demarcatory processes (Hanegraaff, 2012a, 2025). However, the historically situated nature of Western esotericism also means that attempts to provide a precise definition remain problematic – at least to the extent that such efforts would require the foreclosure of an open-ended historiographical horizon (Hanegraaff, 2013b).

More "constructivist" approaches have sought a home in discourse analysis (Granholm, 2013). However, while the adoption of such methodologies has the potential to act as a bracing antidote to the more extreme or naive variants of what has come to be referred to in the academy as "religionism," such radically "anti-essentialist" strategies nonetheless run the risk – if too enthusiastically applied – of defining out of existence the very *topoi* that they originally set out to investigate while simultaneously distorting the historiographical data via the too rigorous application of a methodologically generated "ideological filter" (Hanegraaff, 2013b; Magee [ed.], 2016, p. xx; von Stuckrad, 2015).[48] As Jeffrey Kripal has observed:

> it is just this kind of reductive materialism, usually joined to some retooled form of Marxism (it's all economics and oppression) or Foucauldianism (it's all discourse and power), that now defines so much of the study of religion. By so doing, the field has, in effect, denied its own subject matter, much as the fields of psychology and neuroscience have done with respect to the psyche and the mind, which they now more or less (mostly more) deny even exist . . . Mircea Eliade . . . had it exactly right when he wrote that, "The 'sacred' is an element in the structure of consciousness and not a stage in the history of consciousness." . . . The sacred and the human are two sides of the same coin.
>
> (Kripal, 2010, pp. 254–255)

In order to avoid the excesses arising from the application of a too stringent "reductionism," in tandem with the "grand narratives" approach frequently ascribed to so-called perennialist approaches, the present account is orientated within a critical realist hermeneutic, in which the perspectives opened up by terms such as "ontology," "ideology," "culture" and "history" are viewed as omnipresent and reflexively

---

for contingent historical reasons, they have come to be set apart and imagined as in some sense different or special. . . . I have never defined *esotericism* as "rejected knowledge." . . . Nor have I ever thought of esotericism as a "particular European *historical phenomenon*." . . . The radical historicism that I have always advocated is incompatible with all those positions.

(2024, p. 229)

48 The rubric of "religionism" tends to be associated – sometimes accompanied by a pejorative undertow – with the legacy of Mircea Eliade, perennialism and the notion of religion as a *sui generis* phenomenon – see Hanegraaff (2012, p. 127, n. 174).

interdependent.[49] Moreover, it presumes that such rubrics are themselves subject to processes of *reciprocal* neurological and cultural mediation, in accordance with the findings of transdisciplinary approaches such as *neurotheology.*[50]

While definitions of Western esotericism have been philosophically situated along a continuum ranging from "realism" to "nominalism,"[51] the first widely accepted scholarly definition of the term was formulated by the French esoteric scholar Antoine Faivre in 1992. Based upon an extensive study of Renaissance and early modern sources in particular, Faivre developed a typology consisting of four characteristics that he considered to be intrinsic to Western esoteric "forms of thought," namely those of correspondences, living nature, imagination/mediations and transmutation. In addition to these four intrinsic characteristics, he set forth two further non-intrinsic characteristics, which he termed rituals of transmission and the practice of concordance (Faivre & Needleman [eds.], 1992; Faivre, 1994).[52] Faivre described esotericism as an "ensemble of spiritual currents in modern and contemporary Western history which share a certain *air de famille,* as well as the form of thought which is its common denominator" (Faivre, 1998, p. 2). While Faivre's definition has been subject to various criticisms since this time (indeed, he himself was subsequently to adopt a position of "methodological agnosticism"),[53] his account is nonetheless accepted by most Western esoteric scholars to have set the terms of reference against which most of the ensuing debates around questions of definition and methodology have subsequently taken place.

49 See Schilbrack (2010, pp. 1112–1138). See in particular the following: My critical realism . . . does not deny that "religion" is a product of the European *imaginaire,* nor does it claim that the term is ideologically innocent. On the contrary, it foregrounds the issue of historical context and the purposes of those who developed the terms. Nevertheless, it does not follow that the word is substantively empty or refers to nothing. (p. 1132)

50 At its simplest, the hybrid discipline of *neurotheology* can be thought of as the application of the findings from neurological research to inform our understanding of religious experience – see Newberg (2016). In particular, the "critical realist" ontology outlined above is informed by Newberg's "neurotheological hermeneutic":

> the general functioning of the brain and its structure is amazingly universal on a gross level. . . . Of course, on the microscopic level, each brain is very different since the immense number of neuronal connections in the brain are dependent upon each person's development and experiences . . . our brain shapes the ways in which we can conceive of God and theology.
>
> (Newberg, 2016, pp. 84–85)

See also d'Aquili and Newberg (1999).

51 Hanegraaff (2013b, p. 258). For helpful discussions addressing the use of the term "Western esotericism" within a global context, see Hanegraaff (2015, 2025). In his most recent writings, Hanegraaff has substituted the term "Esotericism in Western Culture" as an alternative to "Western esotericism" (Hanegraaff, 2025, p. 4).

52 One recent paper that addresses questions of definition has identified eighteen "cluster characteristics" of esotericism spread across four discrete dimensions [a. modes of communication/knowledge; b. spiritual goals/techniques; c. views of reality; and d. explicit categorization] (Engler & Gardiner, 2024a).

53 See Hanegraaff (2012, pp. 334ff.) for a more detailed account of these criticisms.

While Faivre's schema has fallen out of favour in more recent times, Glenn Alexander Magee has sought to revive his approach by revitalising the underlying philosophical premises associated with Faivre's original taxonomy.[54] In the course of his revised elaboration of Faivre's typology, Magee puts forward a case for considering mystical *gnosis* to be the central theoretical construct applicable to the study of esotericism (Magee, 2016). Magee considers his approach as steering a judicious course between the binary polarities of methodological agnosticism and the "religionist" positions commonly ascribed to perennialist schools of thought. He does so, in part, by reframing these debates in terms of a distinction he makes between those who consider the study of esotericism to constitute a means for obtaining access to fundamental truths about the universe and human nature and those who regard such ambitions to be inherently incompatible with the requirements of scholarly "objectivity." Magee argues that the tenets of historicism are not "empirically verifiable" and asserts that its assumptions are underpinned by an implicit methodological paradox, whereby "its adherents claim to speak from a privileged, ahistorical perspective that historicism itself declares to be impossible" (Magee, 2016, p. xxxiii, n. 28).

While Magee acknowledges that Faivre's account possesses certain limitations, he also considers the criticisms that have been made of his approach to be ultimately unpersuasive and concludes that Faivre's typology is sufficiently sound in its essentials to constitute a starting point from which to embark upon a deeper and more comprehensive analysis of the term. Magee observes that Faivre's criteria entail a quintessentially "qualitative" approach to understanding that is shared not only by esotericism but also by ancient philosophy.[55] He construes this approach to be fundamentally at variance with modern ideals of objectivity, which he observes extend even to the discipline of modern psychology, wherein "strenuous efforts have been made to banish subjectivity" (Magee, 2016, p. xxiv). Using Faivre's criteria as his starting point, Magee distinguishes four fundamental features he considers to be common to all esoteric currents, namely a qualitative approach to understanding nature; a perceptual reliance on highly rarefied and very subtle modes of subjectivity; knowledge claims regarding other realities that are only accessible by these means; and an acceptance of the authoritative nature of tradition. Magee sums up his own understanding of esotericism as follows:

"Esotericism" refers to a number of theories, practices and approaches to knowledge united by their participation in a premodern, largely pagan world-view. Central to this worldview is commitment to the idea of the unity of existence – that existence is an interrelated whole in which seemingly dissimilar

54 I have given particular attention to Magee's understanding of esotericism, as I draw heavily upon his definition of the term in Chapter 5.
55 Notably, Hanegraaff (2022) has highlighted the idea of "quality" as constituting "arguably the most important and certainly the most neglected key term in the humanities" (p. 349, n. 180).

things exist in qualitative correspondence and vibrant, living sympathy. . . .
These correspondences are discovered through the cultivation of supernormal
aspects of human subjectivity, especially of the imagination. Esotericists typically hold that such knowledge can be utilised to effect changes in the world or
in the self through causal mechanisms that empiricism finds inexplicable (and,
therefore, rejects as impossible). This commitment usually goes hand in hand
with a belief that the same supernormal aspects of the subject can reveal the
existence of other dimensions of reality, usually hidden from view.

(Magee, 2016, pp. xxviii–xxix)

While Magee believes that esotericism is characterised by a certain way of thinking
that was prevalent throughout the ancient world, he also considers that its features
remain ubiquitous to all times and places and have been expressed under various
guises, with "esotericism" acting as one of the most recent of these nomenclatures.
Although he applauds the efforts made by the historicists to rehabilitate major esoteric figures so that their ideas can be more adequately incorporated into intellectual history, he also extends his approbation to include the possibility that their
philosophical contributions could have the potential to provide us with a "richer
and more complete understanding of our world" (Magee, 2016, p. xxxiv).

In a striking instance of conceptual metaphor deployed as a polemic intervention, Hanegraaff has proposed that "Studying Western esotericism is much like
applying psychotherapy to the history of thought" (Hanegraaff, 2005, p. 250, n.
67; Hanegraaff, 2012b, p. vii). One of the more recent developments to which
such a psychotherapeutically informed insight might usefully be applied relates to
the academic demarcations that distinguish competing methodological schools of
thought, such as "methodological agnosticism," "reductionism," "discourse analysis" and "religionism" (Hanegraaff, 2012a, pp. 357–358). However, it is possible to
reframe such developments as entailing both a repetition and a refiguration of the
long-standing problem of *othering* that the academic discipline of Western esotericism originally set itself the task of rectifying. Such symbolic *re-enactments* are
commonly referred to as *parallel processes* in the contemporary psychotherapeutic literature.[56] What is less commonly recognised is that these kinds of processes
can also manifest in historiographical as well as clinical contexts since "histori-
ans, like therapists, unconsciously identify with their objects of study and thus
unwittingly replicate the difficulties present in the object of study" (Kleinberg,
2017, p. 63).[57] Hence, we can sometimes encounter in some of the more polemic

---

56 "*Parallelism phenomena in psychoanalysis and supervision:* a number of psychoanalysts have
noted that psychoanalytic candidates unconsciously enact with their supervisors the very problems
with which they are struggling with their patients" (Akhtar, 2009, p. 202).
57 See also the following: "Paralleling occurs when therapists, in the supervision setting, unconsciously
identify with their patients, enact this identification, and elicit responses from the supervisors that
replicate the difficulties they themselves have encountered – as *therapists* – in the therapy" (H. K.
Gediman & F. Wolkenfeld, cited in Kleinberg (2017, p. 63).

exchanges occurring within academic debates an occasional propensity to engage in the "othering" of those interlocutors perceived to be of a differing theoretical orientation. This is no more than to say that unconscious dynamics constitute an inevitable aspect of the reflexive interplay of reason and emotion in the development and implementation of historiographical methodologies and programmes.[58] However, it is important to add by way of a caveat to this claim the observation that the presence of such processes in historiography does not thereby negate the possibility of a creative dialogue arising between theoretically differing interlocutors as part of a wider shared commitment towards the development of an ever more rigorous and multivalent tertium quid.[59] In this regard, it is notable that Hanegraaff has more recently adopted the term *radical methodological agnosticism* to denote his approach to historiography.[60] Although Hanegraaff's previous prioritisation of "history" over "theory" has been the subject of criticism, his more recent adoption of an explicitly Gadamerian approach to hermeneutics appears to have gone some way towards addressing the concerns of his critics.[61] As he astutely observes,

> The conclusion is that we must neither talk to the text nor sit back and wait for the text to talk to us; rather, the art of hermeneutics involves talking *with* the text and allowing it to talk with us. Texts, like their readers, have agency in the practice of conversation. . . . To perceive what *is* actually there, we must put ourselves on the line and allow for the possibility that as scholars we may simply not know yet *what it would even mean to "understand" these things.*
>
> (Hanegraaff, 2022, pp. 136–137)[62]

Hanegraaff's hermeneutic approach constitutes the inspiration for a brief exegetical excursus undertaken in the final chapter of this book into James Grotstein's *Who is the Dreamer Who Dreams the Dream? A Study of Psychic Presences.*

58
> Psychoanalysis persists in its view that thinking is an emotional matter. . . . Emotions cause some thoughts to be overvalued or denied. Anxiety, guilt and pain lead to defences. Pleasure and excitement can be sought at the expense of reality.
>
> (Mercer, 2008, p. 64)

59 For an exemplary instance of just such a dialogue occurring between two leading contemporary scholars of esotericism (one the leading exponent of *methodological agnosticism* and the other an advocate for a position characterised as *academic gnosticism*), see Hanegraaff (2008, pp. 259–276) and Kripal (2008, pp. 277–279).

60 Hanegraaff (2022) describes his revised approach as being "broadly congenial to the radical empiricism associated with William James" (pp. 4–5).

61 "We should not reject theory to save our sources from oppression; what we need is more sophisticated and systematic theories in order to understand them better" (Asprem, 2021, p. 143).

62 The latter part of this quotation alludes to Hanegraaff's own attempts to engage with the concept of "a supra-rational *gnosis* that can be accessed only by an enigmatic faculty called *nous*" (Hanegraaff, 2022, p. 137).

1.5   Towards a psychoanalytic parapsychology

According to Freud, the essentials of psychoanalytic theory can be reduced to an awareness of the importance of unconscious mental processes in human functioning, an acknowledgement of the phenomena of resistance and repression and an acceptance of the importance of sexuality and the Oedipus complex – "No one who cannot accept them all should count himself a psychoanalyst" (Freud, 1993 [1923], p. 145). However, the austere simplicity of Freud's lapidary expression of psychoanalytical theory stripped to its essentials failed to survive the lifetime of its founder. It is unnecessary in the present context to provide an in-depth account of the complex theoretical disputes that collectively constitute the contested history of what has become an essentially pluralistic endeavour. Nor is it necessary to determine whether these various theoretical developments are to be construed as tending towards a convergent – and possibly integrative – trajectory or as entailing the deconstructing proliferation of increasingly fragmented theories that are ultimately incommensurable with regard to their respective theoretical commitments and assumed frames of reference.[63] While such questions are of undoubted theoretical importance, their significance nonetheless remains tangential to the central preoccupations of this book. Consequently, the following account will limit itself to providing a highly selective outline of those aspects of psychoanalytic theory that are salient to its central concerns. It therefore begins with a brief summary of the features typically associated with a contemporary psychoanalytic model of the mind.[64] This account is subsequently extended to include Elizabeth Mayer's comparative analysis of the implications arising from the "boundaried" and "radically connected" theories of mind developed by Freud and Jung, respectively. Mayer's account is further augmented with reference to her deployment of those findings taken from parapsychological research that possess the potential to enhance our understanding of the more subtle and poorly understood communicative processes commonly encountered in psychoanalysis, such as "unconscious communication," "empathy" and "projective identification" (Mayer, 2002, 2007).

Auchincloss has defined psychoanalysis as that

> branch of psychology that deals most thoroughly and profoundly with understanding human behaviour as the result of the mind . . . [it] attempts to organize

63 For a selection of standard texts on the history of psychoanalytic theories of mind, see Sandler et al. (1997); Fonagy and Target (2003); Greenberg and Mitchell (1983); Mitchell and Black (1995). For a representative selection of synthetic and integrative approaches to psychoanalytic models of the mind, see Pine (1990); Ellman (2010); Auchincloss (2015). For a critique of "common ground" and pluralistic approaches to psychoanalysis, see Green (2005, pp. 627–632). For a useful selection of papers discussing the "ownership" of psychoanalysis viewed from a range of perspectives including the academic, historical, political and scientific, see Casement [ed.] (2004). It has been proposed that there exist at least 20 contemporary psychoanalytic orientations/frameworks – see Hamilton (1996, p. 8).

64 The following account is indebted to Auchincloss (2015) and Britton (2015).

our understanding of how mental phenomena such as feelings, thoughts, memories, wishes and fantasies affect what we experience and do . . . the psychoanalytic model of the mind is an imaginary construction designed to represent a complex system . . . that cannot be observed directly in its entirety. The purpose of any model is to represent a system in such a way that it is easier to talk about and easier to study.

(Auchincloss, 2015, pp. 4–5)

In Auchincloss' estimation, the majority of contemporary psychoanalytic clinicians tend to think of the mind as constituting an emergent property of the brain. This means that while the mind is viewed as being dependent upon the brain, its properties cannot be either described or conceptualised in terms appropriate to the brain alone. From a philosophical perspective, this implies that most clinicians are practising *property dualists* (i.e. they assume that the mind emerges from the brain while nonetheless distinguishing mind from brain for clinical purposes). Dependent upon one's perspective, this default position of property dualism might be thought of as a laudable example of conceptual flexibility employed in the face of clinical complexity. A less charitable reading might view it as a conceptual sleight of hand employed to disguise an obscure but troubling awareness that the mind may be more than a simple epiphenomenon of the brain.[65] Regardless of which of these viewpoints might be taken, Auchincloss is scrupulous in maintaining that until such times as there is a generally accepted integrative framework conjoining brain to mind, explanatory or causal statements lacking a clear evidential basis should be avoided. The implication arising from this is that – for now at least – both realms should be treated as two distinct orders, each with its own particular language, modes of conceptualisation and accepted levels of abstraction (Auchincloss, 2015, p. 101).

Contemporary psychoanalysis is often construed to be an inherently pluralistic endeavour, with each model – whether topographical, structural, object-relational, self-psychological or Lacanian in terms of its orientation – adopting differing perspectives on mental functioning and the significance that should be ascribed to various mental phenomena. Auchincloss advocates employing a two-pronged strategy for the use of specific models, entailing the judicious deployment of a pluralistic approach, even while treating each of the psychoanalytic models encountered as a de facto totalising theory whenever the clinical occasion might appear to require this. While it is generally acknowledged that the concept of the unconscious lies at the heart of all psychoanalytic conceptualisations of the mind, its particular significance from a specifically psychoanalytic perspective lies not so much in its storage function, capacity for subliminal perception or information processing abilities, as in the acknowledgement that thoughts and feelings existing outside of conscious

---

65 For a trenchant yet nuanced account of the associated risks arising from the disavowal of "public" from "private" forms of psychoanalytic knowledge, see Mayer (1996b).

awareness remain alive and active in terms of their subliminal influence upon our everyday experiences and decisions. While the details differ between the various psychoanalytic metapsychologies, Auchincloss' "integrative" account proposes that all psychoanalytic models of the mind seek to address five core dimensions, namely those of topography, motivation, structure/process, development and psychopathology/treatment. Notably, Auchincloss makes positive reference to the use of historical and transcultural perspectives to help make sense of dream phenomena (Auchincloss, 2015, p. 102). She concludes her account with the following cautionary caveat:

> Not everyone agrees that integration of the various psychoanalytic models of the mind is either possible or wise. . . . For now, it is enough to say that we live in an era of psychoanalytic pluralism and that efforts at integration can be seen as efforts to undo this pluralism with a proposed synthesis that is experienced as "too prescriptive" . . . psychoanalytic model making should be an ongoing process.
>
> (Auchincloss, 2015, pp. 255–256)

Ronald Britton begins his account of the various psychoanalytic theories of the mind with an acknowledgement of the emotional energies that underpin our more ostensibly theoretical commitments to any given model. While he observes that excessive tenacity in the retention of one's beliefs might imply an underlying conflict between the pleasure and reality principles, he also observes that the "provisional" and "esoteric" nature of our knowledge means that establishing the "measure of reality testing" is an inherently complex endeavour, particularly when we recall just how difficult it is to learn from experience under circumstances that may require us to change our existing beliefs (Britton, 2015, pp. xiv–xv). These problems are further exacerbated by our difficulties in distinguishing "theories" and "models" from "descriptions."[66] Britton observes that Freud's understanding of brain/mind interaction bears close comparison with the "neutral monism" of William James, whereby mind and matter are construed as differing phenomenal modifications of a shared underlying substantive reality. While Britton delimits the domain of brain neurology to the biological organ of the brain, the central nervous system, the

---

66

So it seems we bring to the psychoanalytic table our theories in the form of models, where they can be mistaken for descriptions of actual events or abstract, logical statements. In fact they are neither of these; they are the products of human imagination that organises experience into a shape that already exists in the human mind.

(Britton, 2015, p. 52)

See also the following:

The formal Freud was strict in understanding his schemas as hypothetical constructs, educated suppositions, inferences. The informal Freud experienced them as living realities. For example, one of his last notes defines understanding mystical experiences as the ego's apprehension or perception of the id. Id, ego, superego: for Freud at once hypothetical concepts and psychic realities.

(Eigen, 2016, pp. 16–17)

autonomic nervous system and its associated hormonal activities, he observes that these biological boundaries cannot be applied to the mind. Hence, he concludes that while neuroscientific theories arise from the study of the brain, psychoanalytic theories are concerned with the study of the mind. Britton proposes that if William James' "neutral monism" is accepted as a working hypothesis, then brain and mind can be conceptualised as existing along a theoretical axis in which brain is located at one end and mind at the other end (the question of *how* exactly they meet constitutes the "hard problem" of consciousness as originally formulated by David Chalmers in 1995).[67] While Freud began his research at one end of this axis as a proponent of the mechanistic Helmholtz school of physiology, he subsequently abandoned his neurological project sometime between 1895 and 1900 in order to shift the focus of his work towards a study of the mind and its derivatives that would come to include dreams, literature, mythology, self-analysis and clinical practice as the basic materials for his research. Although the terms *mind* and *mental* in Strachey's English Standard Edition of Freud's work are translated from the German *Psyche/psychlisch* and *Seele/seelisch* largely interchangeably, the linguistic nuances that distinguish these terms nonetheless help to remind us that Freud's idea of *mind* has *soul* as its historical and conceptual antecedent (Britton, 2015, pp. 6–8).

Mayer has proposed that at the heart of any psychoanalytic theory, there lie two basic premises. The first asserts the power of love and sexuality, while the second asserts the power of unconscious processes as intrinsic to the formation of human subjectivity (Mayer, 2002). The existential consequences arising from these initial premises entail a complex array of unconscious conflicts that distort our capacity to give and receive love. Amidst the vast assemblage of psychological phenomena addressed by psychoanalytic theory, there lies at their heart a fundamental debate concerning the degree of separation versus the degree of connectedness existing between individuals. Consequently, Freudian psychoanalysis – as exemplified, for example, by the quintessentially psychoanalytic phenomenon of transference – can be thought of as a theory concerned with separation and the formation of boundaries, while analytical psychology might conversely be construed to focus upon the principles of complementarity, non-locality and the nature of interconnectedness as exemplified in the Jungian concept of synchronicity. However, while it may follow that to be thoroughly grounded in either of these theories means to

---

67 The difficulties arising from this still unsolved problem are of a sufficient magnitude as to remind one of Sidney Harris' famous cartoon of two mathematicians discussing a complex tripartite equation in which the link between parts one and three consists solely of the words "then a miracle occurs." Frank (2017) provides an intriguing gloss on this theme:

> We know that matter remains mysterious just as mind remains mysterious, and we don't know what the connections between these two mysteries should be. Classifying consciousness as a material problem is tantamount to saying that consciousness, too, remains fundamentally unexplained.
> (cited in McGilchrist, 2021, p. 1048)

For a helpful overview and conceptual reframing of the "hard problem" of consciousness, see Solms (2021, pp. 238–269).

be simultaneously grounded within its tacit world-view, the respective features of both theories nonetheless possess the potential to be conceptualised as complementary rather than antagonistic or competing:

> The Freudian contribution to exploring new conceptualizations of mind lies . . . largely in the territory of offering us a highly refined observational method that vastly extends our observational capacities. Jungian theory, on the other hand . . . [makes] its primary contribution by laying out aspects of conceptual frameworks which can help us newly envision – so we can then further study – a human mind characterized by precisely the forms of radical connectedness that science is starting to suggest. As the two interface, we are likely to learn more not just about the mind, but also how the forms of thinking we've labelled as Freudian verses Jungian do indeed complement and extend each other in the clinical situation, as well as in other spheres.
>
> (Mayer, 2002, p. 97)[68]

Citing the physicist Werner Heisenberg, Mayer observes that the most beneficial developments in any discipline commonly occur where different lines of thought meet. Having argued for the emergence of a consensus that psychoanalysis is quintessentially a subjective and intersubjective endeavour, Mayer proceeds to make a strong case for psychoanalysts to constructively engage with the findings from parapsychological research as a potential source of empirical evidence for some of its most fundamental (albeit most poorly understood) concepts, such as "intuition," "empathic attunement" and "unconscious communication" (Mayer, 2002, 2007). Observing that it was Freud himself who originally established the potential importance of anomalous mental processes for clinical practice, Mayer goes on to advocate for a basic methodological attitude consisting of "maximum open-mindedness as well as maximum scientific rigour" (Mayer, 1996b, p. 724). Mayer summarises her goals as follows. Firstly, she wishes to draw attention to the fact that research into anomalous modes of communication exists. Secondly, she seeks to provide evidence regarding the rigour with which the best of this research has been conducted. Finally, she sets out to demonstrate its potential relevance for arriving at a more adequate conceptualisation of those subtle forms of nonverbal communication that constitute an intrinsic feature of psychoanalytic clinical practice (Mayer, 1996b).[69]

While Mayer's speculations may appear to lie outside the defining "shibboleths" of Freudian psychoanalysis, there are nonetheless grounds for supposing that Freud

---

68 In the estimation of Henderson (2015), "Between them, Freud and Jung set the agenda for the future evolution of psychoanalysis" (p. 3).

69 Mayer's book *Extraordinary Knowing* (2007) notably features many instances in which both patients and analysts have struggled (with varying degrees of success) to integrate their experiences of anomalous phenomena with prevailing cultural norms.

himself may very well have been the first "psychoanalytic parapsychologist."[70] This claim can be illustrated with reference to Freud's dealings with the Italian "astrologer" and "clairvoyant," Francesco Waldner (Pierri, 2022a, pp. 245–246). In his booklet titled *Mes Aventures Surnaturelles*, published in 1962, Waldner provided a touching account of a series of consultations he had with Freud during his time as a young man living in Vienna. It was during the course of these consultations (a central preoccupation of which appears to have concerned unresolved conflicts relating to his deceased father) that we encounter the following exchange as reportedly said by Freud to Waldner during the course of Waldner's treatment: "You must take advantage of this, my boy. I don't expect to live much longer and you really need my help if you want to avoid interference and keep your problems out of your visions" (Pierri, 2022a, p. 247). While the following surmise is of a necessarily speculative cast, it is nonetheless possible to read Waldner's account as providing a description of Freud utilising psychoanalysis as a means for enhancing his patients' "paranormal" capacities rather than as a technique with which to "exorcise" them via a "reductive" process of psychoanalytic "deconstruction."

Having outlined the methodological considerations that constitute the conceptual framework for this book, we can now move on to a consideration of the role that was played in the formation of psychoanalysis by some of its "dark" esoteric precursors.

70 See Chapter 3.

Chapter 2

Dark precursors to an esoteric psychoanalysis[1]

2.1 Introduction

The last chapter set out a framework for conceptualising some of the historical and cultural contexts that contributed to the formation of a "decentred" psychoanalytic subject dialectically conjoined to its occlusive and enigmatic (esoteric) *other*. The present chapter seeks to locate the origins of these "dark precursors" within the various mesmeric, somnambulistic and hypnotic "currents" arising out of the Christian theosophical, German philosophical and Romantic "traditions." It sets out to explore how these developments arose out of a complex genealogical matrix conjoining these "traditions" to mesmerism, animal magnetism, artificial somnambulism and hypnotism, the overlapping features of which bear some comparison with the phenomenologically contiguous state of hypnagogia commonly experienced at the threshold of sleep.[2] It is nevertheless important to preface any such comparative

---

1 "Thunderbolts explode between different intensities, but they are preceded by an invisible, imperceptible *dark precursor,* which determines their path in advance but in reverse . . . every system contains its dark precursor" (Deleuze, 2014, p. 152).

2 For an in-depth account of the research literature on alterations of consciousness, see Baruš (2020). On the phenomenon of hypnagogia, see the following: "Hypnagogic experiences are commonly defined as hallucinatory and quasi-hallucinatory events taking place in the intermediate state between wakefulness and sleep" (Mavromatis, 1987, p. 1). Mavromatis identifies a *hypnagogic syndrome* possessing seven characteristics, which include the following attributes: psychophysical relaxation, "passive volition," parasympathetic predominance, decrease in exteroceptive and proprioceptive stimulation, psychological withdrawal, decreased arousal and need/intention to sleep/dream (p. 77). Notably, in Mavromatis' estimation,

> Several and disparate sources of evidence appear to suggest that hypnagogia is significantly conducive to paranormal events, that spontaneous psi events occur in experimental hypnagogia, that developing psychics experience an increase in hypnagogic phenomena, that hypnagogic visions might be an early form of clairvoyance, and that some hypnagogic images might be precognitive.
>
> (p. 131)

Parallels are drawn between hypnagogia and hypnotic trance (pp. 219ff.), while reference is made to hypnagogic states in the writings of a diverse range of esoteric figures, including Iamblichus (245–325 AD), Emmanuel Swedenborg (1688–1772) and P. D. Ouspensky (1878–1947) (Mavromatis, 1987, pp. 4, 100–103). For an illuminating account of trance and hypnosis, see Baruš (2020, pp. 125–147).

DOI: 10.4324/9781003476733-2

claims with the cautionary caveat that "any attempt to make an epistemological object out of the trance was beset by its variability" (Shamdasani, 2006, p. 12).

Eva Pocs has observed that "ecstatic visionary experience . . . [is] . . . widespread, commonplace and non-culture specific" (cited in Hutton, 2017, p. 78). Such ecstatic experiences can potentially cover a diverse range of cognitive and affective states, including those of trance, dream, hallucination, creativity, delusion and dementia (Hutton, 2017, pp. 78–79; Baruš, 2020).[3] Notably, somnambulistic trance states were associated with a wide and – when viewed from a contemporary perspective – mysterious range of phenomena[4]:

One of Mesmer's many followers, a Marquis de Puységur, discovered that mesmeric treatment could induce a strange condition of sleeplike trance, in which many patients displayed remarkable "paranormal" abilities and entered visionary states in which they claimed to communicate with spiritual beings on other levels of reality. This phenomenon, known as artificial *somnambulism,* has exerted an incalculable influence on the history of Western esotericism during the nineteenth century.

(Hanegraaff, 2013a, p. 38)

This chapter sets out a case for construing these mesmeric and somnambulistic practices as constituting a kind of cultural "conduit" through which the "occult" traditions of the fin de siècle became entangled with a nascent psychoanalysis. Adam Crabtree has identified three distinct currents arising out of the mesmeric and somnambulistic traditions, namely the psychological, the medical and the parapsychological (Crabtree & Osei-Bonsu, 2025). The ensuing conceptual elisions arising from its indebtedness to its mesmeric precursors marked psychoanalysis from its inception. As Henri Ellenberger has remarked:

The case of Breuer's celebrated patient Anna O. (Bertha Pappenheim) actually belonged to those great magnetic diseases that were so much sought after by the early magnetizers. She had unique symptoms, directed her cure, explained it to the physician, and prophesied the date of its termination. Because she chose for her self-directed therapy the procedure of catharsis (which a recent book had made fashionable), Breuer believed that he had discovered the key to the psychogenesis and treatment of hysteria. It was a theoretical misconstruction and therapeutic failure, which, however, stimulated Freud towards the inception of psychoanalysis.

(Ellenberger, 1994 [1970], p. 892)

3 Commenting on the potential dangers associated with the breadth of the "altered states of consciousness" concept, Hutton wryly observes that "The danger is that the umbrella may turn into a dustbin" (p. 79).
4 For an authoritative account of these phenomena, see Etzel Cardina et al. (2014).

In order to map out more clearly the conceptual genealogy that contributed to this original confluence and subsequent demarcation of traditions and disciplines, the chapter begins with an account of the role played by the Silesian Christian theosophist Jacob Boehme (1575–1624) in the ensuing fascination with mesmerism and animal magnetism that arose within German Romantic and idealist circles concerned with *Die Nachtseite der Natur* (the "nightside of nature"). This fascination was exemplified by F.W.J. von Schelling (1775–1854) both in his philosophical writings and through his posthumously published novel *Clara*, and can be further illustrated with reference to the philosophical writings of G.W.F. Hegel (1770–1831) and Arthur Schopenhauer (1788–1860) via their indebtedness to a range of esoteric thinkers, most notably Boehme. It is further proposed that the oblique influence of the esoteric interests of these philosophers upon the formation of psychoanalysis was subsequently "channelled" via the various "esoteric" schools of mesmerism, animal magnetism and somnambulism that rose to prominence during the eighteenth to nineteenth centuries, the "occult" excesses of which were only superficially exorcised under the aegis of a medicalised hypnotism. The significance of this "encryption" of esoteric *enigmatic signifiers* in the formation of a nascent psychoanalytic metapsychology is further illustrated via a highly abbreviated account of Justinus Kerner's monograph on Friederike Hauffe, *The Seeress of Prevorst* (1845), which emphasises its importance, not only as one of the earliest psychiatric monographs but also as an exemplary case of *magnetic gnosis*, the distinctive attributes of which will be elaborated upon in due course.

2.2   The "Three Worlds" of Jacob Boehme

The significance of Boehme's ideas in contemporary thought has often been under-estimated.[5] Paul Tillich (1886–1965) considered Boehme's writings to constitute "one of the most profound and strangest systems of Western thought," while the cultural critic Walter Benjamin deemed him to be "one of the greatest allegorists" (cited in Apetri, 2014, pp. 1–2). One scholarly book-length study has gone so far as to assert that Boehme "through some faculty of super-sensory vision, was able to behold the principle behind the creation and evolution of the cosmos" (Godwin, in Nicolescu, 1991, p. 3). Such ostensibly hyperbolic claims are nonetheless of a piece with the exalted and visionary nature of Boehme's writing:

> One world is in the other, and all are only one. . . . For the earthly body which thou bearest is one body with the whole kindled body of this world, and thy

---

5

Boehme . . . has mattered a great deal in our intellectual history. The interesting issue, though, is not whether we can draw a direct line of influence . . . but is rather the question of how a creative thinker like Boehme is used to create concepts adequate to circumstances after his own time . . . The most interesting Boehme today is the one we don't know is there, the one who has become part of the backdrop against which other concepts strive for manifestation.

(Janz, 2014, pp. 281, 284)

body qualifieth, mixeth or uniteth with the whole body of this world; and there is no difference between the stars and the deep, as also between the earth and thy body: it is all one body. This is the only difference, thy body is a *son* of the whole, and is in itself as the whole being itself is.

(Boehme, cited in Nicolescu, 1991, p. 45)

Andrew Weeks has argued not only that Boehme's "mystical speculation seems to anticipate psychoanalysis" but also that, in his mythopoetic account of the "disso-ciation" of Lucifer from God, we can discern the origins of the nascent philosophi-cal *subject* (Weeks, 1991, p. 181):

The descent into the depths of the spirit attributed to the writings of Jakob Böhme is interpreted . . . as an expression of the principle of *subjectivity.* The withdrawal into the depth of the subject . . . is thus presented as an alternative to the exploration of the outside world . . . Lucifer's rising up against God is . . . the act through which the *I,* subjectivity, emerges for the first time.

Muratori, 2016, pp. 188, 234)

Analogous attempts have been made to construe Boehme's theosophy as a precur-sor to Freudian psychoanalysis (Pruett, 1976–1977, pp. 241–251):

The dark-world and the light-world can be compared to the *id* and the *ego.* These and other parallels have attracted scholarly comparisons with Freudian psychoanalysis. . . . Boehme was led by his own premises to draw the conclu-sions which resemble those of psychoanalysis.

(Weeks, 1991, p. 181)

While there is no evidence to suggest that Freud ever undertook a deliberate study of Boehme's work, traces of Boehme's legacy can nonetheless be discerned both within the corpus of Freud's writings and more broadly across the wider cultural and intellectual milieu within which he participated.[6] The main conduits for the transmission of Boehme's ideas across the wider Germanic culture can be found within the influence that his writings had upon the writers and philosophers of the Romantic period, from whose works Freud's own writings were to take at least

6 See, for example, the humorous allusion made to Boehme in Freud (1976 [1916], p. 128). See also the reference made to Boehme's "paranoidal system" in Kielholz (1924, p. 451). Nonetheless, it remains the case that the pages in the only volume in Freud's library devoted specifically to Boehme's work remained uncut during his lifetime – see *Freud's Library: A Comprehensive Catalogue* [book and CD-ROM] compiled and edited by J. Keith Davies and Gerhard Fichtner (The Freud Museum: London and Tübingen edition discord, 2006). However, in the light of the trenchant criticisms that were subsequently directed towards Kielholz's writings on Boehme, this inadvertent negligence on Freud's part may have constituted a fortunate oversight – see Brown (1977, p. 35, n. 10).

a portion of their inspiration.[7] In the estimation of one commentator, Boehme's theosophical writings constitute "the great well-spring of modern psychodynamic psychotherapy – the thinker who originated the field that was later inhabited by Freud and Jung . . . Boehme . . . defines the larger field within which these later debates took place" (McCullough, 2019, pp. 79–80).

Boehme's texts constituted a vital nexus through which the medieval and Renaissance symbolisations of a transcendental *Spiritus* were reconfigured following the Enlightenment into a self-concept oriented around intramundane and secularised modes of expression:[8]

> Within this context of late Renaissance magico-mystical movements, Boehme . . . was the one who provided the underlying theological justification for the redirection of religious experience. His symbolization of an evolving divine Being and of the theosophic process of reality as a whole was precisely the foundation required for a depiction of the movement towards Innerworldly fulfilment. Moreover, it was Boehme who was probably the most important transmitter of these ideas within modern intellectual history. The mytho-speculative mysticism of the Renaissance was received primarily in its Behmenist formulation by the later generation of Romantic and Idealist thinkers. It was his representation of the unfolding dialectical process that proved of most enduring influence, both in its original theological exposition and in its subsequent secular transformation.
>
> (Walsh, 1983, pp. ix–x)

Once orientated within this particular historio-conceptual matrix, it becomes possible to construe the complex web of cultural and ideological tensions active within the mytho-speculative *Spiritus* of the medieval and Renaissance periods as indirectly contributing to the formation of a secularised, psychoanalytic "trinity" consisting of *id, ego* and *superego*.[9] By the time we arrive at the early Romantic period, it is possible to discern a genealogical trajectory originating within the Medieval–Renaissance *Imago Dei* whose conceptual itinerary leads through the Baroque and early modern periods before arriving at an intellectual "terminus" entailing the

---

7 See Mayer (1999). In Mayer's estimation, "only Friedrich Schlegel and Schelling achieved an active reception of Böhmist material in their philosophical writings" (p. 6). On the cult of *Bildung* (a concept concerned with the combined ideals of education, development and personal cultivation) in Freud's Vienna, see Whitebook (2017, pp. 71–75). On the concept of *Bildung* in early German Romanticism, see the following: "It means literally 'formation,' implying the development of something potential, inchoate, and implicit into something actual, organized, and explicit" (Beiser, 2003, p. 27). It is in this sense that my adoption of the term "formation" (*Bildung*) is utilised in the title for this book. On Freud's debt to Romanticism, see Madeline and Henri Vermorel (1986).

8 For a classic account of these developments, see Taylor (1992).

9 As Kirschner (1996) has remarked, "for Boehme (arguably) and for subsequent thinkers, the discourse of external cosmology starts to look as if it really *is* a symbolic language of the self" (p. 147, n. 54).

Enlightenment apotheosis of an immanentised "inner light of reason." In essence, powers hitherto attributed to a transcendental divinity were reconstituted to provide the components for the proto-subject of depth psychology.[10] Notably, these developments did not lead to the jettisoning of the magico-mystical characteristics previously associated with the divine ground so much as their encrypted re-instantiation – albeit in an attenuated fashion – in a manner analogous to the *Gnostic metalepsis* theorised by Cyril O'Regan, the constituent features of which are described further below. Hence, we find that

> Boehme shifts the locus of transcendence inwards, into the human psyche and the hidden inner life of the world. . . . The dark fire-world and the angelic light world, good and evil, heaven and earth, inner and outer, eternity and time, are said to be "in one another like a single thing."
>
> (Weeks, 2014, pp. 53–54)

On the basis of Boehme's own writings, it is possible to speculate that the core of his theosophy may have originated – to a degree that is necessarily difficult to determine – within the experiential crucible of what Ellenberger has termed a "creative illness," the distinguishing features of which bear comparison with the "initiatory trials" endured by many of the founding figures of the dynamic psychiatries (Ellenberger, 1994, pp. 447–448, 672–673). However, before we can review the evidence that might be adduced in support of this contention, it will be useful to begin with a very brief outline of the conceptual "architecture" of Boehme's "theophany."

It has justly been observed that Boehme's writings are likely to prove "virtually unreadable" to anyone unfamiliar with the basic world-view of Renaissance esotericism, with its associated emblematic and typological modes of representation and expression (Weeks, 1991, pp. 174–175). Moreover, while Boehme's ideas were to have a profound and lasting effect upon the development of German idealism and beyond, it would nonetheless constitute an anachronistic misreading to interpret his writings either as constituting a failed attempt to create a philosophical "system" or as providing a *naïve* "psychological" description of his purportedly "mystical" experiences. Boehme's writings have been described as a Baroque hierophany depicting "the sacramental and absolute mystery of presence and transcendence. . . . Each part contains, or attempts to contain, the whole" (Weeks, 1991, pp. 100, 170).[11] Hence, we find beneath its ornate literary carapace that an

---

10 Kirschner (1996, pp. 152, 185). See also Edel (2018, p. 80).
11 See also Weeks (2014, p. 48) for an account of why Boehme's *Aurora* cannot simply be read as a "psychological report." For a general overview of Boehme's influence upon German Romanticism, see Benz (1983).

experiential substrate of "mystical" encounter is nonetheless discernible. As Arthur Versluis has observed,

> Boehme emphasises his own spiritual authority and direct Gnostic experience. When a secondary author contravenes these claims, he effectively places himself above his subject, claiming in effect to know more than Boehme about Boehme's claims to knowledge. Such implied scholarly claims of supervenience of their subjects come freighted with their own issues.
>
> (Versluis, 2014, p. 265)[12]

A very brief summary of the relevant elements of Boehme's teachings can now be outlined.[13] According to Weeks,

> The overall paradigm (if it can be called that) draws upon meteorological, astrological, alchemical, mechanical, and psychic prototypes. It soon becomes apparent that all these references are subordinated to the overriding theosophical and metaphysical context. The seven qualities are a figure of the Trinity and of the three principles as the *dark-world* (later: "fire-world"), the *light-world,* and *this world* (which is formed in the middle, where the first and second principles overlap.
>
> (Weeks, 1991, p. 109)

While debates continue on how best to categorise Boehme's writings, there nonetheless exists a growing consensus that his theosophical texts inhabit a broad conceptual spectrum spanning the mystical, the philosophical and the esoteric (Versluis, 2014, p. 271; see also Muratori, 2016, pp. 1–56). Boehme's access to the Paracelsian tradition (already firmly established in his hometown of Görlitz at the time of his birth) is evident from the many alchemical references contained throughout his work. Moreover, it has been proposed that his friend and disciple Dr Balthasar Walther (1558–c. 1630) – who was himself a Paracelsian – could have acted as a conduit for the Kabbalistic motifs that pervade Boehme's writings (Weeks, 1991, p. 30).[14] The overarching philosophical significance of Boehme's ideas for future thinkers has been aptly summarised in the following terms:

> Boehme left to philosophy a first principle which becomes creative by generating its own contrary, which it then proceeds to reconcile to itself. He left also

---

12 One commentator has concluded that in relation to Boehme's writings, "each person who reads him would be affected according to their own capacities" (Smith, 2014, p. 101).

13 This account is indebted to the following sources: Goodrick-Clarke (2008, pp. 87–104); Weeks (1991); Deghaye (1993, pp. 210–247). For Boehme's own evaluation of his writings, see his "Letter to an Enquirer" (1621) in Waterfield (ed.) (2001, pp. 78–80).

14 On the difficulties associated with determining the true nature and extent of Kabbalistic influences in Boehme's writings, see Penman (2014, pp. 66–68).

the compelling vision of a fallen universe which is constituted throughout by an opposition of quasi-sexual contraries, at once mutually attractive and repulsive, whose momentary conciliations give way to renewed attempts at mastery by the opponent powers, in a tragic conflict which is at the same time the very essence of life and creativity as well as the necessary condition for sustaining the possibility of progression back to the strenuous peace of the primal equilibrium. The motion into which all things are thus compelled is a circular one, like that of the self-devouring serpent.

(Abrams, 1971, p. 162)

There has been much debate – often of such a kind as to create more heat than light – as to whether, or to what extent, Boehme's writings can be thought of as "gnostic."[15] Many of these discussions have tended to founder from the outset due to the inability of the various interlocutors to arrive at an agreed consensus concerning what exactly it is that the term "gnostic" is intended to convey.[16] Such disputes can be at least partly attributed to the proliferative nature of the early gnostic teachings. Cyril O'Regan, in a theoretically sophisticated – albeit arguably tendentious – reading of Boehme's work, defines Gnosticism as "the haunting of a Christian discourse by its *other,*" which in this instance he prototypically identifies as originating in second-century Valentinian Gnosticism (O'Regan, 2002, p. 5). O'Regan associates Valentinian Gnosticism in particular with the instantiation of the hermeneutic trope of *metalepsis,* which he defines as denoting "the phenomenon of a complex disfiguration-refiguration of biblical narrative, or any first-order interpretation of it," a procedure which he considers to be descriptively typical of Boehme's overall theosophical project (O'Regan, 2002, p. 17). However, while O'Regan's exegesis is deeply informed by a wide knowledge of both the primary gnostic texts and their associated secondary literature, his overall approach is in many respects indebted to Eric Voegelin's (1901–1985) appropriation and extension of the term to denote a complex historical development entailing "transcendentalizing" (Valentinian), "immanentizing" (Marx) and "contemplative" (Schelling and Hegel) "gnostic" variants, in which the cognitive mastery of reality is assumed to be achievable.[17]

15 For a helpful overview of these debates, see van den Broek (2006, pp. 403–416).

16 It is notable that psychoanalysis has been described as possessing an essentially "gnostic view of reality" (McGrath, 2012, p. 183). *Contra* O'Regan, McGrath does not consider Boehme to be a gnostic due to "his emphasis on embodiment as perfection. Nothing could be stranger to ancient gnosticism than to hold such a view" (McGrath, 2012, p. 50).

17 See Voegelin ([1952] 1987, pp. 107–189) for an initial outline of his usage of this term. For an illuminating reference detailing the development of the "gnostic appellation" in Voegelin's writings, see O'Regan (2001, pp. 244–245, n. 5). For a trenchant critique of O'Regan's deployment of the Voegelinian analysis of "gnosticism" in his study of Boehme, see Versluis (2006, pp. 69–84). For a more measured rebuttal, see Hanegraaff (1998, pp. 29–36). With regard to the question of Boehme's purported "gnosticism," It may be worth noting in passing that Boehme himself asserted that he "never desired to know anything of the Divine Mystery" – see Waterfield (2001, p. 63). However,

Aurora (1612) was Boehme's first published work. Its importance was subsequently acknowledged by Schelling and Hegel in particular and by the circle of Jena Romantics more generally (Muratori, 2016; Brown, 1977). Written after a 12-year period of gestation, *Aurora's* origins were, to a large extent, indebted to a period of "creative illness," which Boehme experienced during his earlier years, the effects of which were to subsequently act as the catalyst for an even more profound theophany:

> I at last fell into a severe melancholy and sadness at the sight of the great depths of the world with its sun and stars, clouds, rain and snow. I regarded in my spirit the great creation of this world. In it, I found evil and good in all things, love and anger. . . . Moreover, I regarded the tiny little spark that is the human being and considered what it amounted to before God. . . . This caused me to grow gravely melancholy and deeply troubled. . . . The devil . . . without pause inspired me with heathenish thoughts about which I prefer to remain silent . . . in this deeply troubled state I lifted up my spirit . . . at last, after several firm assaults, my spirit broke through the gates of hell and into the innermost birth of the divinity, there to be embraced by love as a bridegroom embraces his beloved bride. As for my exultation of spirit, I cannot convey it in writing or speech.
>
> (Boehme [1612] 2013, pp. 549–551)[18]

In *Aurora*, Boehme set out to expound his speculations concerning the divine substance, *Salitter* (a term possibly based upon his observations concerning the refined and unrefined forms of nitre); the "qualities" of God as active principles in the world; the notion of a cosmos interpenetrated by seven source-spirits; and the existence of an angelic realm.[19] The striking septenary structure of his theosophical speculations integrates features taken from popular astrology with elements adapted from alchemical lore as part of a highly idiosyncratic attempt to articulate relations among the natural, human and divine worlds. However, it is in its treatment of the fundamental structures of "reality," as encoded in the principles of

---

for the sake of balance, it is also worth observing that as far back as 1835, Ferdinand Christian Bauer had described Hegel as a "modern" gnostic and remarked in this context upon his philosophical contiguity to his precursor, Jacob Boehme (Magee, 2014, p. 240). For a carefully nuanced explication of the term "gnosticism" as applied to Boehme's writings, see McCullough (2019, pp. 120–121, n. 8).

18 See Weeks (1991, pp. 35–60) for an exemplary account of the genesis of Boehme's theophanic vision.

19 Nicolescu (1991) has argued that "Boehme's seven qualities are the intermediate, active, informational energies which give shape to all the various levels of reality" (p. 28). For a more extensive account of this topic, see Weeks (1991, pp. 55–59).

spatiality, temporality and subject–object relations, that the revolutionary originality of *Aurora* is most in evidence:

> To the extent that *Aurora* already surmounts the limits of pictorialism, it does
> so by developing a visionary language. The correspondences which dissolve
> objects also restructure the representation of reality. . . . Eventually, spatial rela-
> tionships are contorted into graphically inconceivable spiritual equivalents, as
> when the prepositions, "*in* sich *aus* gehen," are combined in order to express a
> movement of spirit which unfolds outwards by going into itself. . . . The net effect
> of his usage is the integration of all facets of experience in a non-hierarchical
> vision of the world: a vision in which spatial, moral, and metaphysical precepts
> are related in a new and more complex manner. Angels are explained by the
> same design that accounts for metals or for wild flowers. The angelic and natural
> orders reveal that variety can flourish in harmony.
>
> (Weeks, 1991, p. 90)

In the *Three Principles of Divine Being* (1619), Boehme incorporated the septenary
"holographic" structures of *Aurora* into a complex Trinitarian framework consisting of the "dark world" of the Father, the "light world" of the Holy Spirit and a
"middle world" in which the principles of Christ and Satan are in conflict with
each other.[20] It is in the midst of the tensions existing across these three "worlds"
that human beings are enjoined to work out their salvation. However, while *Aurora*
focuses upon the macrocosmic realms of theogony and cosmogony, the *Three Principles of Divine Being* elaborates a corresponding microcosm that sets out a "cosmogony of will with its drives, emergent spirit, and growth . . . [to create] . . . a map
of the soul's ascent" (Goodrick-Clarke, 2008, p. 96).

In *De Signatura Rerum* (1622), Boehme expounded his theory of *signatures*
as the unfolding of the concealed inner life of all things in the context of a cosmic
process of divine panentheistic emanation into the created universe. It constituted
yet a further elaboration of a key insight of Boehme's, namely that spiritual truths
must be experienced directly and not merely via the reductive mediation of an
immanentising reason:

> All whatever is spoken, written, or taught of God, without the knowledge of
> the signature is dumb and void of understanding; for it proceeds only from an
> historical conjecture, from the mouth of another, wherein the spirit without

---

20

  Many of [Boehme's] writings are only superficially structured as treatises. They are more like
  great series of thematic cycles and epicycles, dominated by briefer expositions, each of which
  treats its topic by bringing the literary equivalents of emblematic symbols to bear upon it. Each
  part contains, or attempts to contain, the whole.

  (Weeks, 1991, p. 170)

knowledge is dumb, but if the spirit opens to him the signature, then he understands the speech of another.

(Boehme, cited in Versluis, 1999, p. 15)

While Weeks has put forward a carefully nuanced argument to support the contention that Boehme's visionary experiences should not be thought of as fundamentally separate from his other sources of creative inspiration, it remains nonetheless
difficult not to conclude that it was precisely these spiritual illuminations that constituted the central inspiration for all of his subsequent literary and spiritual activities (Weeks, 1991, p. 3):

> In this my earnest Christian seeking and desire . . . the gate was opened unto me,
> that in one quarter of an hour I saw and knew more than if I had been many years
> together at a university. . . . For I saw and knew the Being of all Beings, the
> Byss . . . and Abyss . . . also the birth or eternal generation of the holy Trinity;
> the descent, and original of the world, and of all creatures, through the divine
> wisdom: I knew and saw myself in all three worlds; namely, the divine, angeli-
> cal, and paradisical world and then the dark world . . . and then thirdly, the exter-
> nal and visible world. . . . Thus now I have written, not from the instruction of
> knowledge received from men, not from the learning or reading of books; but
> I have written out of my own book which was opened in me. I have no need of
> any other book.
>
> (Boehme, cited in Waterfield [ed.], 2001, pp. 63–66)

Boehme's theosophy manifests itself as a pre-eminently *visionary discipline*
founded upon a "psychology of the imagination," through which cures for the ill-
nesses of the psyche are to be sought through the appropriate "correction of the
imagination" (Versluis, 1999, p. 23). Consequently, his work emphasises the therapeutic value of "penetrating the astral," which he defines as a process of moving
beyond the personal imaginings, fantasies and emotional currents generated by the
"astral cloud," in order to facilitate the individual's entrance into a more profound
spiritual reality (Versluis, 1999, p. 25). Moreover, this movement into a "beyond"
simultaneously entails a "descent" into the *Ungrund* or "abyss":

> God is in himself the *Ungrund*, as the first world, about which no creature knows
> anything, for it [the creature] stands with its body and spirit in the ground alone:
> even God would therefore not be manifest [*offenbar*] to himself in the *Ungrund;*
> but His wisdom has from eternity become His ground [*Grund*], for which the eter-
> nal will of the *Ungrund* has lusted, from which the divine imagination has arisen.
>
> (Boehme, cited in Weeks, 1991, p. 149)

While attempts have been made to elicit parallels between the Behmenist *Ungrund*
and the Freudian *id*, such efforts have tended either to simplify or to simply ignore
the historio-conceptual terrain that has to be traversed before such comparisons

can legitimately be made.[21] Consequently, the ensuing sections of this chapter fore-ground the significance of Boehme's ideas for the development of German Roman-tic and classical philosophical depictions of the "nightside" of human nature, with particular emphasis upon their role as precursors to the drive-haunted unconscious postulated by Freudian psychoanalysis.

2.3 A Romantic interlude

It is outside my remit to provide an in-depth overview of the rich and complex range of philosophical, literary and artistic forms that converge under the rubric of *German Romanticism*.[22] However, some brief background to this term will none-theless be useful as a means for contextualising the role played by Romanticism as a conduit for esoteric traces in psychoanalysis.

The first thing to be remarked upon is the inherent difficulty in establishing a consensus regarding how a "movement" such as Romanticism, which was both complex and diffuse with regard to its antecedents, exemplars and successors, might be defined with any degree of precision. In this respect, M. H. Abrams' description of Romanticism as an "expository convenience" can at least be seen to possess the benefits of clarity and brevity.[23] Within the ambit of early German Romanticism, we encounter an amalgam of cultural milieus – both complementary and oppositional with regard to their effects – that included influences as diverse as Pietism, the Enlightenment, Weimar Classicism and *Sturm und Drang*. With regard to its broader context, the more oblique influence of several "revolutions" can be discerned, including those of the American and the French and the industrial revolution, as well as the epistemological "Copernican Revolution" inaugurated by the philosophy of Immanuel Kant (1724–1804). Although Romanticism has often been construed as having developed out of a critique of Enlightenment values, it constituted a critique whose capacities were nonetheless honed under the aegis of the critical ideals of the Enlightenment (Seyhan, 2009, pp. 2, 7–8). At its apogee, Romanticism "created an anthropology, a cosmology and a theology all rolled into one" (Vermorel & Vermorel, 1986, p. 16). Consequently, while it is important to remain cognisant of the categorical distinctions demarcating Romantic literature from German idealist philosophy, it is equally important to conceptualise their

---

21 See, for example, Pruett (1976–1977), in which intriguing (but ultimately tendentious) parallels are drawn between Freud's concepts of eros and thanatos and their purportedly Behmenist counterparts. See also Weeks (1991, p. 148) for a scholarly exposition of Boehme's use of the term *Ungrund*.

22 For helpful initial orientations to this field, see Beiser (2003) & Saul (ed.) (2009). See also Abrams (1971) for a classic exposition of the subject that focuses upon Romanticism as seen from a Euro-pean perspective.

23 For a critical review of this debate, see Kirschner (1996, pp. 153–156). In its essentials, Lovejoy's classic essay "On the Discrimination of Romanticisms" (1948) argued that the term was so complex and diffuse with respect to its proliferating meanings that its practical value was at best debatable and at worst negligible.

relations as constituting complementary facets of a greater interdependent whole.[24] Despite the disparaging intent of T. E. Hulme's *apercu* that Romanticism was merely "spilt religion," his remark nonetheless aptly encapsulates the role played by the "natural supernaturalism" of Romanticism as a cultural compromise formation mediating between the Christianity of the Medieval–Renaissance periods and the secular cultures of modernity, post-modernity and beyond (Eagleton, 2015, p. 53; Abrams, 1971, pp. 65–70). In many respects, the tensions that were to shape this trajectory were initially articulated by – and subsequently encoded within – the diffuse network of meanings that came to accrue around the competing conceptualisations that circulated around ideas concerning the *unconscious*:

> Many of these languages of the unconscious tend towards the overtly religious or metaphysical – at times the unconscious signals nothing less than the immanent and mysterious power of a divine creator, or of "nature" or the "absolute" which come to stand in for this in only partly secularised ways. But equally, and from early on in the [19th] century, the unconscious is used in a more limited and empirical way to indicate automatic functions such as reflexes . . . from the 1880s onwards there are the new psychiatric and psychological coinages emerging in the work of Pierre Janet, F. W. H. Myers and others, including the subconscious, the subliminal, and the dissociated aspects of the self.
>
> (ffytche, 2012, pp. 8–9)

While the precise nature of the significance of Romanticism for the development of psychoanalysis remains a topic for ongoing debate and reappraisal, the fact of its significance as a formative influence is indisputable.[25] Its pervasive influence can be observed to operate on multiple levels, ranging across those of culture and *habitus* mediated via the idiosyncrasies of individual reception. Moreover, it is evident from even the most cursory examination of Freud's writings that he drew extensively upon the work of Romantic authors and philosophers.[26] Furthermore,

---

24 "Like many Romantic ideas, animal magnetism was a theory of everything" (Bell, 2005, p. 173). For a helpful overview of the relations between Romantic literature and German idealist philosophy, see Eagleton (2015), chapters 2 and 3. See especially the following:

> in its reflections on the unfathomable depths of the subject, Idealism looks towards Romanticism, from which, once more, it can often be distinguished only by the slimmest of borders. There are plenty of occasions when the distinction has little force.
>
> (pp. 93–94)

However, as Eagleton goes on to observe, "Generally speaking, Romanticism is a darker, more troubled affair than Idealism, even if in another of its moods it shares its zest and buoyancy" (p. 96).

25 See Vermorel and Vermorel (1986) & Snell (2013). See also the numerous entries on Romanticism in Ellenberger (1994 [1970]). However, the multifarious historiographical genealogies conjoining Romanticism to psychoanalysis are sufficiently complex as to preclude their convergence under the rubric of a singular "tradition" – see ffytche (2012, p. 9).

26 See Vermorel and Vermorel (1986, p. 17). For an exposition concerning the relevance of Bourdieu's notion of *habitus* as applied to the growth of a specifically psychoanalytic *Bildung*, see Armstrong (2005, pp. 25–32).

there is ample evidence to suggest that Freud did not always explicitly acknowledge or investigate the historical context of those ideas that he subsequently appropriated for use in his own writings (Bettelheim, 1984, pp. 40–41; ffytche, 2012,
pp. 161, 236).

It is from within the ambit of this wider cultural milieu that we can begin to
assess the philosophical contributions made by F. W. J. von Schelling, G. W. F.
Hegel and Arthur Schopenhauer towards the formation of an esoterically inflected
psychoanalytic unconscious.[27] For instance, it is possible to discern in the quest for
a "mythology of reason," as originally proposed in "The Earliest System-Program
of German Idealism" (1797), the nascent beginnings of a psychoanalytic *mythos*
whose cultural ubiquity only came to prominence in the twentieth century and
beyond.[28] While the philosophical writings of Schelling and Hegel drew extensively upon a wide range of esoteric sources and ideas, both philosophers acknowledged in their writings a particular indebtedness to the work of Jacob Boehme
(ffytche, 2012; McGrath, 2012; Magee, 2001, 2008; Horn, 1997). Moreover, both
Hegel and Schelling were indebted to the ideas of Spinoza (1632–1677), with all
three philosophers adopting – to a greater or lesser degree – a de facto dual-aspect
monist ontology.[29]

2.4   Esoteric traces in the writings of F. W. J. Schelling, G. W. F. Hegel and Arthur Schopenhauer

According to Jon Mills, "Schelling was the first to offer a systematic and coherent
theory of the unconscious" (Mills, 2002, p. 45). Sean McGrath has elaborated on
Mill's observation, proposing that "Prototypes for three of the major models of
the unconscious in the twentieth century, the Freudian bio-personal unconscious,
the Jungian collective unconscious, and the Lacanian semiotic unconscious, can
be traced back to Schelling" (McGrath, 2012, p. 1). In the estimation of Gord

---

27 See, for example, ffytche (2012); McGrath (2012); Magee (2001); Mills (2002); Macdonald (2014);
Altman and Coe (2013, pp. 79–91); van Dongen et al. (2014, pp. 42–69).

28 The question of whether this fragment should be attributed to Hegel, Schelling or Hölderlin remains
a matter for scholarly debate. For a translation along with a scholarly exegesis of this "earliest system," see Krell (2005, pp. 16–44). See also Josephson-Storm (2017), pp. 63–67, where the author
contends that the "earliest system" constituted an articulation of the idea that "we have no mythology" (Schegel) – a claim which prefigured the idea of psychoanalysis as a "scientific mythology"
that aspired to become a "science" of mythology. See also Vermorel and Vermorel (1986, p. 26) and
Magee (2001, pp. 84–91).

29 See Atmanspacher and Rickles (2022, pp. 10–13). While the authors observe that the dynamics of
Hegel's "absolute" tacitly reintroduces "something like the Kantian transcendental realm of noumena," they also aver that

> dual-aspect monism offers the option, contrary to Kant, of direct, immanent experiences of the
> psychophysically neutral reality, which avoids the problem of access to a transcendental realm.
> If this reality is primordial enough, like an *Unus Mundus,* it may be aligned with the "absolute"
> and bring us back to Hegel.
>
> (Atmanspacher & Rickles, 2022, pp. 12–13)

Barentsen, "in Schelling's work, there are aspects of both psychoanalysis and analytical psychology, and as such, it sets in relief the theoretical break between Freud
and Jung" (Barentsen, 2020, p. 16). Behind such claims lies the tacit acknowledgement of the indirect contributions made by Boehme's ideas towards these developments.[30] While Freud referred to Schelling on only two occasions in his writings,
extensive parallels have nonetheless been adduced to exist between Schelling's
ideas and those of Freud (Fenichel, 2019).[31] It has been claimed, for example, that
"Freud connects Schelling with *both* occultism and 'clear-sighted' scientific explanation – thus occupying the same territory that Freud himself seeks to lay claim
to in his 'scientific' explanation of the dream work that follows" (Fenichel, 2019,
p. 17, n. 18). Yet, despite these aspirations towards a "scientific" dreamwork, we
nonetheless find lodged within the Freudian metapsychology the enigmatic signifiers of an uncanny, atavistic substrate, from within whose depths there can be
discerned the glimmers of a distinctly Schellingian metaphysics:

> Schubert's expression "the night-side of nature" (*die Nachtseit der Natur*) sums
> up the Schelling school's fascination with intuition, dreams, clairvoyance,
> hypnosis, and somnambulism – phenomena that not only give the lie to the
> self-mastery and self-possession of the Cartesian ego, but also indicate higher
> states of awareness in the unconscious.
>
> (McGrath, 2012, p. 17)

However, we also find that certain concepts whose provenance can be traced back
to Boehme's ideas about "drive" and "desire" were subsequently decoupled from
their theosophical contexts in order to facilitate their integration into an increasingly disenchanted intellectual milieu (McGrath, 2012; ffytche, 2012):

> In Luria, Boehme, Oetinger, and Saint-Martin, an alternative notion of person-
> ality takes shape, strikingly different from the model of representational con-
> sciousness emerging out of late Scholasticism, Descartes and Leibniz. On the
> theosophic view, personality is primarily the product of drive and desire rather
> than representation and knowledge. Both the middle Schelling and Hegel the-
> matize this model in modern philosophical terms, thereby freeing it from its
> visionary and Gnostic frames. Schopenhauer and von Hartmann in turn secu-
> larize the Boehemian-Schellingian will by disentangling it from its religious

---

30 See, for example, the following: "The historical claim of this book is that Jacob Boehme's
    alchemico-theosophical psychology, modified and given metaphysical grounding by Schelling, is
    the origin of the psychodynamic notion of the unconscious" (McGrath, 2012, pp. 1–2). For a useful
    compilation of Schelling's writings, see Berger and Whistler (eds.) (2021).

31 The two texts in which Schelling is explicitly referenced by Freud are chapter 1 of *The Interpreta-
    tion of Dreams* (1899) and his paper on "The Uncanny" (1919) – see Fenichel (2019, pp. 10, 17, n.
    18). Notably, Eduard von Hartmann's *Philosophy of the Unconscious* (1869) privileged Schelling,
    Hegel and Schopenhauer as "forerunners of the unconscious." Hartmann's text was well known both
    to Freud and to Jung – see Barentsen (2020, p. 80).

frame. In this disenchanted form, the psychodynamic unconscious becomes a catch-phrase for late nineteenth-century medical psychiatry.

(McGrath, 2012, p. 46)

For Schelling, the human personality is constitutively "split," thereby creating the need for a pluralistic conceptualisation of personhood entailing "a network of relations among alternative centers of cognition and desire" (McGrath, 2014b, p. 39). In the estimation of McGrath, "Schelling's notion of the unconscious originates in Western esoteric discourses" (McGrath, 2012, p. 21). This is due not only to Schelling's commitment to the idea of a "living nature," prominent as an integral feature of his early work, but also as a result of his long-standing interest in topics such as clairvoyance, theosophy and alchemy, as is evidenced throughout the middle period of his philosophical writings in particular. Moreover, while Schelling's later writings tended to be more critical of his earlier theosophical commitments, such speculations nonetheless tallied with his later evocations of a collective and symbolic unconscious entailing a doctrine of creation structured around a theory of correspondences.[32] Consequently, what we encounter is a version of "the unconscious that is not only beneath the ego but also beside and above it" (McGrath, 2014a, p. 44). In marked contrast to Fichte, and in terms more explicit than those employed by Hegel, Schelling assigned a spirit of subjectivity to nature in a manner that situated its activities within a wider ontological continuum that married its operations to the *microcosmos* of human subjectivity.[33] Consequently, we find his ideas described as "the key node through which Western esoteric notions of will and the spirit-matter relation are transmitted to nineteenth-century medicine and psychology" (McGrath, 2012, pp. 22–23). Schelling transformed the philosophical architecture of post-Kantian idealism by transposing its conceptualisations into a

---

32

Nature for Schelling, as for Isaac of Luria and Jacob Boehme, is a negation of infinity, a contraction (zimzum) of the divine being, which leaves the space, the meontic nothingness, in which something other than God can come to be.

McGrath (2012, p. 204)

See also Dongen et al. (2014, pp. 32 ff). For evidence of Schelling's more critical approach to Boehme's ideas in his later writings, see the following: "Daring mystics or theosophers – like Jakob Böhme – overcome immediate empirical certainties, but in so doing form, as it were, merely a drunken, self-enclosed, conceptless and senseless world" [*Lectures on the System of Positive Philosophy 1832/33*] cited in Berger and Whistler (eds.) (2021, p. 203).

33

Schelling's often fantastic, speculative theogony . . . begins as a Boehmian-inspired narrative of the birth of God from the unground. . . . For Schelling, a person is not one who stands logically in need of recognition by another, but one who is internally self-mediated and hence logically and morally free in their relations to the other.

(McGrath, 2021, p. viii)

McGrath coins the term "non-dialectical personalism" to differentiate Schelling's understanding of personhood from the "dialectic of recognition" proposed by Hegel (McGrath, 2021, p. viii).

realm of Gnostic and Neoplatonically configured cosmological speculation (see ffytche, 2012, pp. 111–112). To this end, he drew upon the writings of figures such as Ficino, Bruno, Proclus, Oetinger and Boehme (ffytche, 2012, pp. 111–112). Schelling first became acquainted with the ideas of Boehme as early as 1799, when Tieck introduced the latter's ideas to Schlegel's intellectual circle. By 1802, Schelling was actively seeking to obtain his own edition of Boehme's writings, although it was only in 1804 that he actually succeeded in doing so (Brown, 1977, pp. 114–116). By 1809, we find Schelling once again seeking to acquire an edition of Boehme's works, having given his previous copy to his friend, the theosopher Franz von Baader (ffytche, 2012, p. 150). Schelling subsequently went on to acquire a further edition of Boehme's writings (Magee, 2001, p. 80).

Six distinctive attributes have been highlighted as integral to Schelling's overarching philosophical project, the specific features of which can be briefly summarised as follows: Schelling posits that reality possesses an intelligible structure; he emphasises the philosophical significance of nature; he highlights the importance of an unconscious dimension to reality; he views the constituent elements of reality as parts of a greater whole; he construes works of art as possessing the potential to exhibit the full truth of reality; and finally, Schelling views reality not as a "substance" or a "thing," so much as a dynamic and a productive process (Berger & Whistler, 2021, pp. 7–8).[34] Schelling developed throughout the course of his philosophical itinerary a fourfold elaboration of the unconscious, beginning with the conjectured instantiation of a pansophic "lost science," the origins of which were purportedly to be found somewhere in the remote epochs of history. To these speculations, he wedded an essentially religious ontology that was indebted to the writings of German medieval mystics such as Meister Eckhart, from whom he took inspiration regarding the existence of a divine abyss (precursor to Boehme's *Ungrund*).[35] Schelling then set about creatively reformulating these attributes so as to simultaneously "ground the self *and* release it from the conceptual closure of the system" (ffytche, 2012, p. 153). Onto this conceptual edifice, Schelling further elaborated a theory of historical repression, which he developed as part of his wider

---

34 However, it is also important to keep in mind the following caveats:

> There is no one closely-knit system which we can call Schelling's system of philosophy . . . though there certainly are distinct phases in Schelling's thought, it would be a mistake to regard these phases as so many independent systems . . . the philosophy of Schelling is a philosophising rather than a finished system or succession of finished systems. In a sense the beginning and the end of his pilgrimage coincide.
>
> (Copleston, 1965a, pp. 125–126)

35

> In his fourth book [*Forty Questions of the Soul*], written in 1620, Boehme took up the term *Ungrund*, which was ordinarily used as a technical term for the status of an argument or proposition that lacked a prior justification or reason (*Grund*). Instead, Boehme used it to designate God as he is in himself. . . . Somewhat similar to the "divine nothingness" of German mysticism, Boehme's *Ungrund* is the primordial aspect of God.
>
> (Brown, 1977, p. 50)

theory of mythology. This account entailed a view of the divine as being active throughout the material world in a manner both hidden and mysterious. Schelling described this divine activity in alchemical-Behmenist terms as "the flash of light concealed in the hard stone" (ffytche, p. 162). During his middle period, Schelling also developed a distinctive teleological theory of libido founded upon the primacy of drive (*trieb*) and desire, the underlying features of which he took from Boehme with very little alteration, thereby effectively abandoning a Greek metaphysics of being (*ousia*) in order to move towards a Kabbalistically inspired metaphysics of life (McGrath, 2012, pp. 180–181). In the estimation of Naomi Fisher,

> Schelling endorses a three-fold absolute: a ground which is discursively external to the system of the world, an absolute essence which is manifested in each individual and can be accessed intuitively, and a *telos* which transcends and guides the development of the world.
>
> (Fisher, 2024, p. 43)

Schelling's *Clara* (1810) has been described as "an exercise of romantic psychotherapy" (Vater, 2023, p. 440). Moreover, it is arguably Schelling's most personal and revealing text when it comes to the depiction of themes of an explicitly mesmeric, clairvoyant and theosophical nature. It is also a work saturated by a profound experience of mourning and loss (Steinkamp [ed.], 2002).[36] Although *Clara* is both thematically and stylistically indebted to a dialectical philosophical tradition stretching back to Plato's *Phaedo,* its implied anthropology is imbued with an explicitly esoteric *Naturphilosophie*, many of the attributes of which he derived from the writings of Swedenborg, Boehme and von Baader, in which nature, human subjectivity and the *Geisterwelt* are viewed as ontologically contiguous and epistemologically permeable. While the human body is conceptualised in terms of its "externality," and the "spirit" is construed in terms of its "thinking" or "consciousness," these two aspects are conjoined by a tertium quid, namely "soul," which Schelling explicitly situates within the Paracelsian tradition of the "astral body," reconfigured so as to meet the requirements of a systematic philosophical exposition. As with Hegel and Schopenhauer, Schelling takes anomalous experiences seriously and makes explicit efforts to integrate them into his wider philosophical vision (Dongen et al., 2014, pp. 35–41). Notably, his depiction of the unconscious

> reflects not simply the attempt to produce an adequate account of the phenomena of interior life, but also a concern with establishing the possibility of a self-caused self, or a self the logic of whose development is irreducibly detached from more systematic forms of explanation.
>
> (ffytche, 2012, p. 23)

---

36 In Karl Jasper's view, it was the crisis induced by the death of his wife Caroline in 1809 that intensified Schelling's interest in theosophy – see ffytche (2012, p. 101).

Despite the philosophical differences that were to lead to the eventual dissolution of their friendship, Schelling's ideas were nonetheless of significance with regard to the development of Hegel's philosophical "system," with both parties sharing an interest in mesmerism and the writings of Jacob Boehme (Magee, 2001). It is to the contributions made by Hegelian thought towards the formation of a psychoanalytic unconscious that our attention shall now turn.

Despite the existence of vast libraries of Hegelian scholarship, a pronounced tendency either to underemphasise or even to dismiss the more explicitly esoteric dimensions present within Hegel's philosophy has been remarked upon.[37] Alongside the writings of Schelling, it is in the works of Hegel that we encounter a version of German idealism in which esoteric ideas are actively deployed in the creation and elaboration of a speculative metaphysics of the human subject. Such claims are not intended to support an erroneous, one-dimensional, "essentialist" reading of Hegel as a hermeticist. As O'Regan has remarked, "Whatever else one can expect of the conceptual object that is Hegelian thought, it is not likely to be available to simple, one-sided description" (O'Regan, 1994, p. 2). Such acts of hermeneutic reductionism and exclusion draw our attention to the extent to which processes of *exdenomination* have been covertly active within certain branches of Hegelian scholarship.[38] However, despite the existence of such tendencies, more recent studies have begun to focus upon the extent to which significant aspects of Hegel's philosophical *oeuvre* are indebted to various esoteric sources; while his most influential work, the *Phenomenology of Spirit* (1807), has been described as "a work of magic" and a "grimoire," the ultimate origins of which are to be found within the gnostic and hermetic traditions:[39]

Hegel was interested in and influenced by strands of thought associated with most, if not all, Hermetic thinkers, such as alchemy, Kabbalism, mesmerism,

37 Notable exceptions to this include Muratori (2016) and Findlay (1962). In the estimation of one commentator,

The non-metaphysical/anti-theological reading relies on ignoring or explaining away the many frankly metaphysical, cosmological, theological, and theosophical passages in Hegel's writings and lectures. Thus, the non-metaphysical reading is less an interpretation of Hegel than a revision. . . . The non-metaphysical reading is simply Hegel shorn of everything offensive to the modern, secular, liberal mind.

(Magee, 2001, p. 15)

For a useful selection of Hegel's writings, see Weiss (ed.) (1974).

38

Barth's notion of "exdomination" is equivalent to ideology where the emphasis is not so much upon ideology as a system of beliefs as ideology as an operation of repression or excision of alternate discursive items. Thus an ideology is just as much constituted by what is excluded as what is included.

(O'Regan, 1994, p. 373, n. 15)

39 See Magee (2001, p. 6). The claim that Hegel was explicitly a *part* of the Hermetic Tradition (rather than merely *influenced* by it) is derived from a polemic essay by Eric Voegelin titled "On Hegel: a study in sorcery" (1971). Voegelin's argument is indebted to Ferdinand Christian Bauer's proposal (originally made in 1835) that Jacob Boehme was a "modern" gnostic and that both Schelling and Hegel (as Boehme's intellectual heirs and epigones) were themselves crypto-gnostics.

extrasensory perception, spiritualism, dowsing, eschatology, *prisca theologia, philosophia perennis,* Lullism, Paracelcism, Joachimism, Rosicrucianism, Free-masonry, Eckhartean mysticism, and doctrines of occult "correspondences" and "cosmic sympathies" . . . Hegel's system . . . is hermetic in both form and content.

(Magee, 2001, pp. 255–257)

In addition to his immersion in and indebtedness to Hermeticism, Hegel has been acknowledged as a major philosophical precursor to psychoanalytical theory:[40]

Hegel anticipated many key psychoanalytic concepts including the unconscious operations of thought, imagination, fantasy, feelings, conflict, and the very conditions that inform psychopathology. He also recognized that the core of character and one's ethical convictions are preserved and emanate from unconscious processes and values internalized from the family and centrally connected with the community. He further recognised many elements of mental activity that are construed by psychoanalysis as defence mechanisms, including the splitting of the ego, fixation, regression, projection and projective identification, repression as significant "forgetting" that manifests itself as a compromise formation – "disease" – primary narcissism as "subjective universality," the primitive thinking and upheaval of the passions – what Freud called "primary process" – associated with derangement, and the notion of sublation as sublimation; not to mention one of the most important discoveries of all – that the *ego* is also unconscious.

(Mills, 2002, p. 191)

While Jon Mills has drawn our attention to the discursive network conjoining Hegel's usage of the terms *Abgrund* (abyss, chasm) and *Schacht* (shaft, pit, mine) to *bewußtlos* (unconscious), it is nonetheless worthwhile observing that, at the heart of this linguistic matrix, its Behmenist precursor and analogue *Ungrund* is made notable by its absence (Mills, 2002, pp. xiii–xiv, 50, 53; Muratori, 2016, pp. 195–198; Magee, 2001, pp. 36–50, 162–163). To some extent, this can be attributed to the fact that Hegel's understanding of *Ungrund* was mediated via a range of philosophical intermediaries that included Neoplatonism, Erigena, Fichte and Schelling (Mills, 2002, p. 16). Hegel's tacit avoidance of the Behmenist *Ungrund* is also the indirect consequence of a polemical dispute with Schelling concerning a perceived lack of dynamism in the latter's conceptualisation of the "Absolute," which Hegel interpreted as arising from Schelling's misguided adoption of the Behmenist conceptualisation in his essay, *On the Essence of Human Freedom* (1809), in which the formulation A=A is adopted as the expression of absolute identity (Muratori, 2016, p. 198). What is especially striking about the Hegelian phenomenology of *Geist* is the extent to which its *mundus imaginalis* is haunted by a preternatural

---

40 "We know . . . from the libraries of each, that both Freud and Jung read and carefully annotated Hegel's work" Hester McFarland Solomon, cited in Henderson (2014, p. 99).

phantasmagoria of gothic and daemonic imagery evocative of the "night-side" of Germanic *Naturphilosophie,* the obscurities of which prefigure the uncanny abyss of the psychoanalytic unconscious:

> The human being is this night, this empty nothing, that contains everything in its simplicity – an unending wealth of many presentations, images, of which none happens to occur to him – or which are not present. This night, the inner of nature, that exists here – pure self – in phantasmagorical presentations, is night all around it, here shoots a bloody head – there another white shape, suddenly here before it, and just so disappears. One catches sight of this night when one looks human beings in the eye – into a night that becomes awful, it suspends the night of the world here in an opposition. In this night being has returned.[41]

In the light of Hegel's explicitly stated and professionally sustained interest in animal magnetism (a nuanced critique of which came to inform his own very particular understanding of "mysticism"), it is possible to speculate that the above account might conceivably document one of his own experiments with the phenomenon of hypnagogia (Muratori, 2016, pp. 29–55, 87–200; Magee, 2001, pp. 215–218; Magee, 2008, pp. 28–31). However, in marked contrast to Schelling's conflation of Boehme's ideas with those of experimental animal magnetism, Hegel developed a more critical view of Boehme's "mysticism," which took his account of "mystical" phenomena on a divergent trajectory from that of the sixth (and final) state of *Hellsehen* ("clairvoyance") reported by percipients subject to the somnambulistic state. More specifically, Hegel sought to develop a *speculative* approach to mysticism characterised by an idea of dialectical progression, whose exemplars included Boehme in particular, as well as by exponents of the Neoplatonic tradition, and against whose teachings he unfavourably compared the purported pseudo-mysticism of the Romantics and the followers of Schelling.[42] In his *Fer-*

---

41 Cited in Magee (2001, pp. 85–86). The text itself is taken from Hegel's *Realphilosophie* manuscript of 1805–06. Cf. the following extract taken from C. G. Jung's *Red Book*:

> Where am I? Are there also cases of death in Hell for those who have never thought about death? I look at my bloodstained hands – as if I were a murderer. . . . Is it not the blood of my brother that sticks to my hands? The moon paints my shadow black on the white walls of the chamber. What am I doing here? Why this horrible drama? . . . But because I do not want to have it, my best becomes a horror to me. Because of that I myself become a horror, a horror to myself and to others, and a bad spirit of torment.
>
> (Jung, 2009, pp. 236–237)

42 The expert on animal magnetism and exponent of Boehme, Johann Karl Passavant, arrived at an opposing viewpoint and concluded that Boehme wrote his works in a state of magnetic *Hellsehen* (Muratori, 2016, p. 41). Despite such differences of opinion, there can be no doubt as to the serious nature of Hegel's engagement with Boehme's writings (especially from 1811 onwards), regarding which Muratori's book arguably constitutes the most comprehensive analysis published to date. Her differences with respect to Magee's analysis are helpfully summarised on p. 65, n. 274, and p. 69, n. 290. In its essentials, while Magee interprets Hegel's interests in Boehme and animal magnetism to constitute convergent signifiers of his esoteric interests, Muratori views them to be conceptually

menta Cognitionis (a text Hegel was deeply familiar with), the theosophist Franz von Baader provided the following pithy definition of animal magnetism – "magnetizing is no more nor less than imagining" (Muratori, 2016, p. 46).[43] In Hegel's estimation, this was precisely the crux of the problem. If the state of *Hellsehen* was susceptible to the vagaries of the imagination, then it constituted a dubious medium for the attainment of any kind of reliable understanding. Moreover, the magnetic state itself entailed a descent into more primitive states of mind, entailing regression and dissociation. The dynamics of this "descent" were of a piece with the prevalent view of *Naturphilosophie*, whereby nature and psyche were conceptualised as discrete polarities situated along a single continuum, whose traversal could potentially transcend the usual limitations of time and space (Magee, 2001, p. 220). While Hegel did not deny the therapeutic effectiveness of animal magnetism, he nonetheless thought it important to distinguish its value as a treatment for "hysteria" from more speculative claims that it could be utilised to access visionary states of consciousness (Muratori, 2016, pp. 68–70). In 1818, Hegel attended mesmeric and spiritualist séances with his friend Franz Joseph Schelver, in response to which he made some intriguing cross-cultural comparisons in his writings concerning mesmerism, "shamanism" and the use of hallucinogens to access what would now commonly be referred to as altered states of consciousness (Magee, 2008, p. 31).[44] Hegel goes so far in his speculations as to claim that it is precisely the ability of his philosophical "system" to give an account of "paranormal" phenomena that constitutes the proof for its veracity:

> Hegel's definition [of "magic"] comprises all those phenomena that we today term "occult" or "paranormal". A magical relationship is one which operates without mediation and which seems to cancel the limitations of time and space. Given this . . . magic is completely inexplicable to the understanding. It can only be comprehended by speculative philosophy . . . Hegel himself essentially argues that only his philosophy can make sense out of the evidence for paranormal phenomena. . . . In other words, animal magnetism constitutes empirical disconfirmation of the materialist model of the mind.
>
> (Magee, 2008, pp. 25, 35–36)

Notably, Magee concludes this paper by aligning his own reading of Hegel's theory of mind with that of the "filter" theory thesis elaborated by Edward F. Kelly and his collaborators in their book *Irreducible Mind* (2007). We will return briefly to

---

divergent, albeit of importance with regard to their significance for the formation of Hegel's own views concerning the nature of authentic mystical experience.

43 Notably, von Baader interpreted animal magnetism as a practice that naturally evolved out of the teachings of Boehme.

44 However, Hanegraaff (2025, p. 126) has expressed a preference for adopting the term "alterations of consciousness" in order to emphasise the idea of "consciousness as a *spectrum* that allows for subtle shifts and gradations."

the work of Kelly and his collaborators on the "filter" theory of mind in the final chapter of this book.

Moving on from Hegel, we shall now conclude this subsection with a brief account of the "weird metaphysics" of Schopenhauer and its significance in the formation of psychoanalysis (Cartwright, 2020). While Schopenhauer's metaphysics have often been treated as a historical curiosity, Bernardo Kastrup has argued that his findings "anticipate salient recent developments in analytic philosophy, circumvent the insoluble problems of mainstream physicalism and constitutive panpsychism, and provide an avenue for making sense of the ontological dilemmas of quantum mechanics" (Kastrup, 2020, p. 1).[45] Although the evaluation of such claims lies outside my current remit, Kastrup's contentions nonetheless serve to highlight the potential value of retrieving Schopenhauer's metaphysics as a historical resource to inform contemporary debates within psychoanalysis concerning questions of ontology and the nature of selfhood.

While certain "family resemblances" have been observed to exist between Schopenhauer's philosophy and the works of other great German idealists (Fichte, Schelling and Hegel), Schopenhauer characteristically tended to minimise the significance of these philosophers for the development of his own ideas, acknowledging only Plato, Kant and the *Upanishads* as the true sources for his inspiration (Copleston, 1965b; Nicholls, 1999). Although Schopenhauer's metaphysical vision has been described as constituting a form of "transcendental voluntaristic idealism,"[46] others have argued that his philosophy is not in fact "transcendental," at least insofar as this term is commonly understood within the Kantian system of thought (Gardner, 1999). While some commentators have discerned in Schopenhauer's metaphysics features of "an explicit dual-aspect theory" (Atmanspacher & Rickles, 2022, p. 14), others have argued that his philosophy is ultimately idealist in terms of its orientation (Kastrup, 2020, pp. 11–13). In contrast to his predecessor Kant, who considered the "thing-in-itself" to be inherently unknowable, Schopenhauer adopted a position in which the will is posited to be that in which the thing-in-itself has "to a great extent cast off its veils," although the precise formulation of Schopenhauer's evolving views on this topic remains as a topic for scholarly debate (Schopenhauer, cited in Cartwright, 2020, p. 181. See also Norman & Welchman, 2020, p. 62 and Cartwright, 2010, pp. 394–395).[47] Schopenhauer argues that the attributes of the will

---

45 In the estimation of McGilchrist (2021, p. 1060), "Schopenhauer was . . . a kind of panpsychist."

46

> It is idealism in the sense that the world is said to be our idea or presentation. It is voluntaristic in the sense that the concept of Will rather than that of Reason or Thought is made the key to reality. And it is transcendental in the sense that the one individual Will is an absolute Will which manifests itself in the multiple phenomena of experience.
>
> (Copleston, 1965b, p. 53)

47 Nicholls (1999) has identified three significant shifts in Schopenhauer's understanding of the "thing-in-itself," the primary impetus for which she argues he received from the growing influence of Eastern thought upon his thinking. In Nicholl's estimation, this resulted in a radical reconceptualisation of his understanding of this idea that extended its theoretical reach to include "other

can be discerned through the kaleidoscope of endogenous volitional and emotional states that each person commonly experiences, including feelings such as "terror, fear, hope, joy, desire, envy, grief, zeal, anger, or courage" (Schopenhauer, cited in Kastrup, 2020, p. 23).[48] However, in the estimation of Copleston, Schopenhauer also held that the "will" is not knowable "in itself, and . . . may have attributes which are unknown by us and indeed incomprehensible to us" (Copleston, 1965b, p. 40). The potential implications arising from this metaphysical lacuna have led one commentator to speculate that if Schopenhauer had lived long enough,

> he may well have embraced the view that the thing-in-itself is not will at all; rather it is the object of awareness of saints, mystics and those who have denied the will. The will, by contrast, is the esoteric but non-noumenal essence of the world.
>
> (Nicholls, 1999, p. 196)

Schopenhauer's superimposition of transcendence, immanence and descent into a metaphysics of "will" can be construed as a refiguration of the Neoplatonic dialectics of reversion and ascent cast into a German philosophical register, the perturbations arising from which can still be dimly discerned within the guise of the initiatory "gateway" to Freud's *The Interpretation of Dreams* (1899): "*Flectere si nequeo superos, acheronta movebo*" (Virgil, *Aeneid* [VII.312]).[49]

Schopenhauer's occult sympathies can be inferred from his likening human experience to "a cryptograph [*Geheimschrift*], and philosophy is the deciphering of it [*Entzifferung*], the correctness of which is confirmed by the connectedness that

---

aspects" that "are the objects of awareness of such persons as mystics, saints, and ascetics, who have denied the will" (p. 174). In this context, it is worth remarking on the parallels that might be adduced between German idealist controversies on the epistemological status of the "thing-in-itself" and late antique disputes between Plotinian and theurgic practitioners concerning the noetic accessibility of the "undescended soul" (Copleston, 1965b; Addey, 2019, pp. 147–157). We will revisit these conceptual resonances in Chapters 5 and 6.

48 In Kastrup's estimation,

> Schopenhauer's metaphysics . . . consists, essentially, of one universal consciousness. Schopenhauer calls it the "will" to (a) highlight the endogenous character of its original experiential states and (b) account for the dynamism of nature by attributing volitional impetus to these states.
>
> (Kastrup, 2020, p. 113)

Intriguingly, conceptual traces that appear to echo these debates can arguably be discerned within contemporary post-Bionian psychoanalysis. See, for example, the following commentary taken from a paper dealing with Bion's concept of *intuition*:

> We do not perceive the thing-in-itself of emotions, or emotions as things in themselves, but we "perceive" them in the form of their various hallucinatory derivatives – hallucinatory precisely because they do not correspond directly to the nature of emotions . . . so *intuition* refers to the derived or indirect visibility of the emotions, which are themselves affections of corporality.
>
> (Civitarese, 2024, p. 28)

49 "If I cannot bend the Higher Powers, I will move the Infernal Regions" (James Strachey's translation). See Shann (2023) for an exemplary exegesis of this epigraph and its relations to the wider Freudian project.

appears everywhere" (Schopenhauer [1844], cited in Cartwright, 2020, p. 179). It was this underlying "connectedness" of all things under the aegis of the "will" that constituted the *nexus metaphysicus* for the various manifestations of "magic" and the "occult" (Cartwright, 2010, p. 446). Yet, despite his "occult" proclivities, "Schopenhauer would tolerate neither a god-enchanted nor demon-haunted world" (Cartwright, 2010, p. 449).

Although Schopenhauer's rhetoric could at times be characteristically intemperate with regard to his criticisms of Schelling's philosophy, it is likely that the excesses of his critique were to some extent driven by the combination of a disavowed "anxiety of influence" coupled with a tacit awareness on Schopenhauer's part of the close conceptual proximities that otherwise underpinned their respective intellectual projects (Norman & Welchman, 2020). While both philosophers found a common source of inspiration in the writings of Boehme – whose ideas they creatively drew upon to inform their respective attempts to overcome the Kantian embargo against metaphysics – their philosophies nonetheless diverged when it came to their differing approaches to understanding the nature of "intellectual intuition" (Norman & Welchman, 2020). While Schopenhauer criticised Schelling's early philosophy for covertly transposing the subject–object distinction into the domain of the thing-in-itself (within whose *noumena* the ideas of temporality, spatiality and causality do not apply), he nonetheless struggled in his own attempts to articulate what might lie beyond the ambit of representational experience. In Schopenhauer's reformulation of this problem, the crux of Schelling's difficulty lay in his conceptualisation of "intellectual intuition" as entailing the existence of a modified *intellectual* capacity capable of directly accessing the noumenal realm. For Schopenhauer, the prioritising of the intellectual in this context is misguided and neglects the fundamental role played by *intuitive* cognition in the formation of concepts (Norman & Welchman, 2020; Cartwright, 2010, pp. 181–182, n. 5). It is from within the philosophical parameters provided by these debates that we can begin to discern the features of the nascent psychoanalytic unconscious penetrated by "traces" of a "higher" mode of intuitive cognition, the historical antecedents to which can arguably be found in the late antique phenomenon of gnosis.[50] Having briefly set out some of the salient features of Schopenhauer's metaphysical "occultism," we shall now consider the influence of Schopenhauer's thought upon Freudian psychoanalysis.

It has been observed that "many of the ideas that constitute the core of Freudianism were set out fully and clearly by Schopenhauer" (Magee, cited in Young & Brook, 1994, p. 103; Gardner, 1999). The extensive nature of these equivalences is such as to have led one commentator to describe Schopenhauer as "the true

---

50 For details of Freud's misgivings concerning the phenomenon of intuition, see Freud (1991 [1933], pp. 194–196). For helpful accounts of the post-Bionian revisioning of *intuition* as an integral clinical concept in psychoanalysis, see Civitarese (2024) and Sandler (2005, pp. 347–359). On the influence of Bergson and Whitehead's ideas upon Bion's approach to intuition, see Torres (2013a). For an exemplary overview of more recent research into intuition in both its empirical and philosophical aspects, see McGilchrist (2021, pp. 673–776).

philosophical father of psychoanalysis," while another has asserted that "no one should deal with psychoanalysis before having thoroughly studied Schopenhauer" (Gardner, 1999, p. 379; Foerster, cited in Ellenberger [1970], 1994, p. 542).[51] Freud's intellectual indebtedness to Schopenhauer is considerable, with the latter's influence being discernible upon a wide range of key ideas integral to Freudian metapsychology:[52]

> Schopenhauer's concept of the will contains the foundations of what in Freud became the concepts of the unconscious and the id. Schopenhauer's writings on madness anticipate Freud's theory of repression and his first theory of the aetiology of neurosis. Schopenhauer's work contains aspects of what became the theory of free association. And most importantly, Schopenhauer articulates major parts of the Freudian theory of sexuality.
>
> (Young & Brook, 1994, p. 101)

However, although Freud initially assigned the role of "forerunner" to Schopenhauer, claiming that his "unconscious 'will' is equivalent to the mental instincts of psycho-analysis," he subsequently came to view these parallels as being coincidental in nature, asserting they were "not to be traced to my [Freud's] acquaintance with his [Schopenhauer's] teaching," since he [Freud] "read Schopenhauer very late in life."[53] While Freud's motives for adopting this position are disputed, what is evident from Freud's correspondence with Lou Andreas-Salomé is that he read Schopenhauer for the first time in 1919 (Atzert, 2012; Bishop, 2020). Be that as it may, there are still grounds for supposing it was "Freud [who] became the true heir of Schopenhauer's philosophy of the will" (Atzert, 2020, p. 498). Atzert's contention could conceivably be extended to include within its ambit the "encryption" of an "occult" metaphysics located within an ostensibly "materialist" Freudian metapsychology.[54]

51 However, Gardner has also concluded that "Schopenhauer and Freud do not share a concept of the unconscious" (Gardner, 1999, p. 386). For helpful summaries of Freud's theoretical divergences from Schopenhauer, see Dean (2016) and Gardner (1999).

52 For a detailed explication of Schopenhauer's influence upon Freud's *Jokes and Their Relation to the Unconscious* (1905), *Beyond the Pleasure Principle* (1920) and *The Future of an Illusion* (1927), see Atzert (2012, pp. 321–331).

53 Freud, "A Difficulty in the Path of Psychoanalysis" (1916–17); "An Autobiographical Study" (1925), cited in Janaway (2010, pp. 142–143). Freud read Eduard von Hartmann's *Philosophy of the Unconscious* (1869), a work that is deeply influenced by the ideas of Schopenhauer (Copleston, 1965b, p. 57). Notably, Hartmann's account of the unconscious extends to a detailed historiographical investigation into the relations he believed to exist among the phenomena of mysticism, intellectual intuition, philosophical genius, instinct and the concept of the unconscious (Hartmann, 2010 [1868], v.1, pp. 362–365).

54 If we accept Kastrup's contention that Jung's metaphysical "system" is "particularly consistent with that of Arthur Schopenhauer" (Kastrup, 2021, pp. 7–8), then the conceptual reach of Schopenhauer's influence can be seen to extend across the ambit of the wider dynamic psychologies. See also Shamdasani (2003, pp. 173–174, 197–199) for an account of Schopenhauer's influence upon Jung.

While the question of Freud's indebtedness to his philosophical precursors is complex and multifaceted (Altman & Coe, 2013), it is nonetheless apparent there were occasions when he sought to obscure his indebtedness to his philosophical precursors by providing "revisionist readings . . . that seemed to annihilate all trace of influence," while simultaneously seeking to invoke "the authority of their faded signatures" (Grimwade, 2012, p. 143). Although it has been argued that Freud's reluctance to acknowledge the extent of his indebtedness to Schopenhauer was at least partially motivated by a desire to emphasise the originality of his own ideas (Atzert, 2012), it is also possible that this propensity may have been further exacerbated by a desire on Freud's part to obscure the implications arising from his reliance upon the ideas of a philosophical precursor who utilised "occult" phenomena as "evidence" to support his metaphysical speculations (Grimwade, 2012; Dongen et al., 2014).[55] In the uncompromising estimation of Schopenhauer:

> Whoever at the present time doubts the facts of animal magnetism and its clairvoyance should be called not a sceptic but an ignoramus . . . the phenomena we are discussing are . . . incomparably the most important of all the facts that are presented to us by the whole of experience. It is, therefore, the duty of every scholar and man of science to become thoroughly acquainted with them.
>
> (Schopenhauer [1851], cited in Dongen et al., 2014, p. 68)

In Chapter 3, we will examine in more detail the conflicts and ambivalences that typified Freud's engagement with such anomalous "facts." However, for my current purposes, it will be sufficient to conclude this subsection with a very brief overview of Schopenhauer's deployment of "occult" ideas as part of the evidential basis in support of his metaphysical world-view.[56]

Schopenhauer's investigations into the significance of anomalous phenomena as a form of "evidence" that could be utilised to support his "theoretical metaphysics" are explicitly explored in three of his writings, the details of which are as follows: a brief text titled "Suggestion of an Explanation of Animal Magnetism" (1815)

---

55 Despite the parallels which he adduces to exist between their respective dream theories, Grimwade notes the brevity of Freud's allusions to Schopenhauer's "Essay on Spirit Seeing" (1851), which the former references in *The Interpretation of Dreams* (1899). Grimwade uses this lacuna as the basis for embarking upon the following speculative commentary, which he concludes with a telling rhetorical question:

> If Freud had discussed Schopenhauer's "Essay on Spirit Seeing" in *The Interpretation of Dreams*, he would have been forced to confront a series of questions concerning the occult, which might have amounted to a lethal combination for a *Wissenschaft* in its infancy. Did Freud defer this discussion of Schopenhauer's dream theory because he was not ready to address the fact that psychoanalysis opened the door to questions far beyond the limited purview of late nineteenth-century positivism?
>
> (Grimwade, 2012, p. 365)

56 As supporting evidence of Schopenhauer's "occult" interests, it is worth remarking that his posthumous library is known to have contained more than a hundred books on "paranormal" phenomena (Cartwright, 2020, p. 187, n. 8).

that was published posthumously; a chapter titled "Animal magnetism and magic," which is to be found in his work *On Will in Nature* (1836); and in his "Essay on spirit-seeing and related issues" published in *Parerga and Paralipomena* (1851) (Segala, 2021, p. 5; Garcia-Alandete, 2025). The second of these three studies sets out a carefully constructed argument for construing the Schopenhauerian "will" to be the only metaphysical entity capable of both explaining anomalous phenomena and accounting for their various manifestations (Segala, 2021, pp. 4–8). These forms not only included animal magnetism, telepathy and magic but also extended to phenomena such as clairvoyance and even ghosts (although the latter "troubled . . . [Schopenhauer] metaphysically") (Cartwright, 2020, p. 184).

Notably, Schopenhauer claimed to have had some personal experience of the "occult," including precognition and the experience of apparitions (Cartwright, 2010, pp. 436–437). For Schopenhauer, "It is through the activity of the dream organ that intuition is possible in the phenomena of somnambulism, clairvoyance, second sight, and visions" (Garcia-Alandete, 2025, p. 26). While Schopenhauer possessed an acute awareness of the potential for fraudulent behaviour among "occult" practitioners, he was nonetheless impressed by the extensive cross-cultural history of "magic," the preternatural attributes of which led him to affirm the existence of a metaphysical form of causality that existed alongside physical causality (Garcia-Alandete, 2025, p. 14; Cartwright, 2020, pp. 176–177; Cartwright, 2010, p. 439). During the course of his research, Schopenhauer consulted a wide range of esoteric authors, including figures such as Jacob Boehme, Theophrastus Paracelsus, Johann Baptist van Helmont, Cornelius Agrippa von Nettlesheim, Jane Leade and Justinus Kerner (Cartwright, 2010, pp. 437, 449; Bishop, 2023, p. 32). Schopenhauer sought to utilise the findings from these researches to provide "evidence" for his metaphysics of the will.[57]

Although Schopenhauer and Freud both shared a deep interest in hypnosis, their respective approaches towards understanding the various aspects of this phenomenon were informed by differing currents active within the mesmeric, somnambulistic and hypnotic traditions. While Schopenhauer drew heavily upon the teachings of the Marquis de Puységur (1751–1825), his contacts with his teacher Dr Karl Christian Wolfart (1788–1832) and the ganglionic theory associated with the writings of Johann Christian Reil (1753–1813), Freud's understanding of the phenomenon of hypnotism was primarily indebted to the ideas of Jean-Martin Charcot (1825–1893) and Hippolyte Bernheim (1840–1919) (Garcia-Alandete, 2025; Mayer, 2013). While Schopenhauer conceived of "magic" and animal magnetism as being essentially synonymous with regard to their shared metaphysical substrate, Freud's understanding of trance states diverged from the metaphysical

---

57 With regards to the importance that should be attached to the differing historical contexts, it is worthwhile remembering Segala's caveat that

> Bergson's interest in hypnotism in the 1880s cannot be examined and assessed by the conceptual instruments we would use in the case of Kant's analysis of Swedenborg's magic one century before or Schopenhauer's chapter on magic in *On Will in Nature* in 1836.
>
> (Segala, 2021, p. 3)

extremes of the mesmeric and somnambulistic traditions, substituting in their place the medicalised model of hypnosis developed by James Braid (1795–1860) (Garcia-Alandete, 2025; Crabtree, 1993). However, in order to gain a better understanding of how these ostensibly divergent trajectories came to be both sublated and encrypted within the conceptual ambit of psychoanalytic theory, it will be helpful to set out a brief historical itinerary charting the esoteric currents that existed within the mesmeric, somnambulistic and hypnotic traditions, which were to contribute to the formation of an occluded "psychoanalytic parapsychology."

2.5   From magnetic gnosis to hypnotic trance

It was Freud himself who emphasised the importance of hypnotism in the formation of psychoanalysis.[58] Yet it has also been remarked that hypnotism is itself "an enigma, a phenomenon without a theory" (Borch-Jacobsen, 2005, p. 5). Nor are its historical antecedents, as embodied in the shifting manifestations of mesmerism, animal magnetism, artificial somnambulism and magnetic gnosis, any less mysterious. Indeed, they may arguably be more so, particularly if we accept that the practices associated with the induction of somnambulistic trance states were more complex and varied than is usually supposed.[59] While standard psychoanalytic historiographies have tended to present the arrival of Freudian psychoanalysis as instantiating a radical break from earlier approaches to the unconscious, a cogent case can nonetheless be made for concluding that "it cannot be plausibly maintained that hypnosis was ultimately superseded by psychoanalysis" (Meyer, 2013, p. 225).[60] In this regard, it is telling that McGrath has remarked how:

"The first magnetizers were immensely struck by the fact that, when they induced magnetic sleep in a person, a new life manifested itself of which the subject was unaware, and that a new and often more brilliant personality emerged with a continuous life of its own" [Ellenberger, 1994/1970, p. 145]. The second personality, showing itself in dreams and under hypnosis, seemed to compete with the first. Some anticipating Freud, argued that the second self was closed, containing only memories, representations that were once conscious. Others, anticipating Jung, held it to be open, in communication with other selves, with other levels of reality, with the inner life of nature, even with the souls of the departed.

(McGrath, 2015, p. 57)

58

It is not easy to overestimate the importance of the part played by hypnotism in the history of the origin of psychoanalysis. From a theoretical as well as from a therapeutic point of view, psychoanalysis has at its command a legacy which it has inherited from hypnotism.

(Freud, 1993 [1923], p. 163)

59   As evidence for this, see, for example, the passage from Emma Hardinge Britten's *Ghost Land* (1876) cited by Hanegraaff in "Magnetic Gnosis" (2010; p. 123), where the induction of trance states is attributed to various methods, including drugs, spells, crystal gazing, music and dancing.

60   For a trenchant critique of the excesses of the Freudian "hagiography," see Borch-Jacobson and Shamdasani (2012).

It is unnecessary in the present context to set out a comprehensive history of the mesmeric "currents" or "traditions" that preceded psychoanalysis. Each of the diverse cultural movements thereby denoted is sufficiently complex when considered individually as to require a lengthy monograph in its own right.[61] Even so, a brief overview of the wider historical context within which they can be located will be useful as a means for mapping out the itinerary through which the various forms of esoteric mesmerism were gradually transformed into a medicalised hypnosis, and from there, into a nascent psychoanalysis.

Animal magnetism was the most widely known and influential form of therapy available to the practitioners of Romantic medicine. Its origins lay in the work of Franz Anton Mesmer (1734–1815), who from 1774 onwards developed his eponymous theory of animal magnetism, in which "magnetic passes" were therapeutically utilised under the aegis of a highly speculative cosmological fluid theory. Although Mesmer viewed himself as a mechanist and a materialist, his laudatory allusions to Enlightenment savants such as Newton ("the last of the magicians" according to the economist John Maynard Keynes) and Descartes (a one-time aspiring Rosicrucian adept, some of whose philosophical insights came to him in the form of dreams) were nonetheless underwritten by hermetic theories of magical healing, the teachings of which he originally encountered in the writings of figures such as Paracelsus, Athanasius Kircher, Robert Fludd and Johannes Baptista van Helmont.[62] Mesmer's account of his experiences leading up to the founding of his own school of therapeutics reads like an amalgam of Ellenberger's concept of "creative illness" intensified by the more ecstatic elements of a visionary theosophy:

A devouring fire filled my entire soul. I was searching for the truth no longer full of tender devotion – I was searching for it full of extremest unrest. Only field, woods and the most remote wildernesses still appealed to me . . . I must really have resembled a madman. All other occupations became hateful to me . . . I regretted the time that I needed to give expression to my thoughts. I found that we are used to clothing each thought immediately, without long reflection, in the language best known to us: and so I made the strange decision to free myself from this slavery. . . . For three months I thought without words.

When I ended this deep thinking, I looked round in amazement. My senses no longer betrayed me as before. All things looked different to me. . . . Gradually

61 The standard histories are Gauld (1992) and Crabtree (1993). Ellenberger (1994 [1970]) provides an extensive account of the mesmeric prehistory of the depth psychologies. See also Charet (1993, pp. 27–58) and Barkhoff (2009). For esoteric perspectives on the history of the mesmeric traditions, see Hanegraaff (2010, pp. 118–134), (2012a, pp. 260–277) and Méheust (2006, pp. 75–82). All of these sources have been extensively utilised throughout the following pages.

62 Mesmer's propensity to self-interpret his teachings as a form of "materialism" despite their imbrication with esoteric modes of thinking arguably bears comparison with similarly problematic readings of Freudian psychoanalysis as being unambiguously "materialist" with regard to its metaphysical orientation.

peace returned to my soul, for now it was wholly convinced that the truth I had been pursuing so vehemently really existed. . . . Now a long and difficult journey through the realm of other people's experiences lay ahead of me.[63]

As might be inferred from the words of Mesmer just cited, it would appear that even a self-designated "mechanist" and "materialist" could, on occasion, embody a predisposition towards "an ecstatic state beyond rational discourse" (Hanegraaff, 2012a, p. 261). After experiencing some initial success in the treatment of patients by using actual magnets, Mesmer had discovered by 1774 that he was able to bring about cures in their absence. Consequently, he speculated that these curative properties did not originate in the magnets themselves but were attributable to the "animal magnetism" issuing from the person of the magnetiser. With regard to their essentials, Mesmer's teachings can be distilled into four basic principles: that there exists a subtle fluid filling the universe, which forms a connecting medium among humanity, the earth and the celestial bodies; that illness is caused by the unequal distribution of this mysterious fluid in the human body, while health is restored once its equilibrium has been restored; that certain techniques can be utilised to convey this fluid to other people; and that "magnetic crises" can be invoked in others as a means for restoring them to health. However, the holistic conception of "animal magnetism" was underpinned by a complex matrix of psychological, anthropological and cosmological theories entailing an intricate web of correspondences hypothesised to conjoin humankind to the universe, the therapeutic techniques practiced by the magnetiser, the phenomenon of magnetic somnambulism (the specific attributes of which are described further below) and the various cultural currents that were set in motion by Mesmer's activities (Méheust, 2006, p. 76).

In 1784, the Marquis de Puységur induced a somnambulist trance (subsequently described as *artificial somnambulism* to distinguish its more dreamlike qualities from the therapeutic "crises" associated with mesmerism) in one of his subjects that reportedly produced a series of "paranormal" phenomena analogous to those that were subsequently to be described under terms such as telepathy and clairvoyance.[64] Further experiments involving other participants duplicated many of these original findings. Although Mesmer did not refer to any personal experiences of the

---

63 Mesmer, cited in Hanegraaff (2012a), p. 260. On the role of "creative illness" in the founding of dynamic psychiatry, see Ellenberger (1994 [1970]):

> A creative illness succeeds a period of intense preoccupation with an idea and search for a certain truth. It is a polymorphous condition that can take the shape of depression, neurosis, psychosomatic ailments, or even psychosis. . . . The termination is often rapid and marked by a phase of exhilaration. The subject emerges from his ordeal with a permanent transformation in his personality and the conviction that he has discovered a great truth or a new spiritual world.
>
> (pp. 447–448)

64 See the Marquis de Puységur's *Memoirs to Serve the History and Establishment of Animal Magnetism* (Crabtree & Osei-Bonsu [eds. & trans.], 2025). For a helpful account of the socio-historical dynamics that contributed to the shift from mesmerism to somnambulism, and then to hypnotism, see Ellenberger (1965).

"paranormal" in his own writings, there has been speculation that he may nonetheless have encountered such phenomena during the course of his therapeutic practice, which he neglected to aver to due to his materialist commitments (Méheust, 2006, p. 77). Although animal magnetism subsequently fell into disrepute at an institutional level (largely in response to a series of highly disputed inquiries, the most significant of which took place in France between 1826 and 1842), it nonetheless continued to flourish across the wider cultural milieu.[65] By 1843, the progressive "psychologization" of mesmerism was exemplified through the introduction of the term "hypnosis" by the Scottish doctor James Braid (1795–1860) to denote a therapeutic practice inspired by animal magnetism, albeit one more modestly reformulated so as to fit the requirements of orthodox medical practice. Notably, although Braid remained non-committal with regard to the anomalous effects that were historically associated with animal magnetism, he did not unequivocally reject the possibility that such phenomena could actually occur, as has often been assumed (Méheust, 2006).

Following its re-theorisation under the rubric of "hypnotism," a diminished range of trance phenomena was once again readmitted into the hallowed portals of official French medicine under the auspices of the famous Jean-Martin Charcot (1825–1893). As a consequence of Charcot's patronage, hypnosis rose rapidly to prominence as a technique for investigating hysteria in particular and as a tool of depth psychology more generally. Towards the end of the nineteenth century, animal magnetism underwent a resurgence in academia, albeit one now coloured by the prevailing assumptions of the ascendant materialist paradigm of the period. Along with this resurgence, there arose a series of comparative research programmes that were pursued in England under the rubric of "psychical research" and in France as *métapsychique*.[66] Yet, despite this reframing of somnambulistic phenomena under a more scientifically acceptable nomenclature, we find in 1886 the young Pierre Janet (1859–1947) delivering a report to the Parisian Société de Psychologie Physiologique recounting a series of experiments in which a woman referred to as Léonie B was placed into a somnambulistic trance by means, so it seemed, of mental suggestion alone (Ellenberger, 1993, p. 247).[67] Although the phenomenon of "provoked somnambulism at a distance" was well known to the early magnetists, it nonetheless presented itself as something extraordinary to the assembled members of the society. While Janet was careful to maintain a neutral tone throughout the course of his exposition, it is a matter of record that cases of

---

65 Notably, the sexual component to the "magnetic crisis" was emphasised in a secret report on animal magnetism made by J. S. Bailly to Louis XVI in 1784. See De Saussure (1943) for more on this.

66 "Metapsychists used séances in their attempt to develop a new science of the mind, which they hoped would be incorporated into the scientific corpus" (Lachapelle, 2011, p. 6).

67

Although these experiments . . . [with Léonie] gave Janet instant fame, he soon realised that many reports of his work were inaccurate. He became suspicious of parapsychological research, preferring instead to pursue systematic investigation of the phenomena of hysteria, hypnosis and suggestion.

(van der Hart & Friedman, 2019, p. 6)

a similar nature were reported by a wide range of credible investigators, including Charles Richet, Henri Beaunis and Jules Hericourt (Brower, 2010, pp. 27–28).[68] However, important figures such as Wilhelm Wundt (1832–1920) considered the purportedly excessive attention given to trance phenomena by the nascent discipline of psychology to be antithetical to its development as a science (von Stuckrad, 2022, pp. 18–19). By the time we arrive at the annual review of French thought published in the *Philosophical Review* (1922–1923), a marked divergence of opinion on such matters is emphasised as a means for distinguishing the views of the educated professional from those of the public at large:

> a strong movement . . . manifest among psychologists and psychiatrists, against all that concerns hypnosis, "secondary personalities," intelligent psychological automatism, one could almost say against all that deviates from the mental functions recognised for centuries by commonsense. To this is doubtless due the persistent lack of success of Freudianism in our country. *On the contrary,* on the part of the public at large, in the broadest sense of the term, there is to be noted a very lively success by all that touches on the marvellous, in philosophy or in psychology: occultism, telepathy, spiritism, theosophy.
>
> (Lalande, cited in Brower, 2010, p. 139)

It is important to bear in mind that the various magnetic movements that developed across France, Germany, Britain and America throughout this period contained many – occasionally conflicting – schools of thought and practice. Nevertheless, stripped to their essentials, this proliferation of approaches can broadly be grouped under three categories, the respective teachings of which can be briefly outlined as follows. Firstly, there was the "materialist" school of mesmerism, as exemplified by the founding figure of Mesmer himself. A second "school" consisted of the disciples of Puységur and Deleuze, otherwise known as the *psycho-fluidists.* Despite its spiritualist proclivities, this "school" maintained that while artificial somnambulism disclosed the existence of a "hidden self," such knowledge did not extend to providing proof for the existence of discarnate "entities" external to human consciousness. A third category – which itself devolved into a series of subcategories – operated under a range of rubrics which have come, in more recent times, to be referred to by terms such as "esoteric magnetism" (Méheust) and "magnetic gnosis" (Hanegraaff), thereby highlighting their "mystical" attributes. The study and practice of "esoteric magnetism" had its nucleus in the city of Lyon (at one time the reputed esoteric capital of France). Its adepts tended to mix ideas of progress with those of eschatology, alchemy and Kabbalah in ways that were in many respects highly subversive to notions of a unilinear historical progressivism. Some practitioners, such as the Chevalier de Barberin, did not subscribe to the idea of

---

68 Notably, Janet later compared the role of Freudian psychoanalysis with that of animal magnetism; see Brower (2010, p. 139).

entities external to human consciousness, choosing to interpret the efficacy of their activities as being dependent upon a combination of willpower and prayer. Others, such as Jeanne Rochette, purportedly contacted "angelic entities" while in a state of somnambulistic trance (Méheust, 2006, p. 79).

However, it was in Germany that esoteric magnetism was to achieve its apotheosis. Building upon the pre-romantic theologies of light and electricity developed as early as 1765 by figures such as Prokop Diviš, Friedrich Christoph Oetinger and Johann Ludwig Fricker, magnetism was frequently adopted by many of the proponents of *Naturphilosophie* as the means by which the somnambulist could be put into a state of rapport with the totality of nature and its contiguous transcendental realms.[69] Noted theorists included Gotthilf Heinrich von Schubert (1780–1860), author of *Views from the Night Side of Natural Science* (1808) and *The Symbolism of Dreams* (1814).[70] Somnambulistic researchers sought to identify an underlying physiological mechanism responsible for the trance state, which they located in a hypothesised opposition between the cerebro-spinal system (believed to be the organ of wakeful rationality purportedly predominant in men) and the ganglion system (associated with the feminine and the realm of the nocturnal). The particular form that mesmerism took in German Romanticism was based almost entirely upon this latter theory, which was originally proposed by the physician Johann Christian Reil prior to its appearance in an influential textbook on animal magnetism published by Carl Alexander Ferdinand Kluge in 1811 (Bell, 2005, pp. 167–170, 176). This theory proposed the existence of two separate, but complementary, nervous systems referred to as the "cerebral system" (brain and spinal marrow) and the "ganglion system" (centred round the solar plexus), which together constituted the organic basis for the conscious and unconscious dimensions of the soul:

> According to Reil, two antagonistic nervous systems are simultaneously at work in our body. The cerebral system with the brain as its centre dominates during our waking hours, clearly differentiating between individual senses, coordinating perception and guaranteeing overall rational control. During sleep and related

---

69 *Naturphilosophie* became prominent as a philosophical outlook from around the end of the eighteenth century to the middle of the nineteenth century. It has been described as a form of "sacred physics," and its exemplars included figures such as F. W. J. Schelling, Franz von Baader, Carl August von Eschenmayer, Joseph Ennemoser, Gustav Theodor Fechner and Justinus Kerner. Most *Naturphilosophen* tended to share three common beliefs: that nature possesses a history of a mythical order, that spirit and nature are ultimately identical and that nature as a whole is made up of a web of living correspondences that can be deciphered and integrated into a holistic world-view (Faivre, 2006, pp. 822–826). In Fenichel's estimation, "Freud inherited, directly and indirectly, fundamental aspects of Schelling's *Naturphilosophie*, particularly his articulation of unconscious drives" (Fenichel, 2019, p. 13). For an account of both Freud and Jung's indebtedness to Schelling's *Naturphilosophie*, see Barentsen (2020, pp. 41–77).

70 This latter text was cited by Freud in the bibliography for *The Interpretation of Dreams* (1899). Schubert was a Christian theosopher (in the lineage of Jacob Boehme) and an exponent of *Naturphilosophie*, whose work has been described as "a precursor of psychoanalysis" (Valette, 2006, p. 1043).

states like the magnetic trance, however, the other, so-called ganglionic system with the solar plexus as its centre takes over, subdues the individual senses and mobilises a synthetic sixth sense, not controlled by reason, but led by intuition and seen as particularly receptive to the overall harmony of the world soul.

(Barkhoff, 2009, p. 215)

This guiding concept was widely adopted by a range of writers and philosophers including G. W. F. Hegel, Gotthilf Heinrich von Schubert and Justinus Kerner, each of whom accepted on the basis of this theory that it was possible for the percipient, via the ganglion system, to have access to the mysterious "nightside" of nature. However, it was only while subject to the artificial state of somnambulistic sleep that the percipient could access the full potential of this "nightside" state of consciousness. Notably, many contemporary observers left accounts of somnambulistic subjects reportedly displaying a wide range of "anomalous" phenomena, including action at a distance, precognition, clairvoyance, the perception of spirits and angelic beings, speaking and writing in archaic and unknown languages and mystical visions of divine realities (Hanegraaff, 2012a, pp. 261–262). It was from within this context that "somnambulism and somnambules became a strange theological tool, a means of investigating extraterrestrial worlds, a machine for answering metaphysical questions" (Hanegraaff, 2010, p. 120).

Arguably, the most influential Germanic exemplar of esoteric magnetism was the Swabian somnambulist Friederike Hauffe (1801–1829), whose story was immortalised by her biographer, the physician and poet Justinus Kerner (1786–1862), in his book, *The Seeress of Prevorst* (1829).[71]

Living in a semi-permanent state of somnambulistic trance, Hauffe presented the whole gamut of magnetic endowments: the gifts of second sight and precognition, predicting deaths, revealing maladies, prescribing remedies, and being extremely sensitive to certain substances. She even saw spirits of the dead and maintained a semi-permanent communication with them.

(Méheust, 2006, p. 80)[72]

---

71 Kerner (2011 [1829]). For additional background, see Hanegraaff (2001). For a helpful overview of Kerner's life and work, see also Hanegraaff (2006c). In Hanegraaff's estimation,

> There can be little doubt . . . about the status of *Die Seherin von Prevorst* as almost certainly the most highly developed representative of a specific perspective on superior or even absolute knowledge that emerged in the context of German Romantic mesmerism in the first half of the 19th century . . . to which I have been referring as magnetic gnosis.
>
> (Hanegraaff, 2010, p. 132)

72 As Gauld has observed:

> Whether or not one believes in such phenomena, there is no escaping the fact that they were, and for upwards of fifty years remained, a central feature of the animal magnetic scene. Nor did they by any means wholly disappear with the advent of hypnotism.
>
> (Gauld, 1992, p. 62)

Kerner's book was not only in its day a prodigious literary success, but it was also "the first monograph devoted to an individual patient in the field of dynamic psychiatry" (Ellenberger, 1994 [1970], p. 81). Yet, for Schopenhauer, the true value of Kerner's work lay in his compilation of "the most detailed and authentic reports on spirit seeing that have appeared in print" (Schopenhauer, cited in Cartwright, 2010, p. 437). With reference to Kripal's hypothesis that trauma may have the potential to act as the catalyst for inducing transcendent alterations in consciousness (Kripal, 2024, p. 226), it is worth observing that there is evidence to suggest that Hauffe may have been the victim of childhood sexual abuse (Hanegraaff, 2001).

Kerner himself had a keen interest in the occult and was the first person to make a systematic attempt to investigate Mesmer's life. In his medical practice, Kerner reportedly encountered cases of what he construed to be possession, which he categorised under the hybrid typology of "demonic-magnetic disease," and for the treatment of which he proposed a therapy consisting of a peculiar combination of exorcism and magnetism (Crabtree, 1993, pp. 201–202).

Kerner conceptualised magnetic somnambulism as existing on a continuum ranging from the occluded and barely perceptible to transcendental states of *magnetic gnosis* whose nature he elucidated in the following quasi-visionary terms:

> In the clearest and highest magnetic condition, there is neither seeing, hearing, nor feeling; they are superseded by something more than all three together – an unerring perception, and the truest penetration into our own life and nature.
>
> (Kerner, 2011 [1829], p. 25)

As might be expected, Kerner adhered to the ganglionic theory of somnambulism and cited Jacob Boehme as one of the sources of inspiration for his own insights (Kerner, 2011 [1829], pp. 4, 26). Kerner argued against a traditional religious supernaturalism insofar as he viewed somnambulism to be a part of *Naturphilosophie* and as therefore constituting a phenomenon that was not inherently "supernatural." On the other hand, he also emphasised that the "occult" powers of nature could not be grasped via a reductive form of rationalism (Hanegraaff, 2006c, p. 660). In Ellenberger's estimation, "In spite of their shortcomings, Kerner's investigations of the seeress were a milestone in the history of dynamic psychiatry" (Ellenberger, 1994 [1970], p. 79). Kerner himself has received recognition as a pioneer through his emphasis on the therapeutic importance of empathy, while his work on the *Kleksographien* in the 1850s prefigures – and may indeed have influenced – Rorschach's psychological "inkblot" tests (1921) (Hanegraaff, 2001, p. 233; Hanegraaff, 2006c, p. 661). At the same time, his work has also been cited as one of the earliest attempts to undertake an empirical investigation into the paranormal via his book-length account of a case of "magnetic illness" acting as the catalyst for an experience of spiritual "realities" (Hanegraaff, 2006c).

Hauffe's case aroused enormous interest throughout Germany, and she was visited by a range of esoteric and philosophical luminaries such as Baader, Schelling and von Schubert, as well as by theologians such as David Strauss and Friedrich

Schleiermacher, all of whom took her revelations quite seriously (Hanegraaff, 2006c). In the estimation of Hanegraaff, "Without for a moment denying the critical and hermeneutical issues involved, we can safely assume that those who were present at Friederike Hauffe's sickbed did indeed witness strange and unusual things happening on a regular basis" (Hanegraaff, 2001, p. 216). Consequently, it is perhaps not so surprising to find that Kerner's writings have been described as "the ultimate in the spiritistic magnetic tradition" (Crabtree, 1993, p. 202). Kerner's work also exemplifies Asprem's claims concerning the seminal role played by the "philosophy of the unconscious" as a matrix for the "epistemological concerns in German *Naturphilosophie*, psychological research, and the practices of occultists and spiritualists" (Asprem, 2014b, p. 442).[73] Méheust has correctly emphasised that

> For mainstream Western culture, animal magnetism was a shock and a challenge, whose magnitude and effects are too often forgotten today. . . . While the phenomena of somnambulism have never been completely objectified or explained in a satisfying manner, they have certainly stimulated and/or disquieted all aspects of culture. Psychiatry, psychoanalysis, the psychology of altered states of consciousness, philosophy, the history of religion, ethnology, art, literature, and theories of education – all have been affected by this current and still bear its mark.
>
> (Méheust, 2006, p. 81)

It is from within the reverberations arising out of this wider cultural amnesia that psychoanalysis has persisted in its struggle to come to terms with the implications arising from its coincident indebtedness to and disavowal of these earlier mesmeric traditions. As Freud observed in 1888 in a review addressing the work of the Austrian neuroanatomist Heinrich Obersteiner,

> If we accept that a magnet is made to work by the influence of a state of a person then it is not weird to suppose that this person can influence another person, like a magnetised iron rod passes over its influence to another one. This analogy does not reduce the miraculous nature of the fact that a nervous system is able to influence another nervous system through as yet unknown sensory organs. We must admit that proving this idea will contribute something new, as yet unknown to our world-view, and will subvert the so-called borders of the personality.
>
> (cited in Gyimesi, 2016a, p. 51)

73 Notably, it was a copy of Kerner's *The Seeress of Prevorst* that C.G. Jung chose to present to his mediumistic subject – and cousin – Hélèn Preiswerk for her fifteenth birthday in March 1896 (Bair, 2004, p. 50).

Much as in Freud's own dealings with telepathy (discussed in the next chapter), psychoanalysis has similarly been "set on swallowing *and* simultaneously rejecting the foreign body named Telepathy [or animal magnetism, or somnambulism], for assimilating it and vomiting it without being able to make up its mind to do one or the other" (Derrida, 1988, p. 38).[74] It is worthwhile considering at this point to what extent Freud's decision to nominate free association as the exemplary psychoanalytic technique could be attributed to his deficits as a hypnotist. Hence, we find that the instantiation of the free association technique in psychoanalysis simultaneously marked its divergence from the work of figures such as Frederic Myers, who actively utilised trance states to provide "the springboard for diving into the deepest states of the (transformational) unconscious" (Parsons, 2021, p. 212). As we shall see, while the impact of the early mesmeric traditions was initially *encrypted* within psychoanalysis under the guise of hypnosis, the transference and the use of the couch, the ensuing transformation of these conceptual *hieroglyphs* under the aegis of the Hungarian and post-Bionian schools of psychoanalysis entailed a de facto re-instantiation and refiguration of these earlier mesmeric "traditions" translated into a psychoanalytic register.

---

74 The interpolated references to animal magnetism and somnambulism have been added by me to Derrida's quote on telepathy in order to further extend the reach of his original argument.

Chapter 3

Before and After Science

3.1 Introduction

Freudian psychoanalysis can be situated within an extensive "pre-history," whose *longue durée* traverses a diverse range of historical influences, including those of shamanism, the therapeutic schools of Ancient Greece, the Christian practice of spiritual direction, Christian theosophy, German Romanticism and mesmerism. (Ellenberger, 1994 [1970]), pp. 110–181). Henri Ellenberger has described the various schools of psychology that prefigured the rise of psychoanalysis as constituting "the First Dynamic Psychiatry," chronologically situating its activities between the years of 1775 and 1900. Its primary characteristics included the use of hypnotism as a means for accessing the unconscious and treating mental illness; a preoccupation with disorders such as somnambulism, multiple personality and hysteria; and a model of the mind founded upon ideas of dual consciousness (*dédoublement de la personnalité*) and the existence of subconscious personalities:

> During this time [1882–1900], the main tool of psychological research and therapy was hypnosis; the main psychological phenomenon of interest was somnambulism, of which multiple personality and spiritualism were varieties; and the main psychological disorder was hysteria. Hypnosis, hysteria and spiritualism are all variants of somnambulism, which, in psychological parlance at the turn of the century, referred to *any* rather complex act performed while asleep, in trance, or in some other "altered state of consciousness" – to use the expression in vogue today.
>
> (Haule, 1984, p. 638)

What is perhaps most notable about Ellenberger's periodisation of the psychoanalytic *longue durée* is that it establishes the "First Dynamic Psychiatry" as the overarching, pre-existing "orthodoxy" out of which – and in tension with – the theories of Freud and Jung (among others) were eventually to make their way to international prominence.

The complex interplay of synergistic, ambivalent and agonistic dynamics that typified relations between the First Dynamic Psychiatry and its successors is

DOI: 10.4324/9781003476733-3

exemplified by the respective roles played by F. W. H. Myers (1843–1901) and William James (1842–1910) in the introduction of Breuer and Freud's ideas on the nature of hysteria to the Anglophone world. However, the difficulties that arose during the course of initial attempts to distinguish the *subliminal self* of Myers and James from the Freudian unconscious have tended to be overlooked (Kuhn, 2017, pp. 5–6, 26–28, 294).[1] In the estimation of T. W. Mitchell (1869–1944):

> Freud's Unconscious is in truth not very different from Myers' Subliminal, but it seems to be more acceptable to the scientific world, in so far as it has been invoked to account for normal and abnormal phenomena only, and does not lay its supporters open to the implication of belief in supernormal happenings.[2]

The process of establishing the context to this confusion will require some comparison to be made between Freud's paper, "A Note on the Unconscious in Psychoanalysis" (1912), and the more expansive concept of the *subliminal self* that was initially developed by Myers and subsequently taken forward in the writings of his friend and colleague, William James (Taylor, 1996; Knapp, 2017).

It is notable that Freud chose to publish his first major theorisation of the unconscious in the *Proceedings of the Society for Psychical Research* (Freud, 1958 [1912], pp. 255–266).[3] While the hypothesis that Freud tacitly construed his conceptualisation of a specifically psychoanalytic unconscious to be in competition with Myers' pre-existing theorisation of the *subliminal self* remains subject to debate, it is nonetheless evident that disciplinary anxieties regarding boundary

---

1 However, Kuhn dates the actual introduction of Freudian psychoanalysis to the membership of the Society for Psychical Research to 1909, noting that this initial confusion took the form of a misreading in which Breuer, Freud and Myers' theories were consistently misaligned with each other. In Kuhn's estimation, an undue emphasis upon the links conjoining Myers to Freud has contributed to a misreading of the latter's significance to the detriment of the former while obscuring the greater significance that Janet's work had for Myers. In Myers' estimation, Freud was something of a "late entrant" into a field already explored in some depth by figures such as Gurney, Janet and Myers himself – see Hamilton (2009, p. 190). Unfortunately, Myers' untimely demise meant that a two-volume work he had intended to call *Human Personality in the Light of Recent Research* was posthumously titled *Human Personality and Its Survival of Bodily Death* (1903), a textual redescription that "undoubtedly deterred scientific readers" (Newman, 2021, p. 276).

2 Cited in Gyimesi (2009, p. 467). I am indebted to Gyimesi's paper for drawing my attention to the significance of demarcatory disputes in highlighting the infiltration of the psychoanalytic unconscious by its occluded "esoteric" *other*.

3 The request for Freud to submit his paper appears to have been instigated by T. W. Mitchell, primarily for the purpose of providing clarification concerning the distinctive features of the Freudian unconscious, as contrasted with those competing models of the "subconscious" that were prevalent at the time – see Kuhn (2017, p. 323). Kuhn is notably critical of Keely's contention that Freud's submission of this paper was motivated by a perceived rivalry on his part with the deceased Myers' theory of the subliminal mind (Kuhn, 2017, pp. 327–328).

demarcations remained prominent throughout the professional politics of this period (Gyimesi, 2009):

> The beginning of the twentieth century witnessed the most intense activity of scientific psychology through giant symposia, where, notably, terms like "unconscious" and "subconscious" were defined . . . on one side stood (at least) Jean Martin Charcot, Janet, and Freud, for all of whom the content of the unconscious and subconscious was negative and therefore had to be rejected. On the other side stood (at least) Myers, William James, Théodore Flournoy, and Jung, for whom the content of the subconscious was positive since it allowed a form of awareness beyond consciousness.
>
> (Pilard, 2018, p. 67)

Such disagreements constituted but one variant of more long-standing attempts to delegitimise the "nightside" of psychological research as part of a wider agenda to bolster the discipline's scientific credibility. These efforts included strategies of genealogical occlusion to which the various magnetic traditions were subjected during the course of their "de-occultization" into the medicalised and secularised practice of hypnosis.[4]

While such developments were presented by their exponents as being ideologically "progressive" in nature, it is nonetheless possible to speculate that their underlying motivations may have been – to a degree that is necessarily difficult to assess – concurrently motivated by a disavowed melange of fears, anxieties and repressions of a more fundamentally irrational nature:[5]

> the boundary disputes between psychology and the study of the paranormal . . . increasingly involved the "psychologization" and "pathologisation" of psychical research in the Imperial and inter-war periods. . . . Unable to come to terms with the paranormal ontologically . . . German psychologists attempted to transform paranormal phenomena and those who studied them into legitimate objects of research, thereby, undermining their threat not only to psychology, but also to stable notions of history and self.
>
> (Wolffram, 2009, p. 30, n. 54)

Moreover, this polemic dispute mirrored wider debates concerning the strategic implementation of a psychologised world-view to promote the secularisation of

---

4 See Keeley (2001, pp. 767–791); Kuhn (2017, pp. 327–330); Thurschwell (2001, pp. 40–41). On the role of the "nightside" in German Romantic psychology and its relation to the origins of Jungian analytical psychology, see Hanegraaff (2012, pp. 262–264, 285–289).

5 Or in the honest (albeit not very "rational") words of the American neurologist George M. Beard, for "logical, well-trained, truth-loving minds, the only security against spiritism is hiding or running away" (Beard, 1879), cited in Sommer (2016, p. 114).

earlier modes of thinking historically aligned to "spiritist" ontologies (Hayward, 2007).

It was during this period that figures such as Charcot and his associates "rediscovered" the associations between hypnotism and the purportedly "occult" phenomena previously explored by the mesmerists and subsequently "forgotten" by their successors (Raia, 2019). Although Freud made scant reference to these earlier developments in his own writings, the milieu of Charcot's Salpêtrière was nonetheless rife with speculations concerning the alleged links between hypnotism and "occult" phenomena, the literature of animal magnetism and mesmerism being otherwise well known to him (Reichbart, 2019, p. 82).[6] This confluence of "nightside" currents evoked powerful emotional reactions in many of the more avowedly scientifically minded interlocutors. Their ensuing responses not infrequently gravitated around an affective mosaic made up of fascination, uncanniness and secrecy, resulting in disavowed feelings of shame, accompanied by a concomitant fear of "contamination" should the unwary visitant draw too close to the flame (Rabeyron & Evrard, 2012, p. 108).

In order to contextualise these developments more thoroughly, it will be helpful to undertake a brief excursus into some of the more recent revisionist histories that seek to explicitly situate the development of Freudian psychoanalysis within the "nightside" milieu of the so-called dark enlightenment (Whitebook, 2017; Roudinesco, 2016).

3.2 "A gnosis of symbols" – the role of the "Nightside" in the formation of Freudian psychoanalysis[7]

While not seeking to dispute either the accuracy – or the legitimacy – of Freud's self-identification as a partisan of the *Aufklärung,* to the extent that he was simultaneously heir to the mesmeric, Romantic and (to a markedly more ambiguous degree) Roman Catholic traditions, he can also be construed as an exemplar of the "dark enlightenment" (Whitebook, 2017, p. 11; Roudinesco, 2016, pp. 215–232).[8] This

6 For a detailed historical account of the alleged associations between hypnotic trance and paranormal phenomena, see Dingwall (ed.) (1968). A search of the CD-ROM catalogue of Freud's library returned 23 books/articles dealing with "animal magnetism" and five books/articles dealing with "mesmerism." A total of 47 books/articles on hypnotism (excluding items beginning with "hypnotism and") were also identified: see Davies and Fichtner (eds.) (2006). It is notable that as early as 1887, Freud referred in a review to the experimental use of hypnosis as a means for dramatically improving the hearing capacity of a number of young boys who were suffering from deafness (Solms, 1990, pp. 365–366).

7 "When psychoanalysis 'forgets' its own historicity, that is, its internal relation to conflicts of power and position, it becomes either a mechanism of drives, a dogmatism of discourse, or a gnosis of symbols" (de Certeau, 1986, p. 10).

8 For a lucid account of the "genealogy of the myth of the Enlightenment," see Josephson-Storm (2017, pp. 71–72). On the topic of Freud's "positivism" and its limitations, see Whitebook (2017, pp. 398–399). In the estimation of Cornelius Castoriadis, Freud's "scientific mirage was a vital and even fertile illusion," cited in Whitebook, 2017, p. 96. On the subliminal "influence" of Roman Catholicism on Freud, see Vitz (1988).

term was originally coined by the philosopher Yirmiyahu Yovel to denote "a deeper, conflicted, disconsolate, and even tragic yet still emancipatory tradition within the broader movement of the Enlightenment" (Whitebook, 2017, p. 11). Viewed from this perspective, Freud's ambivalent engagement with Counter-Enlightenment currents can be construed as a part of a wider creative struggle to navigate a tertium quid that sought to transcend a polarised understanding of Romantic and Enlightenment world-views:

> Recent research into esotericism sees . . . a general structural element of Enlightenment discourse, in which the fascination with the dark and irrational, as well as its resolution in the light of understanding, represents a crucial point. . . . It shows that the glorification of enlightenment and knowledge as it was practiced by many intellectuals in the eighteenth century in fact did not link up primarily with Descartes' models of reason or Kant's limits of reason, but rather to Renaissance authors' search for the "Light of Truth." Through the linking of esotericism and enlightenment we can see the entanglement of discourses of reason with discourses of *higher* knowledge, perfect knowledge, and a truth that transcended simple understanding for those who participated in it.
>
> (von Stuckrad, 2015, p. 69)

This underlying imbrication of ostensibly divergent intellectual currents can be thought of as serving – at times – an apotropaic purpose, insofar as the "irrational" elements thereby invoked could – by virtue of this process of conceptual superimposition – subsequently become sublated into a more expansive and less reified conception of reason. In this respect, it is striking how, in spite of the "hagiographical" efforts that have been made to portray Freud as the quintessential Victorian gentleman-scientist (*pace* Ernest Jones), psychoanalysis has itself nonetheless managed to take on some of the attributes of a syncretic tertium quid in which the tensional energies of Enlightenment *and* Counter-Enlightenment discourses are brought into a rapprochement with each other through the bringing together of conscious "rationality" with its "nightside" *other*.[9]

While it is true that Freud's publications on telepathy drew upon the paradigm of a dynamic unconscious powered by instinctual drives, it is also evident that his private views on such topics could be at considerable variance with his more public avowals of an explanatory reductionism (Vitz, 1988, p. 157).[10] Consequently, he remained cognisant of the extent to which his conscious aims could potentially

---

9 See, for example, Jones (1957, p. 408), in which Jones describes a series of late-night discussions with Freud on topics of an occult or uncanny nature. At the conclusion of one of these discussions, Freud's rejoinder to Jones' scepticism was as follows: "I don't like it at all myself, but there is some truth in it." What is striking throughout these exchanges is the impression of Jones' barely concealed anxiety that Freud's ostensible jocularity might disguise a more serious underlying intent.

10 See Vitz (1988, p. 157). See also Whitebook (2017, p. 159) for an account of Loewald's seminal distinction between Freud's adoption of "official" and "unofficial" positions.

be undermined by his only partially repressed attraction towards the "occult" (Roudinesco, 2016, pp. 229–232).[11] Freud maintained a lucid awareness of his own ambivalence on the matter of publishing on such topics (Reichbart, 2019, p. 108).[12] Indeed, his insights on this issue could be recruited to support the hypothesis that his motives for embarking upon his 1912 paper on the unconscious not only constituted a theoretical intervention intended to distinguish his approach from those of his competitors but also served the more oblique function of erecting a conceptual *bulwark against the black [tide of mud] of occultism*.[13] Otto Rank adumbrated on this theme in the following terms:

> Freud essentially eliminated the soul. By acknowledging the unconscious he acknowledged the realm of the soul; but by his materialistic explanation of the unconscious he denied the soul. Consciousness, obviously, contains *something* more, as well as something different, than just the data of the external world. Freud attempted to explain this "something more" out of the unconscious; but he takes the unconscious itself again to be merely a reflection of reality, a remnant of the external world. But the unconscious, too, contains more than past reality; it contains and encompasses something unreal, extra-sensory, which from the start was inherent in the concept of soul.
>
> (cited in Nelson, 2001, pp. 128–129)

From the 1920s onwards, Freud's research gradually came to orient themselves around three specific areas of enquiry, namely his speculative investigations into *eros* and *thanatos,* which he uneasily sought to align with his development of a structural model of the psyche; an exploration into the social dynamics of power in groups; and a conflicted attempt to delve into the "nightside" phenomenon of telepathy (Roudinesco, 2016, p. 211). Despite his allegiance to Enlightenment values, Freud nonetheless formed multiple identifications with a range of Counter-Enlightenment tropes and exemplars, including those of the Faustian drama of the Mephistophelian "pact," the penumbra of mystery surrounding

---

11 Notably, Freud identified thought-transference as being one of only two themes (the second being counter-transference) that "always discomposed" him – see Roazen (1975, p. 232).

12 While Freud had initially intended to present his first paper on "thought-transference" to a select group of his colleagues at a meeting in the Hartz Mountains in 1921, he somehow managed to misplace his notes. While a subsequent version of the paper was eventually published in 1933, the original draft only came to light again in 2010 after its discovery by Maria Pierri – see Skues (2021); see also Hewitt (2014, p. 100). As Derrida remarked, it was not merely coincidental that none of Freud's telepathy "lectures" were ever in fact "delivered" and were not infrequently "lost" – see Reichbart (2019, p. 107). This sense of Freud's underlying ambivalence is further compounded when we consider that he could never quite bring himself to pay his membership dues to the Society for Psychical Research – see Luckhurst (1999, p. 68, n. 39).

13 See Jung (1995, p. 173).

ancient mythologies and the dangers thereby encountered through the surmounting of reason by the passions:

> [Freud] belonged to the tradition of "dark Enlightenment" through his ability to let himself be haunted by the demoniacal, the occult, the *pharmakon,* or the "uncanny" (*Unheimliche*) and then immediately distance himself from it by invoking the ideal of science . . . it is within this dialectic play between darkness and light that we can situate . . . a will to transform Romanticism into science.
>
> (Roudinesco, 2016, p. 215)

However, it remains a matter of debate as to whether, or to what extent, such a transformation was ever in fact achieved. Moreover, it has been proposed that Freud suffered from a series of neurotic fantasies featuring the Devil that concluded with a fantasised "demonic pact," the contents of which drew upon an amalgam of sources, including those of Goethe's *Faust*, as well as the documentary materials provided by the European witch trials of the seventeenth century.[14] As early as 1897, Freud wrote to his friend Wilhelm Fliess in the following evocative terms:

> I am beginning to grasp an idea: it is as though in the perversions, of which hysteria is the negative, we have before us a remnant of a primeval sexual cult, which once was – perhaps still is – a religion in the Semitic East [Moloch, Astarte] . . . I dream, therefore, of a primeval devil religion with rites that are carried on secretly, and understand the harsh therapy of the witches' judges. Connecting links abound.
>
> (Masson, 1985, p. 227)[15]

Moreover, Freud explicitly identified with the figure of Goethe (actualising this identification to the extent of winning the Goethe prize in 1930) and drew upon Goethe's *Faust* as a primal *ur*-text, or thematic *palimpsest*, traces of which may be discerned throughout the *corpus* of his own writings (Prokhoris, 1995, pp. 33–34; Bishop, 2009, pp. 9–32).[16] More specifically, parallel relations between the "witch theme" in Freud's work and what has been described as his personal "witch psychology" have been remarked upon at length in the scholarly literature (Vitz, 1988, p. 148, pp. 101–171). It has been suggested that it was Freud's use of cocaine that acted as one of the major catalysts through which he was able to subvert by chemical means the order of his own rationality, thereby bringing into the foreground of his consciousness the "nightside" of the daimonic and the *unheimlich*

---

14 "I propose that Freud had neurotic fantasies about the Devil and that at some time, whilst fantasizing, he concluded a pact" (Vitz, 1988, p. 155).
15 See also Duffy (2020, pp. 16–17ff) for an exegesis of this passage and its subsequent implications for the early development of psychoanalytic theory and practice.
16 Jung, too, was profoundly influenced by Goethe's *oeuvre* (Bishop, 2009). Indeed, Jung was even rumoured to be a direct descendant of Goethe – see Bair (2004, p. 8).

in psychoanalysis (Roudinesco, 2016, pp. 39–40).[17] Intriguingly, Freud first took cocaine on 30 April 1884, which is to say, *Walpurgisnacht*. Like Faust, Freud too was enamoured by the idea of a drug-induced rejuvenation that intensified the libido (Vitz, 1988; Roudinesco, 2016, p. 39).

If we can accept the extent to which theory "is always first and foremost local emotional politics" and that "sexuality and the unconscious were the new, scientifically prestigious words for the occult," then we can begin to grasp the importance of the highly charged exchanges that took place between Freud, Jung and Ferenczi from 1908 to 1914 over the precise meaning of the "occult" and the significance that should be ascribed to it with regard to the future of psychoanalysis (Phillips, 1995, pp. 23, 19; Rabeyron & Evrard, 2012; Keve, 2015; Thurschwell, 2001, p. 118). Consequently, it is to these exchanges that our attention shall now turn.

3.3 The "occulted" relations of Freud, Jung and Ferenczi (1908–1914)

The dissolution of relations between Freud, Jung and Ferenczi were to prove momentous for the future of psychoanalysis. Indeed, there are grounds for supposing that the combined effects of these ruptures upon future generations of psychoanalysts and analytical psychologists led to their becoming the inheritors of a transgenerational trauma, the encrypted symptomatic expression of which was enacted under the guise of "theory."[18] In the estimation of one commentator, "The parting broke Freud's heart, but it broke Jung's spirit" (Fodor, 1971, p. 111).[19] If the initial relations between Freud and Jung were not of an already sufficient intensity, these tensions were further exacerbated due to the combination of Oedipal and sibling rivalry arising between Carl Jung ("the Crown Prince") and Sándor Ferenczi ("the son-in-law Freud wished he had") (Keve, 2015, p. 99). As early as 1907, Jung had written to Ferenczi to advise him that he had been "made Honorary Fellow of the American Institute for Scientific Research, a society that primarily studies psychology and occult phenomena" (Keve, 2015, p. 96). By 1908, Jung was providing Ferenczi with an outline of his experiments with hypnogogic states (his account of which might arguably constitute an early reference to the embryonic concept of "active imagination"). In 1910, Ferenczi actually consulted a somnambulistic medium – rather than, say, a psychoanalyst – for advice on how to manage his relations with Jung (Rabeyron & Evrard, 2012, p. 102). By 1911, Freud, Jung and

17 It has been remarked that "The white power contained both the magic that tempted and excited [Freud] and the antidote to the anxiety that the magic aroused" (Whitebook, 2017, p. 116).
18 On my use of the term *encrypted* in this context, see the following: Abraham and Torok view the unintelligibility they encounter in their patients as psychically motivated disturbances of meaning. . . . One of these mechanisms, which they call cryptonymy, inhibits the emergence of meaning by concealing the significant link within a chain of words. (Rand, 1994, p. 17)
19 On the topic of Jung's purported "psychosis" as constituting a de facto "trance illness," see Obeyesekere (2012, pp. 409–439).

Ferenczi were in regular correspondence with each other on matters relating to the occult (Keve, 2015, pp. 98, 100).

Tom Keve has argued that a complex series of disputes concerning the nature of sexuality and the meaning of the occult (exacerbated by an unresolved negative paternal transference on Jung's part) lay at the heart of the eventual rupture between Freud and Jung (Keve, 2015; see also Fodor, 1971, pp. 110–113).[20] Notably, many of their respective differences concerning the meaning and significance of the libido concept were fought on the basis of data drawn from occultism, religion and mythology (Charet, 1993, p. 199). While the elder Jung retrospectively interpreted Freud as treating sexuality as though it were a kind of *numinosum,* it is nonetheless evident that during this earlier period, it was Jung himself who was struggling with the "numinous" powers of sexuality, as embodied in the vicissitudes of his erotic relationship with his ex-patient, Sabina Spielrein, with regard to which Freud – somewhat reluctantly – found himself assigned to the role of "mediator" between the various disputants embroiled in this saga.[21] Moreover, these disagreements may have evoked within Freud anxieties around questions of demarcation and legitimation. By emphasising sexuality as one of the linchpins to his theory of the unconscious, Freud firmly grounded his model of the mind within biology, thereby demarcating its *modus operandi* from the various "spiritualist" schools active within the milieu of the dangerously contiguous discipline of psychical research (Gyimesi, 2009, p. 460; Wolffram, 2009, pp. 54–62; Oppenheim, 1985, pp. 238–239). It was in the midst of these interpersonal tensions that Freud continued to wrestle with his own internal struggles arising from his conflicted fascination with the occult (Fodor, 1971, p. 110; Rabeyron & Evrard, 2012, p. 108). As Borch-Jacobson has acutely observed,

> Their [psychiatrists' and therapists'] intervention is part of the "etiological equation" of the syndromes that they claim to observe from the outside. [As well as the historians of psychiatry] they must, if they want to remain faithful to their improbable "object," study the complex interactions from which those syndromes and those theories emerge, somewhere between the doctors, the patients and the society that surrounds them. In short, they must study the making of psychiatric history, and understand that they participate in it.
>
> (Borch-Jacobson, cited in Pilard, 2018, p. 71)

For Jung, psychoanalysis seemed to offer an opportunity to deepen the quest for his elusive "second self," a task he had initially embarked upon under the auspices

---

20 See also the following: "In psychoanalysis the supernatural returns as the erotic" (Phillips, 1995, p. 19).
21 See Kerr (2012, pp. 221–231 ff.). The reference to Jung's assertion that Freud treated sexuality as a *numinosum* is an allusion to the account given by Jung in his *Memories, Dreams, Reflections,* referenced later in this chapter. For an account of the cautions and caveats that should be applied to the material contained in this text, see Shamdasani (2003, pp. 22–26).

of his research into the occult (Kerr, 2012, pp. 111–112; Jung, 1970 [1902]). In his correspondence with Freud, Jung referred to the evidence from psychical research that might be utilised to provide confirmatory evidence for Freud's own findings. (McGuire, 1991, p. 85 [letter 50J, 02/11/1907]). Eventually (in response to a request initially made by Jung), Freud delegated to Jung and Ferenczi the task of taking psychoanalysis into the realm of the occult. On 11 May 1909, Freud wrote to Ferenczi as follows:

> Jung writes that we must also conquer occultism and requests permission to undertake a campaign in the realm of mysticism. I see that both of you can't be restrained. You should at least proceed in harmony with each other; these are dangerous expeditions, and I can't go along there.
>
> (Keve, 2015, p. 100)

Despite this disclaimer, in 1911, Freud joined the British Society for Psychical Research and attended a series of séances accompanied by Ferenczi. That same year, Freud wrote to Jung about his own experience of the "occult" in the following emotive terms:

> In matters of occultism I have grown humble since the great lesson Ferenczi's experiences gave me. I promise to believe anything that can be made to look reasonable. I shall not do so gladly, that you know. But my hubris has been shattered.[22]

Regardless of this purported "humbling" on Freud's part, his exquisite oscillations on this topic nonetheless remained as a recurrent feature throughout these exchanges and beyond, with incipient tensions between Freud and Jung regarding the significance that should be ascribed to the "occult" exemplified by their respective reactions to a series of poltergeist-like phenomena (memorably articulated by Jung in his impromptu neologism, *catalytic exteriorisation phenomenon*) that reportedly occurred during the course of a visit made by Jung to Freud's home in March 1909 (McGuire, 1991, pp. 143–146; Jung, 1995, pp. 178–179). Nevertheless, despite these difficulties, we can discern throughout the course of this three-way correspondence the nascent stirrings of fundamental psychoanalytic conceptualisations concerning counter-transference and intersubjectivity (Rabeyron & Evrard, 2012, p. 103). Moreover, as Freud remarked in his correspondence with Ferenczi, once it is accepted that the telepathic "receiver" must necessarily be subject to unconscious processes of distortion, then the application of psychoanalytic hermeneutics

---

22 McGuire (1991, p. 227 [260f, 15/06/1911]). Freud's remarks may also allude to certain experiments pertaining to "clairvoyance" and "telepathy" conducted by Ferenczi in 1909 on a Berlin psychic called Frau Seidler and a "somnambulist" named Mrs Jelinek. For more on this episode, see Josephson-Storm (2017, pp. 198–199).

will necessarily be required if the true meaning of any psychical transmission from "sender" to "receiver" is to be accurately deciphered (Rabeyron & Evrard, 2012, p. 101).[23]

While the much-debated significance of the so-called Kreuzlingen gesture has entered into analytical mythology as the proximate "flashpoint" marking the end of Freud and Jung's friendship, in retrospect, Jung came to consider that it was their fundamental divergence on questions concerning sexuality and the occult that constituted the decisive factor leading to their eventual estrangement:

> I can still recall vividly how Freud said to me, "My dear Jung, promise me never to abandon the sexual theory. That is the most essential thing of all. You see, we must make a dogma of it, an unshakeable bulwark." He said that to me with great emotion, in the tone of a father saying, "And promise me this one thing, my dear son: that you will go to church every Sunday." In some astonishment I asked him, "A bulwark – against what?" To which he replied, "Against the black tide of mud" – and here he hesitated for a moment, then added – "of occultism."[24]

It is evident from Jung's retrospective account that he associated "occultism" not only with those forms of knowledge that he considered psychoanalysis to be incapable of digesting but also as constituting a "threat" against which Freud felt he had to defend himself:

> What Freud seemed to mean by "occultism" was virtually everything that philosophy and religion, including the rising contemporary science of parapsychology, had learned about the psyche. . . . Although I did not properly understand it then, I had observed in Freud the eruption of unconscious religious factors. Evidently he wanted my aid in erecting a barrier against these threatening unconscious contents.
>
> (Jung. 1995, pp. 173–174)[25]

---

23 For a critique of the "sender-receiver" model of telepathy in psychoanalysis, see Reichbart (2019, pp. 111–112).

24 Jung (1995, p. 173). As has been observed, "Freud is fascinating . . . because he hesitated between both revelation and concealment . . . we can learn much about the mechanisms of occult repression from the master theorist of repression himself" (Josephson-Storm, 2017, p. 181). For the background to the "Kreuzlingen gesture," see Maguire, *Freud/Jung Letters,* pp. 273, 275, 278, 279, 283, 295 and Kerr (2012, pp. 410, 413, 423, 428, 438).

25 For a more sceptical reading of the wider context to this dispute as reported by Jung, see Fodor (1971, p. 110), in which Fodor comments that "It is hard to believe this statement as Jung reported it in *Memories.* Freud did not consider occultism a black tide, nor did he want to make a canonic theory about sex."

One notable feature of Jung's remark concerns his passing reference to parapsychology as a "rising contemporary science," an observation that identifies psychical research as constituting a significant academic discipline during the time when this dispute originally occurred. Moreover, his remarks highlight the extent to which Freud's attitude towards the occult was highly conflicted and subject to a plethora of defensive processes. In Jung's estimation:

> the sexual theory was just as occult, that is to say, just as unproven a hypothesis, as many other speculative views. . . . Although, for Freud, sexuality was undoubtedly a *numinosum,* his terminology and theory seemed to define it exclusively as a biological function. It was only the emotionality with which he spoke of it that revealed the deeper elements reverberating within him.
>
> (Jung, 1995, pp. 173–175)

Following his break with Freud, Jung set out on an initiatory journey (charted in his *Black* and *Red* books) that arguably paralleled – at least in some of its aspects – the intellectual itinerary undertaken by his friend and mentor Theodore Flournoy (1854–1920), whose own work on psychical research had traversed a comparable trajectory, beginning with a process of psychological demystification and ending in a renewed commitment to a reconstituted idea of "occult forces" (Luckhurst, 1999, p. 59). Jung was subsequently to emphasise (citing William James) that in his estimation, it was Myers who in 1886 "discovered" the unconscious (Jung, 1969 [1947; rev, 1954], pp. 237–279, n. 23). Indeed, echoes of Myers' influence on Jung can be discerned in an account of the concept of Jungian "intuition" that has highlighted the presence of a fourfold psychological hermeneutic in which the Jungian concept of the *unterbewusst* (an intermediate region located between the unconscious and consciousness) is identified as the realm associated with "paranormal" intuitions (Pilard, 2018, pp. 66–68).[26]

3.4   Freud and psychical research

Recent studies have tended to present nineteenth-century psychical research as an emergent discipline inhabiting a hybrid realm conjoining religion, literature, philosophy and the nascent discipline of psychology to empirical science (Wolffram, 2009).[27] It is from within the tensional matrix arising out of these respective dis-

---

26 Notably, Pilard's ideas on intuition additionally draw upon a threefold typology provided by Antoine Faivre (2008), in which the latter outlines a hierarchical "occult" epistemology beginning with phenomena associated with paranormal research, through to "higher" faculties enabling contact with realms of the angelic, the demonic and the dead, before culminating in the highest "visionary" faculties of a purportedly "gnostic" character. On the significance of Myers' work for Jung, see Shamdasani (2003, pp. 125–128, 261).

27 Other useful histories of psychical research, the findings from which have been drawn upon in the following pages, include Treitel (2004) and Oppenheim (1985).

ciplines that we can begin to discern the trajectory of a materialist ideology active in both French and German fin-de-siècle psychology, which sought to bring about the programmatic "reduction" of *psychical* phenomena (including its experimental "subjects" such as somnambulists and mediums) into the pathologised "objects" of scientific research, thereby obviating any potential dangers posed by competing notions of a "transcendental subject" extraterritorially "decentred" outside the parameters of a materialist ontology.[28]

Newly evolved disciplines, such as Carl du Prel's "transcendental psychology," utilised trance states to access unconscious mental capacities construed as being "transcendental" in nature due to the hypothesised existence of an implied organising intelligence known as the "transcendental subject" (du Prel, 2022 [1885]). However, by the middle of the 1890s, the desire on the part of the "physiological" psychologists to create a clearer demarcation that would assist in distinguishing their own research agendas from those of the more outré variants of fin de siècle occultism led to the formation of a hybrid approach known as "critical occultism," the axioms of which were premised upon more naturalistic modes of explanation.[29] This development contributed to a retreat from the animist paradigm hitherto characteristic of German psychical research, leading to a shift towards a materialistic psychology operationalised to establish a series of "reductive" explanations for paranormal phenomena (Wolffram, 2009, pp. 71, 84). The process of genealogical occlusion that ensued has been aptly summarised as follows:

> Automatic writing, initially the stuff of the séance, also became early on central to the psychological experiment. The medium was the first and perhaps best experimental subject for the early interests of subliminal psychology such as that of F. W. H. Myers. The Freudian eclipse of these early studies succeeded in sweeping mediumship under the umbrella of sexuality. Clearly the séance was a space in which sexually transgressive desires could be enacted, but the collapse of the medium into the hysteric, and the apparent historical disappearance of them both, does a disservice to the complicated dynamics of mediumship.
>
> (Thurschwell, 2001, p. 107)

---

28 For German developments, see Wolffram (2009, p. 30, n. 54, p. 50). For a very helpful overview of the French *Psychologie Physiologique* (as well as its countercurrents in French psychiatry), see Raia (2019, pp. 181ff).

29 "Physiological" psychology referred to a development in the latter part of the nineteenth century that sought to transform psychology from a subdiscipline of philosophy into a fully fledged empirical science by emphasising research into the physiological correlates of mental events. Its method of research was pre-eminently laboratory-based, and its overall orientation was antipathetic to the legacy of Friedrich Schelling and the Romantic form of science known as *Naturphilosophie*. Its leading exponent was the German psychologist Wilhelm Wundt (1832–1920), who founded the first psychological laboratory in 1879. However, its critics declared it to be "a psychology without a soul" (Wolffram, 2009, pp. 38–39).

The existence of multiple points of contact among psychoanalysis, psychical research and psychology was a conspicuous feature throughout this period, when the nascent boundary demarcations separating these disciplines were especially permeable. In his 1899 masterpiece *The Interpretation of Dreams,* Freud made a number of laudatory remarks concerning the "transcendental psychologist," Carl du Prel.[30] In du Prel's estimation, it is the "transcendental subject" who constitutes the metaphysical source of personhood, with the everyday phenomenological self merely acting as the holographic facsimile of this deeper source of subjectivity. Consequently, we might surmise from this a complex interplay of parallels and divergences arising among du Prel's "transcendental subject," Myers' "subliminal self" and the drive-haunted Freudian unconscious (Sommer, 2009). In contrast to the comparative lack of interest shown in Freud's "dream book" by the medical doctors and scientists of his day (due, in part, to the negative associations his early work had already acquired among his Viennese peers as a consequence of his interest in hypnotism), Freud's most sympathetically inclined early readers were initially to be found among the German psychical researchers (Treitel, 2004, pp. 48, 71–72).[31] Moreover, the liminal role of psychoanalysis active as a de facto nexus between occultism and the wider modernist movement can be illustrated via the work undertaken by a leading spiritualist press owned by Oswald Mutze (founded in Leipzig in 1872), which published a diverse range of texts on spiritualism, psychical research and psychology, including works by Carl du Prel, Jung's 1902 doctoral dissertation on the occult and Daniel Paul Schreber's *Memoirs of my Nervous Illness* (1903) (Treitel, 2004, pp. 71–72).[32] In general, while theoretical divergences remained prominent, there nonetheless existed an occluded contiguity of thematic concerns conjoining psychoanalysis to fin de siècle occultism.

By 1912, Freud had become a "corresponding member" of the Society for Psychical Research (SPR) in London (his work on hysteria having previously been

30 In a footnote to the 1914 edition (out of a total of six that were devoted to du Prel), he was described by Freud as a "brilliant mystic" who had recognised that "the gateway to metaphysics, so far as men are concerned, lies not in waking life but in the dream," cited in Treitel (2004, p. 48). For more on Freud's usage of du Prel's ideas (and on du Prel's mystical proclivities), see Josephson-Storm (2017, pp. 179–180, 189–191).

31 See also Marinelli and Mayer (2003) for a detailed account of the early reception of Freud's "Dream Book" by his first readers. On the gradual inclusion of material on telepathy in the 1925 edition (subsequently to be excised from the 1930 edition following an intervention by Ernest Jones), see Grubrich-Simitis (2004, p. 30).

32 It has been remarked how, in a secular age, a common reaction to the supernatural may entail the supplanting of "sacred terror with psychological pathology" (Tobin Siebers). Viewed from this perspective, a reading of Schreber's memoir as an account of a "modern Western psychotic . . . overwhelmed by Hermetic visions of the macrocosm" becomes increasingly plausible – see Nelson (2001, pp. 126–129) and Schreber (2000 [1903]). See also Obeyesekere (2012, pp. 62–74). Approaching Schreber's memoir from an anthropological perspective, Obeyesekere emphasises the contextual basis upon which value judgements such as "visionary" or "psychotic" are applied in order to maintain the normative assumptions of the respective host cultures.

brought to the attention of the British public by the SPR in 1893), and he was sub-sequently to acquire honorary memberships with the American and Greek Socie-ties for Psychical Research (Jones, 1957, p. 425; Hinshelwood, 1995). However, his initial decision to diverge from Breuer's theory of hypnoid states, compounded by his comparative neglect of the phenomenon of dissociation, meant that Freud had effectively set himself in opposition to a body of then influential theories that drew upon an "alternate consciousness" paradigm associated with the work of fig-ures such as Richet, Myers and James, each of whom explicitly sought to synergise relations between academic psychology and psychical research (Luckhurst, 1999, p. 58).[33]

By 1921, we find Freud writing to the psychical researcher Hereward Carrington in the following unequivocal terms that were subsequently to be made subject to more obscure processes of unconscious disavowal: "If I had my life to live over again I should devote my life to psychical research rather than to psychoanalysis" (Jones, 1957, p. 419).[34] We have already noted a marked proclivity on Freud's part to experience occult phenomena as a potential source of both fear *and* fascination. In this respect, Freud's forgetfulness in the context of his 1921 communication with Hereward Harrington constitutes an exemplary instance of the conflicts that can be experienced by those who find themselves in contact with the "paranormal."[35] Since it is in Freud's papers on telepathy that we find his most sustained expression of these tensions, it is to these papers that our attention shall now turn. It is outside my remit to provide an exhaustive account of Freud's views on the phenomenon of telepathy and its place in psychoanalytic theory (see Devereux [ed.], 1974 [1953]). For my present purposes, it will be sufficient to outline the origins of the telepathy concept before embarking on a highly compressed examination of Freud's complex and (at times) difficult-to-determine views on this subject.

33 On Freud's divergence from the alternate conscious tradition, see Crabtree (1993, pp. 351–360).

34 However, there are slight but significant differences between Jones' account of this correspondence and Fodor's (who was the original source for Jones). Fodor's transcription of the original Photostat of Freud's letter reads as follows: Dear Sir, I am not one of those who, from the outset, disapprove of the study of so-called occult psychological phenomena as unscientific, as unworthy, or even as dangerous. If I were at the beginning of a scientific career, instead of, as now, at its end I would perhaps chooses no other field of work, in spite of all difficulties. cited in Fodor (1971, p. 84) Notably, eight years later, when Freud was questioned regarding the accuracy of this assertion, he initially denied its veracity, only to have his denial disproved by a photostat provided by Hereward Carrington.

35 This term derives from "parapsychology," originally coined by Max Dessoir in 1889 to denote the science of phenomena that "go beyond the everyday [but nonetheless] come out of the normal life of the psyche" (Treitel, 2004, p. 46). It was around this same time (1885) that F. W. H. Myers coined the term "supernormal" to demarcate anomalous phenomena that could at least potentially be made subject to a scientific explanation from those accounts that sought to evoke an explicitly "supernatural" provenance – see Pilard (2018) and Kripal (2010). See also Sommer (2016) for a lucid discussion as to why both the "will to believe" and the "will to disbelieve" in the existence of paranormal phenomena can prove equally problematic for the researcher.

The term *telepathy* was coined in December 1882 in the first volume of the *Proceedings for the Society for Psychical Research*: "we venture to introduce the words *Telaesthesia* and *Telepathy* to cover all cases of impressions received at a distance" (Luckhurst, 2002, p. 60). The term itself drew upon a diverse amalgam of meanings, ranging from the then cuttingedge technologies of telegraphy and the telegram to the feeling-toned resonances of the ancient Greek *pathos* (Kripal, 2010, p. 81). It arose during a time and within a culture where advances in communicative technologies coupled with evolving ideas concerning the nature of the mind (and of the "supernatural") were closely aligned to changing notions about intimacy and communication (Thurschwell, 2001, p. 14). For Myers, the concept of telepathy constituted the vital conceptual matrix that bound together a wide array of disparate phenomena, ranging from poetic and philosophical genius to "spirit communication" and "crisis apparitions" incorporated into a metaphysical world-view which, while methodologically aligned to science, nonetheless drew upon the earlier discourses of mesmerism and animal magnetism and ultimately from ancient Platonic notions of a "world-soul." Yet, despite its implicit reliance upon earlier modes of "esoteric" discourse, it nonetheless sought to supersede these by substituting in their place a category of human psychical potential that was theoretically accessible to everyone (Kripal, 2010, p. 81).[36] It was (in parallel with the Freudian concept of the "transference") closely aligned with the experience of the erotic: "Love is a kind of exalted, but unspecialised telepathy" (Myers, *Human Personality,* 1903: cited in Kripal, 2010, p. 85). It was the mesmeric phenomenon of the *rapport* that constituted the clinical context for telepathy and for the transference, both of which can thereby be traced to a common ancestral origin (Kuhn, 2017, pp. 54–55).[37]

In the estimation of Marsha Aileen Hewitt, "telepathy is the axis that connects psychoanalysis and mystical spirituality, science mysticism, parapsychoanalysis, and religion" (Hewitt, 2020, p. 158). For Jeffrey Kripal, it is trauma that constitutes the "technology" of telepathy – an assertion that has corresponding implications with regard to the ethics of undertaking research into this phenomenon within a laboratory setting (Kripal, 2024). Parallels have been drawn between Freud's description of "telepathy" (*Gedankenübertragung*) and the concepts of "transference" (*Ubertragung*)/"countertransference" (*Gegenübertragung*), leading one commentator to describe the former as "an extreme, rebellious form of transference" (Lana Lin, cited in Zeavin, 2018, p. 57). Indeed, these terms seemed almost,

---

36 For an excellent overview of Myers' theory of the *subliminal self,* see Raia (2019, pp. 141–204).

37 As far back as 1818, a Parisian doctor called Jean Jacques Virey observed the following: "Magnetism is nothing more than the result of natural, nervous emotions produced by imagination and affection between different individuals and principally by those which arise from sexual relations," cited in De Saussure (1943, p. 199). It was roughly during this same period that Joseph Philippe Deleuze (1753–1835) observed how both the magnetiser and his subject could experience sexual feelings as a consequence of the effects arising from the rapport – see Crabtree (2008, p. 563).

at times, to converge upon each other, as though driven by an involutive process possessive of a discrete hauntological resonance:

> One may say that the central psychoanalytic concept of "transference" would be inconceivable without the prior theorization of telepathy. Transference, like the dead, operates as a haunting return: the "stereotype plates" of first love turn everyone who comes after as ghostly: "All my friends have in a certain sense been reincarnations of this first figure . . . they have been *revenants*." It was the analytic interaction in which transference and telepathy repeatedly touched on each other.
>
> (Luckhurst, 2002, p. 275)[38]

The phenomenon of transference evolved out of a cultural matrix in which mesmerism, hypnotic suggestion and telepathic transfer feature as constitutive elements integral to the nascent conceptualisation of the therapeutic rapport (Raia, 2019, p. 276).[39] Freud conducted his own experiments into telepathy with his colleague Sándor Ferenczi and his daughter Anna, the success of which came to have a "persuasive power" sufficient to relegate "diplomatic considerations . . . to . . . a back seat," much to Ernest Jones' chagrin (Gay, 1989, p. 445). Freud also participated in at least two telepathic séances over a brief period in 1913 (Roazen, 1975, p. 237; Zeavin, 2018, pp. 57–58).[40] Freud was notably impressed by Gilbert Murray's account of a series of telepathic experiments published in the *Proceedings of the SPR* in December 1924. He subsequently disseminated his views on these experiments in the form of a circular letter, which he distributed to the membership of the Secret Committee on 19 February 1925 in terms that were sufficiently laudatory for him to assert that he "would even be prepared to lend support to the cause of telepathy through psychoanalysis" (cited in Evrard et al., 2017, p. 13).[41]

Freud himself was highly conscious of the negative implications that recurrent accusations of "occultism" could potentially have for psychoanalysis while remaining sympathetic to their respective synergistic potential. Both disciplines were frequently perceived as having disreputable origins, and both shared an aspiration towards establishing their scientific credentials (Jones, 1957; Phillips, 1995).

---

38 The citations from Freud referenced in this extract are taken from "The Dynamics of Transference" (1912) and *The Interpretation of Dreams* (1899).

39 There is evidence to suggest that as early as 1888, Freud was aware of the associations between the phenomenon of "trance" and that of "telepathy" via the then-famous experiment of Babinski with Charcot – see Solms (1989, pp. 401–403). See also Raia (2019, pp. 179–186).

40 Perhaps unsurprisingly, we find that "All records of the day that the Vienna Psychoanalytic Society spent with the mediums are missing" (Zeavin, 2018, p. 58).

41 It is worthwhile remarking that a number of Murray's contemporaries observed a series of methodological flaws in his work that were subsequently acknowledged by the author. However, these limitations may not have been of so much interest to Freud compared to the opportunities provided by his excursions into telepathy as a means for furthering his psychoanalytic theorising.

Regarding their potential for synergy, Freud was of the opinion that dream analysis could be of particular value for research on telepathy, insofar as it provided the tools and concepts for unearthing latent telepathic communications from the distracting babel of the manifest dream content. Freud also speculated that the dream state could potentially be conducive to the reception of telepathic communications.[42] Freud was notably wary of the idea of precognition and went to considerable – not to say ingenuous – lengths in his deployment of psychoanalytic hermeneutics to ensure that it remained discounted as a theoretical possibility.[43] However, Freud also believed that the psychoanalytic concept of the transference potentially offered a new approach to the study of telepathic and associated parapsychological phenomena (Ellenberger, 1994 [1970], p. 534). Indeed, it is possible to see their linguistic and clinical contiguity as playing a contributory role in subsequent attempts to theorise the transgenerational transmission of trauma and the unconscious circulation of affect. It is these aspects of their entwined interaction that have led some commentators to identify Freud's work on telepathy as being foundational to psychoanalysis and as integral to its metapsychology (Hewitt, 2014, pp. 86–89; Frosh, 2013, pp. 5–6).

Freud provided his own pithy definition of telepathy as " the reception of a mental process by one person from another by means other than sensory perception," before going on to argue that "it provides the kernel of truth in many other hypotheses that would otherwise be incredible" (Freud, 1922, in Devereux [ed.], 1974 [1953]). Freud subsequently speculated (1933) that such phenomena constituted the original archaic method of communication between individuals that, during the course of phylogenetic evolution, was replaced by sensory communication. However, he also proposed that this older method of communication could still persist in the background and might potentially, under certain conditions, become active again (Freud, 1933). Moreover, by locating his speculations on the origins of telepathy within an atavistic and bio-mechanistic frame of reference, Freud distinguishes his approach to this phenomenon from that of Myers, who construed its origins and activities as existing within a more expansive world-view (Thurschwell, 2001, pp. 124–125; Kripal, 2010, pp. 66–75).

---

42 Freud (1922), in Devereux (ed.) (1974 [1953]). This volume consists of a series of very useful primary sources addressing the topic of psychoanalysis and telepathy, covering the period from 1899 to 1953. While the editor of this volume has included a total of six texts by Freud consisting of a combination of individual papers and book excerpts, more recent commentators, such as Evrard et al. (2017) and Reichbart (2019), have tended to focus upon the following four key texts: "Psychoanalysis and Telepathy" SE 18 (1921), pp. 177–193; "Dreams and Telepathy," SE 18 (1922), pp. 197–220; "The Occult Significance of Dreams," SE 19 (1925), pp. 125–138; and "Dreams and the Occult," SE 22 (1933), pp. 31–56. Notably, Freud refers in three of these papers (1921, 1925 and 1933) to a single patient called Frau Hirschfield, who evoked in him "those two unsettling and intertwined phenomena that always made him uneasy: countertransference and thought-transference." Falzeder (2015, p. 45).

43 Freud's misgivings on the topic of precognition were not shared by all of his psychoanalytic successors – see, for example, Eisenbud (1982).

Freud could be intriguingly (and at times disingenuously) equivocal in his attitude towards telepathy, concluding one paper in which the topic is discussed at
some length with the following nugatory remark: "I have no opinion; I know nothing about it" (Freud [1922], in Devereux [ed.], 1974 [1953]). Yet, despite these
disclaimers, he initially felt sufficiently constrained to treat the topic of telepathy
as a "psychoanalytic secret" to be shared only with his most select and trusted colleagues.[44] Freud's fluctuating attitude towards telepathy charted a complex path
over the course of nearly a quarter of a century, oscillating between an enthusiastic
advocacy in support of the views propounded by its most vocal supporters, Jung
and Ferenczi; the persistent antipathy displayed by senior analysts such as Abraham and Jones towards the disputed phenomenon; and the middle ground in this
debate, which was inhabited by figures such as Eitingon, Rank and Sachs (Roazen,
1975). In the course of these discussions, associated concepts such as "empathy"
became the subject of heated debate, due in part to what Freud described in his correspondence with Ferenczi as its "mystical character" and the absence of satisfac-
tory criteria to distinguish its unique characteristics from those of telepathy (Kakar,
2003, pp. 667–669).

While Freud's equivocations on this subject are suggestive of a sensitivity to
political nuances coupled with a strong undertow of psychological conflict, he
nonetheless evidenced in his writings on the topic a highly sophisticated understanding of the "psychopathology" of paranormal phenomena (vestiges of infantile omnipotence, hallucination, subliminal perception, fraud, etc.) alongside a
judicious and nuanced appreciation of the evidence that might be adduced in its
favour. Nevertheless, despite his dealings with the Society of Psychical Research,
his knowledge of the associated literature, his experiments with telepathy, and his
participation in telepathic séances, Freud nonetheless remained keen to promote
an idea of psychoanalysis that made it seem more akin to a medical procedure than
a séance (Phillips, 1995, p. 19). The deployment of such a strategy evidently made
good sense in the context of a political climate in which Freud and his disciples
found it necessary to clearly demarcate their nascent discipline from its "occult"
rivals and competitors (Gyimesi, 2009). Yet, despite these political equivocations,
it is evident that the trajectory Freud followed from "Dreams and Telepathy"
(1922) through to "Dreams and Occultism" (1933) is one marked by an increasing
sense of conviction concerning the reality of the phenomenon under investigation.

Notably, a number of more recent commentators have speculated that Freud
himself may have displayed signs of a "repressed" telepathic sensitivity that was
experienced by him during the course of his own clinical practice.[45] In the Forsyth

44 Yet, despite these strategically motivated constraints, Freud was nonetheless sufficiently self-aware
    'to observe that "If one regards oneself as a sceptic, it is a good plan to have occasional doubts about
    one's scepticism too. It may be that I too have a secret inclination towards the miraculous which thus
    goes half way to meet the creation of occult facts'" (Freud, 1933 [1932], cited in Monk, 2023, p. 24).
45 See, for example, Wargo (2018). Since this hypothesis is based on the psychological significance
    that such anomalous processes may have had for Freud, its validity is therefore not dependent upon
    such arguments as might be adduced either to support or to refute the existence of such phenomena.

case, for example (in "Dreams and Occultism" [1933]), it has been argued that the telepathic phenomena purportedly manifested by Freud's patient, Herr P., could have originated from within Freud himself (Reichbart, 2019, pp. 109–111).[46] It has even been conjectured that Freud's "Irma" dream, the founding "specimen" dream of psychoanalysis subsequently immortalised by him in *The Interpretation of Dreams*, may have been "precognitive" with regard to its foretelling the type of cancer Freud would eventually die from in 1939 (Wargo, 2018, pp. 222–230; Resnik, 2000, pp. 119–120). Freud's adoption of a de facto dual-aspect monist theory of mind, entailing an ontologically ambiguous unconscious, was theoretically capable of incorporating the possibility of telepathic phenomena originating from an as yet unidentified archaic phylogenetic process (Solms & Turnbull, 2011, pp. 4–6; Kripal, 2019). However, the uncanny possibilities evoked by the precognitive hypothesis brought in its wake the spectre of a non-materialist world-view sufficiently disconcerting as to require the invocation of apotropaic "stop-concepts" (Bertrand Méheust) in order to prevent the emergence of an acute "metaphysical emergency" (Kripal, 2010, p. 222). A poignant and enigmatic gloss to these speculations can be found in the text of Lou Andreas-Salomé's *Freud Journal,* where she writes as follows:

> The day after the congress, September 9 [1913], with Freud in the Hofgarten. The long conversation (in confidence) on these rare occasions of thought-transference which certainly torment him. This is a point which he hopes need never again be touched in his lifetime; I hope the contrary. In a recent case the situation goes like this . . . the mother had indeed abreacted that which had retained its intensity in the daughter, quite as though it were her own, far beyond her own experience.
>
> (Andreas-Salomé, 1987, pp. 169–170)

As matters so transpired, Freud's hopes in this regard were to be largely unfulfilled, as, over time, this *primal scene* instantiated a trans-generationally *encrypted* trauma possessing its own spectrally transmissible qualities. As a consequence, the metapsychological "carapace" that classical psychoanalytic theory sought to erect in response to this unconsciously perceived threat of an ontological *Outside* gradually began to take on the aspect of a psychoanalytic metapsychology "haunted" by the revenants and survivals signified by its own telepathic "ghost."[47]

---

46 For an exemplary book-length exegesis of the Forsyth case, see Pierri (2022b).
47 See also Jung's remarks on the role of psychoanalytic theory as a defensive formation cited in Kingsley (2018, p. 508, n. 74).

3.5   "This is gold" – Freud and Kabbalistic hermeneutics

The parallels that can be drawn between psychoanalysis and the Jewish Kabbalah have been described as "profound," with psychoanalysis itself being construed as "a secular extension of Kabbalah" (Berke, 2015, p. xi). Jung himself declared that

> a real understanding of the Jewish component in Freud's outlook . . . would carry us beyond Jewish orthodoxy into the subterranean workings of Hasidism, and then into the intricacies of the Kabbalah, which still remains unexplored psychologically.[48]

Even so, no less a figure than the great scholar of Kabbalism Gershom Scholem (1897–1982) was dismissive of Freud and psychoanalysis, opining that he had "read dozens of better mythological concepts of the soul than his." As a historian, Scholem was similarly critical of the ahistorical and essentialist propensities of Jung and his followers (Scholem, 1991 [1962], pp. 6–7). Yet, in spite of the arguments that can be adduced against undertaking such a comparison, a strong case has nonetheless been made for construing the conceptual metaphors provided by psychoanalysis and analytical psychology as providing two of the best contemporary frameworks that we have for engaging with the concepts of the theosophical Kabbalah (Drob, 2000, p. 47).[49] However, such endeavours are not without their associated challenges. As Sanford Drob has astutely observed,

> By "projecting" the kabbalist's myths into the realm of reason and philosophy, two things occur. The first is that the principles of logic and reason begin to deconstruct in the face of the antinimous [sic] nature of the Kabbalistic symbols. The second is that there is a moment where we are able to understand the myths for the first time in a perspicacious fashion, before the vehicle of this understanding (reason) itself begins to fall apart before our eyes . . . the very rational concepts, elements, and structures that we use in order to make the Kabbalistic symbols comprehensible begin to lose their own normal sense in the process of being applied to the Kabbalah.
>
> (Drob, 2000a, pp. 35–37)

Definitional and methodological difficulties notwithstanding, the following account attempts to undertake the admittedly impossible task of providing a very brief and

---

48 C.G. Jung, "Letter to Edith Schröder" (April 1957), in: *C.G. Jung Letters*, 2 vols., [ed. Gerhard Adler, trans. R.F.C. Hull] (New York: Routledge & Kegan Paul, 1976), 1: 358–359.

49 For arguments in support of construing psychoanalysis and analytical psychology as essentially convergent disciplines, see Jacoby (2000), Henderson (2015) and Brown (ed.) (2018).

highly selective overview of the Kabbalah insofar as this might be deemed perti-nent for the purposes of this book.[50]

The Kabbalah reflects five elements within Jewish tradition: *Aggadah*, the nar-rative traditions of the Talmud and Midrash; *halacha,* Jewish law; liturgy, including poetry and prayer; *Merkavah,* or "chariot" mysticism, which predated the Kabba-lah and was based upon the prophetic visions of Ezekiel; and the *Sefer Yetzirah,* a proto-Kabbalistic work that introduced the doctrines of the *sefirot,* the attributes of God and the mystical contemplation of numbers and letters (Starr, 2008, pp. 4–5). Scholem regarded both the *Merkavah* and *Hekhaloth* ("throne") literature as con-stituting a Jewish type of Gnosticism that had parallels with (but was not identical to) the other variants of Gnosticism that existed in the Middle and Near East in the second century AD. For my current purposes, it will be sufficient to focus upon the *Lurianic* Kabbalah, since there are reasons to suppose it is this particular version of the Kabbalah that has provided a "basic metaphor" for elucidating Kabbalistic thought within a contemporary psychoanalytic context.[51]

It was in the sixteenth century in the town of Safed in Israel that Moses Cor-dovero and Isaac Luria developed a strikingly original theosophical system based upon ideas originally articulated in the *Zohar.* Luria's oral teachings were written down by his disciple Chaim Vital (1543–1620) and can be briefly summarised as follows.

According to the Lurianic Kabbalah, God consists of a paradoxical conjunction of *Ein-sof* (being without end) and *ayin* ("nothingness"), in which creation was made possible through an act of withdrawal known as *tzimtzum,* which created a void from which the *sefirot* emanated. However, the vessels that were meant to contain these emanations shattered (*Shevirat Hakelim*), entrapping shards of light in "husks" known as *klippot* that form the lower worlds, including the world of evil, referred to in the Lurianic tradition as the *sitra achra.* In the higher worlds, the masculine and feminine aspects were driven apart by this shattering of the ves-sels, resulting in a disruption of the flow of erotic energy throughout all the worlds. Nevertheless, some of the divine light that was not trapped in *klippot* returned to its source, thereby beginning a process of repair known as *tikkun.* Humanity's role in this cosmic drama is to support this process of *tikkun.*[52]

---

50 I am indebted to the following sources: Scholem (1946/1995); Scholem (1978). However, while these texts possess their deservedly classic status, I should state that the perspectives taken here are primarily indebted to the writings of Sanford L. Drob due, in large part, to the subtlety of his com-parative readings across the disciplines of Kabbalah, philosophy and psychology.

51 For a discussion on Lurianic Kabbalah as constituting a "basic metaphor," see Drob (2000b, pp. xviii–xxi). For examples of Lurianic Kabbalah deployed in post-Freudian psychoanalysis, see Eigen (2012); Berke and Schneider (2003, 2008); Kutzky (1989). It is important to note that Jung was apparently unaware of Luria's ideas prior to 1954 and viewed his belated encounter with them as constituting confirmation of his own ideas – see Drob (2000b, p. 336).

52 See Starr (2008, p. 6). See also the very helpful tabulations of the Lurianic system in Drob (2000a, pp. 18–19) and Drob (2010, pp. 17–18). The intricacies of the Lurianic system, considered in its entirety, are such as to lead to its being described by both Scholem and Idel as one of the most

The potential relevance of the Lurianic Kabbalah to psychoanalysis has been lucidly summarised in the following terms:

> One more schema of spiritual transformation is the Tree of Life, in the Kabbalistic tradition of Jewish spirituality. This is a remarkable diagram which sets out ten sepiroth, or centres of energy, to describe different elements in the nature of man. It is of potentially special interest to psychoanalysts, because more than any other spiritual tradition that I know of, this offers a clearly worked out, indeed a highly elaborated, account of psychic structure. To compare psychoanalytic conceptualisations of psychic change with the dynamics of the Kabbalistic Tree of Life would be a fascinating enterprise. By studying the multifaceted meanings of each centre, and their relation to each other within the structure of the Tree of Life, the student of Kabbalah is led to a deepening understanding of what it means to be human.
>
> (Parsons, 2006, pp. 124–125)

While various studies have been made concerning the Jewish contexts of Freudian psychoanalysis, comparatively few of these have specifically addressed the topic of the Jewish Kabbalah in any detail.[53] David Bakan's *Sigmund Freud and the Jewish Mystical Tradition* was the first serious attempt to establish a connection between Freud's familial background and his purported use of Kabbalistic ideas in the formulation of his theories (Bakan, 2004 [1958]). Unfortunately, the general critical consensus was that certain key aspects of Bakan's thesis remained largely unproven.[54] Bakan was able to demonstrate that Freud self-identified as a Jew in an increasingly anti-Semitic milieu. He also presented a convincing argument to support his contention that this increasing atmosphere of hostility contributed to Freud's strategic denial of any Jewish origin to psychoanalysis. Moreover, Bakan set out a strong case for linking psychoanalytic interpretation to the Talmudic exegesis of the Torah.[55] However, his proposal that Freud identified with the militant messianism of Shabbatai Tzvi (1626–1676) has generally been viewed as being speculative to the point of being untenable.

More convincing in this regard is Karen Starr's review of the biographical data, in which she concludes it is unlikely that Freud consciously incorporated Jewish mystical ideas into his writings. However, Starr does accept that Freud was almost certainly exposed to Kabbalistic ideas via his familial and cultural milieu and that he was therefore correspondingly influenced by these sources, albeit at an unconscious level of awareness (Starr, 2008, p. 18).

---

complex intellectual systems ever produced by the human mind (Drob, 2000b, p. xviii, n. 8). For a helpful contemporary philosophical and psychological interpretation of the Lurianic Kabbalah, see Drob (2000a).

53 See, for example, Frosh (2006, pp. 205–222).

54 For criticisms of Bakan's theses, see Drob (2000b, pp. 242–243, 2010, pp. 18–19). See also Starr (2008, p. 17).

55 See Frieden (1990) for a book-length exposition of the role played by Talmudic hermeneutics in the formation of Freudian dream interpretation.

The above criticisms notwithstanding, Bakan does describe in the preface to the second edition of *Sigmund Freud and the Jewish Mystical Tradition* an intriguing encounter between Freud and Chaim Bloch, in which Freud, having been requested by Bloch to write a foreword to a work on the Lurianic Kabbalist Chaim Vital, reportedly exclaimed on reading the manuscript that "This is gold" and queried why Vital's work had never been brought to his attention before (Bakan, 2004 [1958], pp. xvi–xviii). Unfortunately, a disagreement that ensued between both parties shortly thereafter as to the relative merits of publishing Freud's *Moses and Monotheism* in a climate of anti-Semitism resulted in the proposed foreword never being written. Nevertheless, it is notable that when Bloch perused Freud's library during the course of his visit, he reportedly found a copy of a French translation of the *Zohar,* as well as a number of German books on the Kabbalah.[56]

It is worth remarking on the fact that Freud, in spite of his adherence to a scientific *Weltanschauung,* was in fact highly superstitious.[57] These superstitions included a conviction of the significance and predictive powers of numbers that may not have been all that different (at least in some of its aspects) from the Kabbalistic number mysticism of *Gematria,* as well as a belief (to the point sometimes of dread) in such notions as the *Doppelganger*, which may have had its counterpart in the Kabbalistic concept of the *Tzelem* (or celestial twin). It has been proposed that these beliefs might have constituted a form of "the return of the repressed" that functioned as a counterpoint to Freud's avowed naturalism and that may even have contributed a dynamic impetus to his work (Drob, 2000b, p. 247). Be that as it may, while Freud frankly acknowledged on his part the existence of strong political motives for keeping psychoanalysis separate from the occult, he also continued to aver in private that the occult was in fact inextricably bound to psychoanalysis (Brottman, 2011, p. 6).

While Freud does not appear to have made any explicit references to the Lurianic Kabbalah in his written works, there is nonetheless some evidence in his correspondence with Karl Abraham of an explicit (and sympathetic) awareness on the part of both correspondents as to the parallels that might be adduced to exist between psychoanalytic and Talmudic modes of interpretation (Kradin, 2016, p. 12). On 11 May 1908, Abraham wrote to Freud as follows:

> I freely admit that I find it easier than Jung does to go along with you. I, too, have always felt this intellectual kinship. After all, the Talmudic ways of thinking cannot disappear in us just like that. Some days ago a small paragraph in

56 Bakan's text also refers to a large collection of *Judaica* in Freud's library that was apparently absent from the presumptive "Freud library" housed at that time in the library of the New York Psychiatric Institute. Searches made on the CD-ROM catalogue of Freud's library (Davies & Fichtner, 2006) using the search terms "Kabbalah" and "Zohar" came back with no results. Consequently, it appears that the implications of Bakan's anecdote remain as no more than an intriguing possibility.

57 See chapter XIV ("Occultism") in Jones (1957, pp. 402–436) for extensive evidence in support of this assertion.

Jokes strangely attracted me. When I looked at it more closely, I found that, in the technique of apposition and in its whole structure, it was completely Talmudic.[58]

As we saw earlier, Jung came to believe that a full understanding of Freud would eventually lead "into the intricacies of the Kabbalah, which still remains unexplored psychologically" (cited in Drob, 2000b, p. 249). Consequently, the parallels that Drob adduces between the Lurianic Kabbalah and Freudian psychoanalysis are not quite as tendentious as they might initially appear to be at first glance (Drob, 2010, pp. 20–22).[59]

Shifting our attention momentarily to the work of an influential early twentieth-century occultist, it is worth observing that the esotericist, Kabbalist and "psycho-analyst" Dion Fortune (1890–1946) had great respect for Freudian theory, to the extent that she recommended Freud's *The Interpretation of Dreams* to her esoteric students as "occultism on a sound scientific basis" (cited in Greene, 2012, p. 393).[60] Through her deployment of Freudian psychoanalysis (she published a book on the topic under her birth name of Violet Firth titled *The Machinery of the Mind* that was unfavourably reviewed in *The International Journal of Psychoanalysis*), it has been proposed that Fortune was in fact appropriating to her own brand of occultism a psychological school of thought that was itself imbued with esoteric elements originating in Freud's Hasidic background, as well as the Kabbalistic currents (both Lurianic and ecstatic) that were already imbricated within the tenets of this movement:

> In Fortune's work, a curious ouroboric circle may be observed: an early-twentieth-century occultist "psychologises" esoteric ideas through the use of a psychological system which is itself a "secularised" expression of those same ideas, and likewise "sacralises" that psychological system through the framework of the same esoteric ideas that infused it to begin with.
>
> (Greene, 2012, pp. 396–397)

The extent to which psychoanalytic theory is suffused by Kabbalistic traces has become increasingly apparent within some of the more recent scholarly literature on the topic (Greene, 2012, pp. 398–399; Berke & Schneider, 2008, p. 6). Consequently, it is perhaps not so surprising to encounter in Freud's dream interpretation

---

58 Abraham to Freud, 11 May 1908, letter 30A, in: Falzeder [ed.] (2002), p. 40. Notably, Freud wrote to Jung in 1909 concerning his superstitious feelings regarding numbers as follows: "You will see in this another confirmation of the specifically Jewish nature of my mysticism" (McGuire (ed.) (1991, p. 146) [139F 16th April 1909]).

59 These parallels include primary procreative energy/*Ein-sof*/the Libido, negation of energy/*Tzimtzum*/primary repression and deconstruction/*Shevirah*/splitting of ego-structures.

60 On Fortune's time as a student of psychoanalysis at The Medico-Psychological Clinic in Brunswick Square, see Knight (2000, pp. 29–35).

a hermeneutic approach that treats dreams as though they were oneiric "texts" that needed to be decoded if the secret workings of the psyche were to be revealed:

> There is a psychological technique which makes it possible to interpret dreams, and . . . if that procedure is employed, every dream reveals itself as a psychical structure which has a meaning . . . I shall further endeavour to elucidate the process to which the strangeness and obscurity of dreams are due and to deduce from those processes the nature of the psychical forces by whose concurrent or mutually opposing action dreams are generated.
>
> (Freud, *The Interpretation of Dreams*)

It has been remarked that if in the above passage the phrase "psychical forces" was to be replaced by "ten *sefirot*," then this Freudian text could easily be read as an illustration of traditional Kabbalistic hermeneutics.[61] Such instances serve to exemplify the extent to which it is possible for certain elements of the Freudian *corpus* to operate as a palimpsest, beneath whose superficially mechanistic surface the glimmers of older, pre-Enlightenment traditions of the "preternatural" can dimly be discerned:

> When Freud discovered (really, *re*discovered) the unconscious, he blended the logical positivistic notion of absolute science and the German Romantic conception of the mysterious preternatural powers of Nature. The result was a lexicon of ontic, mechanistic, dehumanised entities such as "drive" and "object," rather than "homunculi," "chimerae," "monsters," "demons," "angels," "ghosts," or "revenants."
>
> (Grotstein, 2000, p. 144)

Having summarised the Freudian context to these developments, the subsequent chapters of this book set out the evidence for adducing the existence of an *Orphic trajectory* active within psychoanalysis since its inception, through which a number of influential post-Freudian psychoanalysts have engaged – both tacitly and more explicitly – in the project of transforming "the positivistic-mechanistic drive unconscious into a numinous, mystical unconscious" (Grotstein, 2007, p. 331).

Acknowledgement

An earlier version of this chapter first appeared in the article 'Before and after Science: Esoteric Traces in the Formation of the Freudian Psychoanalytic Subject,' *Journal of the Irish Society for the Academic Study of Religions*, Volume 7 (2019). I acknowledge the use of these materials in this chapter.

---

61 I am indebted to Greene (2012, p. 400) both for the quotation from Freud and for the suggested parallels with Kabbalistic hermeneutics.

Chapter 4

From metapsychology to magnetic gnosis

4.1 Introduction: the Budapest School of Psychoanalysis

Sándor Ferenczi (1873–1933) was the single major catalyst for the reception and development of psychoanalysis within Budapest in particular and across Hungary more generally. Five years after his initial meeting with Freud, Ferenczi established the Hungarian Psychoanalytical Society on 19 May 1913. Moreover, his tireless efforts as a speaker, writer and teacher of psychoanalytic topics facilitated the dissemination of these ideas to a wide and varied range of modernist intellectuals across Hungary. By 1918, Freud was writing to Karl Abraham of his expectation that "Budapest will now become the headquarters of our movement" (Falzeder [ed.], 2002, p. 382). The role that Ferenczi came to play in the development of psychoanalysis cannot be under-estimated, even if, in the words of Lou Andreas-Salomé, it came about that – for reasons that shall become apparent – "his was not the present but the future" (see Rudnytsky, 2018, p. xiii). Ferenczi's influence upon his roster of analysands and students was substantial and included figures such as Melanie Klein, Ernest Jones, Franz Alexander, Michael and Enid Balint, John Rickman, Margaret Mahler and Otto Rank.[1] Ferenczi's writings (at least prior to his [in] famous "Confusion of Tongues" paper [1932]) were deemed by Freud to be "pure gold" (Moreau-Ricaud, 2018, p. 87). For many years, Ferenczi occupied the multiple roles of "a disciple, a patient, a friend and a confidant" of Freud's before eventually ending his days as a "dissident" who was rumoured by his detractors to have descended into "madness" shortly before his death (Bokanowski, 2018, p. 3).

The receptivity to psychoanalytic thinking within the Budapest school was manifested across a wide range of disciplines, including those of literature, ethnography, education and economics. Moreover, its influence extended across the wider socio-cultural milieu to the extent that its pervasiveness could be discerned even in café conversations and folk song parodies (Meszaros, 2010, p. 71). Psychoanalytic ideas were promulgated across a range of publications, including medical journals

---

1 Szekacs-Weisz (2018, p. xxi). See also Falzeder (2015, p. 60) for a more substantial listing of Ferenczi's most influential students and analysands.

DOI: 10.4324/9781003476733-4

such as *Gyógyászat* (*Therapy*), journals on literary criticism such as *Nyugat* (*The West*) and sociological journals such as *A Huszadik Század* (*The Twentieth Century*). These links were further strengthened by the decision to locate the fifth International Psychoanalytic Congress in Budapest. Furthermore, during the course of this Congress, a wealthy benefactor named Antal Freund pledged the equivalent of half a million dollars to set up a publishing house and a library in Budapest. Then, on 25 April 1919, Ferenczi was appointed (albeit for only a brief period) as the first-ever professor of psychoanalysis, an event which occurred in tandem with the establishment of the first-ever department of psychoanalysis located within a medical university. In the light of such developments, it is not so surprising to find Freud making unfavourable comparisons between "the hostile indifference of the learned and educated . . . in Vienna" (1914) with the notably more receptive response to his teachings that he encountered in Budapest (Meszaros, 2010, pp. 71–72).[2]

However, these initial gains were subsequently to come under serious attack on a number of fronts. Ferenczi's professorship was revoked on 8 August 1919, in the context of the much wider unrest that occurred following the right-wing White Terror under Admiral Miklós Horthy. The repercussions that ensued from these events included the cancellation of plans to set up a university clinic in Budapest and the transfer of Freund's donation from Budapest to Vienna. The early 1920s also saw the first wave of emigration undertaken by those psychoanalysts who sought to flee the rise of the Soviet republic and the increase in anti-Semitism, as well as by those who did not wish to live under the White Terror, with its associated disregard for liberal values, descent into economic chaos and general civic disorder. A further wave of emigration among the psychoanalytic community took place between the years of 1938 and 1941 in response to the devastating political, social and economic consequences that ensued following the rise of National Socialism (Meszaros, 2014).

It has been observed that the combined effects of these disastrous events meant that "important Hungarian ideas and plans on both the institutional and theoretical levels were realised somewhere else, in another country or on another continent" (Meszaros, 2014, p. 49). Moreover, there are reasons to suppose that the cumulative effects of these destructive processes were further exacerbated *within* the environs of institutionalised psychoanalysis due to the covertly administered dynamics of *Todschweigen* ("death by silence") that were surreptitiously deployed by the proponents of a psychoanalytic "orthodoxy" against the "heterodox" teachings put forward by "dissident" figures such as Ferenczi and Severn.[3]

---

2 For a more detailed exposition of these contextual themes, to which the above account is indebted, see Meszaros (2014), chapters 1 and 2.
3 See Rachman (2018), chapter 7, for more on this theme. However, by way of providing a balance to this perspective, it is worth noting that a case has been put forward for the existence of a de facto Ferenczi "cult" – see Erös (2004, pp. 121–128).

4.2   The occult milieu of the Budapest School of Psychoanalysis

Having briefly set out the broader socio-historical context that shaped the formation of the Budapest School of Psychoanalysis, we can now shift our attention to the fin de siècle milieu of late nineteenth- and early twentieth-century Hungarian "occultism," the tenets of which were to prove a more fertile source of inspiration for the Budapest School of Psychoanalysis than is commonly supposed.[4] This imbrication of secular with religious modes of discourse can be construed as merely the latest iteration of an earlier thematic active within psychoanalysis since at least 1895:[5]

> The trance states of mediums, the encrypted memories that came to the surface in several mediumistic manifestoes, the mysterious psychological and physical occurrences mediums produced were leading to further questions about altered states of consciousness, the functioning of the unconsciousness or subliminal layers, the theory of hypnotism and suggestion, and about the as yet unknown capacities of the human psyche in general . . . through the experiments of Freud and Ferenczi in the field of thought-transference the forming ideas of intersubjectivity, transference, countertransference, introjection and projection emerged . . . In this sense the occupation of early psychoanalysts with the so-called "occult" was an important complement to the evolution of psychoanalysis.
>
> (Gyimesi, 2016b, pp. 366–367)[6]

"Spiritualism" (or "spiritism") was introduced to Hungary in the late 1800s during the course of its diffusion across Europe more generally. While its proximate origins are attributed to the activities of the Fox sisters beginning in 1848 in the United States, its more distal antecedents can be traced back to major esoteric figures such as Emmanuel Swedenborg (1688–1772) and Anton Mesmer (1734–1815).[7]

In Hungary, two of the main contributors to the rise of spiritualism were Count Ferenc Szapáry and the Austrian Baron Lázár von Hellenbach, whose

---

4 See, for example, the following: "By the concepts of introjection and projection Ferenczi created a potential bridge between psychoanalysis and psychical research" (Gyimesi 2012, p. 141). For an illuminating account of the role played by animal magnetism upon psychological thinking in Hungary, see Gyimesi (2021).

5 "Freud's materialistic discourse and naturalistic framework for psychoanalysis . . . was increasingly infiltrated by a stream of religious metaphors and images starting in 1895, although they remained mostly below the surface" (Bonomi 2018, p. 86).

6 The author explicitly acknowledges her indebtedness to the work of André Haynal in this context.

7 It is worth remarking at this point that in Hungarian, the same term is used to denote both "spiritualism" and "spiritism" – see Gyimesi (2012, p. 145, n. 2). However, the latter term was more usually associated with the overtly "metaphysical" system of Allan Kardec, while the former tended to denote the more "experimental" type of mediumship practiced in England and North America – see Gyimesi (2016b, p. 358, n. 2).

popularisation of mesmerism and spiritism extended to Hungary. The first Hungarian spiritualist society – the Budapest Association of Spiritual Investigators – was founded in 1871 under the auspices of the physician Adolf Grünhut and the Baroness Adelma Vay, who expounded a version of the spiritist teachings of Allan Kardec (1804–1869). The latter of these two instigators rose to prominence through the combination of her numerous publishing activities, as well as her acquaintance with the famous Hungarian magnetiser, János Gárdos (whose reputation was sufficiently well known as to be referenced by Ferenczi in his correspondence with Freud). Over time, various other spiritualist organisations followed, such as the Hungarian Metapsychical Society, founded in 1932, which explicitly aligned its activities with the French Nobel Prize winner Charles Richet. Yet, despite such efforts, a lack of scientific rigour with regard to its investigative processes was noted to persist as a more general feature of Hungarian spiritualism – a state of affairs which put its "spiritist" activities at variance with the more empirically orientated approaches adopted in countries such as France, Germany and England.[8]

Having briefly introduced the wider socio-political context and the cultural "occult milieu," from within which the activities of the Budapest School of Psychoanalysis were situated, we can now move on to consider some of the contributions made by two of its most prominent representatives, namely Sándor Ferenczi and Elizabeth Severn (1879–1959). This chapter then concludes with a brief account of the work of one of the neglected pioneers of "psychoanalytic parapsychology" – and the only psychoanalytic "heir" to Elizabeth Severn – Nandor Fodor (1895–1964).

Like many of the early analysts, Ferenczi possessed both a professional interest and a personal interest in the occult, while Severn herself was an active exponent of a "secularising mysticism" (Rachman, 2018, pp. 260–261; Bonomi, 2018, p. 202). It was from within this context that the Budapest School acted as a significant conduit for the introjection, encryption and transmission of esoteric *traces* across the wider conceptual fabric of psychoanalytic metapsychology.[9] In order to foreground these processes of encrypted transmission, a discourse analytic approach will assist us in establishing the occluded theoretical itinerary conjoining Ferenczi's investigations into trance and telepathy to some of their contemporary conceptual avatars, notably *reverie* and *projective identification*.[10] By way of a preamble, some brief contextual background is provided in the form of a summary account of Ferenczi's early paper on "Spiritism" (1963 [1899]) and the correspondence exchanged between Freud and Ferenczi on the role of telepathy and "occultism" in psychoanalysis. However, its central focus is devoted to those sections of Ferenczi's

8 See Gyimesi (2016b) for a more elaborate account of this historical background to which this brief exposition is indebted.
9 For an in-depth exegesis of the concept of introjection in Ferenczi's writings, see Chan (2015).
10 For useful accounts of the use of discourse analysis as applied to the study of esotericism, see Granholm (2013); von Stuckrad (2013, pp. 5–25); and von Stuckrad (2014, pp. 226–243).

Clinical Diary (1995 [1932]) that address the more explicitly "esoteric" aspects of *Orpha* and *astra.* Ferenczi's account of these enigmatic agencies is augmented by drawing upon the complementary perspectives provided by Severn in her book *The Discovery of the Self* (1933).

A number of commentators have alluded to the "occult" aspects of "Orpha."[11] The present chapter seeks to build on these accounts by foregrounding the more explicitly "esoteric" elements of Orpha and astra, thereby highlighting their comparative discontinuity with the tenets of classic Freudian metapsychology by emphasising their contiguity with the alternate consciousness tradition associated with figures such as F.W.H. Myers (1843–1901), William James (1842–1910) and Freud's one-time collaborator Josef Breuer (1842–1925) (Crabtree, 1993, 2008). As we shall see, the researches of Myers and James in particular into the *subliminal self* both drew upon and were in thematic resonance with the earlier mesmeric traditions of Romantic psychology, within whose cultural milieu Freudian metapsychology came to occupy a "defensive" position, the robustness of which was both destabilised by and imbricated with a persistent underlying sense of ambiguous contiguity vis-à-vis its ostensibly discredited Romantic predecessors.

4.3   "Remaining friends with the spirits" – Sándor Ferenczi on spiritism and telepathy

Following the conclusion of his studies at the University of Vienna, Ferenczi returned to Budapest in 1898, where he began military service as a junior physician attending to the treatment of venereal diseases in Rókus Hospital. In order to provide himself with some intellectual stimulation during his spare time, he embarked upon a series of informal investigations into spiritualistic phenomena. These included his attendance at séances run by the well-known professor of chemistry, Emil Felletár.[12] Ferenczi's interest in such matters identified him as a tacit participant in the alternate consciousness tradition within psychiatry.[13] Ferenczi's own experiments with automatic writing were to lead to some interesting consequences:

> I went to the junior physicians' room and engaged in "automatic writing," frequently discussed by the spiritualists of the time; Janet had already published interesting observations on this phenomenon . . . I picked up a pencil and, holding it loosely in my hand, I pressed against a blank piece of paper. I decided to let the pencil "move on its own," letting it write "on its own," letting it write

11 See, for example, Hristeva (2019, pp. 517–539); Kalsched (2013); and Soreanu (2019, pp. 132–153).
12 See Gyimesi (2014, 2016) for some very useful background on the various sources of Hungarian spiritualism that were active both prior to and subsequent to the fin de siècle period. Spiritualism, in particular, constituted an important nexus for the transmission of esoteric trance phenomena into the wider cultural milieu (Gutierrez, 2016, pp. 240–242).
13 Ferenczi explicitly referenced Myers' work in his correspondence with Freud – see Rabeyron and Evrard (2012, p. 106).

whatever it wished. Senseless scribbles came first, then letters, words . . . and finally whole sentences. . . . Finally the pencil suggested the following: "Write an article on spiritualism for *Gyogyaszat* [*Healing Arts*], the editor will be interested." . . . The next day I wrote my first medical paper entitled "On spiritualism". I started off from the phenomenon of automatism which I had observed in myself. My conclusion . . . was that the so-called occult phenomena do not contain anything supernatural and should be viewed as manifestations of the functioning of the unconscious. I sent the article to the *Gyogyaszat*.

(Ferenczi, 1993 [1917], p. 430)

This was the initiatory context to Ferenczi's first academic publication, "Spiritism" (1899), which also marked the beginnings of his friendship with the editor of the medical journal *Gyogyaszat*, Mika Schächter (Ferenczi, 1963 [1899]). Ferenczi's subsequent publications for this journal included a review of Leopold Löwenfeld's *Somnambulismus und Spiritismus*, as well as a translation of Sante de Sanctis' essay, "The miraculous element in dreaming." In a footnote to this latter work, Ferenczi strongly emphasised the importance of employing a rigorous scientific methodology in psychical research, a matter in respect to which Ferenczi – in a review written by him in 1900 concerning a book by the physician and spiritist Lajos Wajdits titled *Essays on the Field of Spiritism* – took the author to task for his perceived methodological deficiencies. However, despite his advocacy for methodological rigour, it was Ferenczi himself who subsequently became the subject of a critical review, during the course of which he was roundly criticised by its anonymous author for his confused account of the theories of Alexander N. Aksakof (1832–1903), whose work Ferenczi had cited in his 1899 paper on spiritism (Gyimesi, 2016b, pp. 372–373). It was in the context of debates such as these that Ferenczi's early interest in occult topics became intertwined with his deepening commitment to psychoanalysis.[14]

Although Ferenczi did not subscribe to a spiritualistic world-view, his later writings judiciously utilise the terminology of psychical research while mapping out a complex bio-psycho-esoteric *bricolage*, whose tenets entailed an engagement with "the non-materialistic reality of spiritualistic phenomena, which he tried to interpret with psychological concepts" (Gyimesi, 2012, p. 134). This can be inferred, for example, from the various discourse entanglements encountered in the *Clinical Diary*, in which Lamarckian biology is invoked to provide a "scientific" scaffolding to be erected alongside the purported phenomenon of *teleplasty* – a term coined by Frederic Myers to denote the supposed materialisation of psychical

---

14

I believe that the special interest of the early writings comes not so much from their scientific content but from the occultist, vitalist and mystic tendencies which are part and parcel of Ferenczi's life-work, and contributes to the creation of mythologies – through his own sexual-philogenetic [sic] mythology described most consistently and at the same time with poetic erudition in Thalassa.

Erös (2004, p. 126)

phenomena (Ferenczi, 1995 [1932], p. 117; Johnson, 2015). Ferenczi himself possessed a sophisticated awareness of the complex emotional and intellectual tensions aroused by his deployment of such conceptually disparate terminologies, the ambiguities arising from which he discussed with Freud in their correspondence:

> My "inclination towards occult matters" is not "secret" but rather quite obvious – it is also not actually an inclination towards the occult, but rather an urge towards de-occultization, at the base of which there may be, in the final analysis, magic-religious strivings, which I am defending myself against by wanting to bring clarity to these matters. I am convinced of the actuality of thought transference. I believe, incidentally, that even an indication that *prophecies* are possible, could or should not force one to abandon the scientific basis. Certainly I know of no proven case of foretelling the future.
>
> (Falzeder & Brabant, 1996, pp. 70–71)

While Ferenczi was willing to consider the possibility of precognition, such speculations were decidedly antipathetical to Freud's world-view (Brabant et al., 1993, p. 79). Yet, despite their disparity of outlook on this particular topic, their respective approaches to occult matters more generally were often in harmony with each other. Both drew heavily on their clinical experiences as the basis for their discussions.[15] As early as 1909, for example, we find Ferenczi alluding to the clinical phenomenon of "psychic induction," which he appears to reference as a conceptual precursor to his subsequent speculations on telepathy and clairvoyance (Brabant et al., 1993, p. 77). By 1910, we find Ferenczi writing to Freud in the following highly excitable terms:

> Interesting news in the transference story. Imagine, *I am a great soothsayer, that is to say, a reader of thoughts!* I am reading my patients' thoughts (in my free associations). The future methodology of ψA [psychoanalysis] must make use of this. . . . This method will be suitable to catch the patient's *most active* complexes at work. – It can be refined even more!
>
> When I come to Vienna, I will introduce myself as "court astrologer to the psychoanalysts."
>
> (Brabant et al., 1993, pp. 235–236)

Due to the complex array of intellectual and emotional conflicts evoked within Freud and Ferenczi by the "occult" during the course of their voluminous

---

15 See, for example, the following:

> A breakthrough came when Ferenczi started to work with his masochistic, homosexual patient who referred quite often to Ferenczi's hidden thoughts in his free associations. This case seemed to be reliable for Freud, too, and turned both of them to the question of thought-transference.
>
> (Gyimesi, 2016b, pp. 367–368)

For a helpful overview of occult themes in the Freud–Ferenczi correspondence, see Rabeyron and Evrard (2012).

correspondence, it is perhaps not so surprising to find that flights of "manic excitement" are recurrently interspersed by reactive retreats into caution. We see this, for example, in the guise of Ferenczi's assurances to Freud that he is "not in danger of lapsing into occultism," a remark that he rather incongruously appends as an addendum to a series of speculations, which include the following appositely ambiguous remark: "Finally, the time would come for the assumption of a real clairvoyance, telepathy, etc." (Brabant et al., 1993, p. 77). As we saw in Chapter 3, throughout this period (1908–1913), Jung too appeared as an active participant in what amounted – at times – to being a three-way colloquium on psychoanalysis and the occult. By 1914, we find that Ferenczi's emotional conflicts on these topics have become subject to a triune process of "splitting," the nature of which he describes to Freud in the following terms: "My 'Occultism' is very distinctly separated from my other knowledge and doesn't disturb it in any way; it is completely free of *mysticism*" (Falzeder & Brabant, 1996, p. 33). In the light of Ferenczi's subsequent researches into psychic permeability, his desire on this occasion to construct a rigid epistemological bulwark constitutes an intriguing development, whose origins might conceivably be entangled with his avowed "urge towards de-occultization." Moreover, his deployment of what amounts to an *ad hoc* idiolect structured around an idiosyncratic deployment of the rubrics of "occultism," "mysticism" and "other knowledge" is highly suggestive of a defensively appropriated semiotic *encryption* typified by processes of *enigmatic signification* as outlined in Chapter 1.

In contrast to Ferenczi's (not to mention Myers') view of anomalous phenomena as constituting an expression of latent human potentialities, Freud initially pursued an alternative avenue of enquiry, in which he sought to develop a theory of "thought transference" that reduced it from being a phenomenon of potential psychoanalytic interest to "a purely somatic one" (Brabant et al., 1993, p. 80; Roazen, 1975, p. 235). In an exemplary instance of boundary demarcation operating as an ironic art form, we find Freud opining to Ferenczi the following disclaimer during the course of their deliberations regarding a purported instance of "mind reading," which the latter experienced with the "medium" Frau Seidler – "Should one now, as a result of this experience, commit oneself to occultism? Certainly not; it is only a matter of thought transference." Freud immediately follows this shift from an "occult" into a "psychical research" register by counselling Ferenczi – "Let us keep absolute silence with regard to it." Shortly thereafter, in the same letter, Freud goes on to remark – "We want to initiate Jung at a later date, when we have more to go on" (Brabant et al., 1993, p. 81).

The combined tropes of "secrecy" and "initiation" are thematically prominent throughout this exchange, thereby imbuing its contents with a decidedly esoteric penumbra.[16] Yet, despite this epistolary web of occlusions and evasions, we can still discern in these exchanges Freud taking his first tentative steps towards the development of a specifically psychoanalytic view of telepathy, which included

16 On the topic of "secrecy" in esotericism, see Faivre (2006b, pp. 1050–1060).

the proposal that psychoanalytic hermeneutics could be applied to this phe-nomenon as a means for decoding the inevitable communicative "distortions" that would colour such communications due to the accompanying unconscious processes of symbolisation, displacement and condensation (Freud, 1922, in Devereux, 1974 [1953], pp. 69–86). In his 1922 paper, Freud maintained a posi-tion of strategic neutrality in which an undertow of emotional conflict is nonethe-less discernible.[17] While Freud's views on thought-transference fluctuated over time, its potential theoretical importance for psychoanalysis was nonetheless deemed by him to be of sufficient importance as to justify its inclusion as a topic for discussion in his *New Introductory Lectures in Psychoanalysis* (1933). As for Ferenczi, it has been remarked that he arrived at a position whereby he no longer sought to "differentiate the essence of telepathy and psychoanalysis. He is incorporating Seidler, or what she represents, into his psychoanalytic think-ing" (Chan, 2015, p. 160). Such exchanges paralleled wider debates within the international community of psychologists, which centred around a controversy that initially arose during the Fourth Psychological Congress (1900) concern-ing questions of disciplinary boundary demarcation (Taves, 2015). The impact of these discussions not only led to heated debates concerning the validity of "occultism" as a legitimate subject matter for academic research but also threw into question the professional parameters that should be applied to the discipline of psychology itself. Attempts to distinguish the boundaries separating "psychol-ogy," "psychical research," "mysticism," "magic" and the "occult" became a focus for controversy. Notably, some of these disputes centred around diverging conceptualisations of the phenomenon of dissociation, the distinctive attributes of which were located across a spectrum ranging from the pathological (Janet) to the exceptional (Myers, James and Richet) (Taves, 2015).

Ferenczi went so far in his investigations as to draw up a detailed plan for a never-to-be-written research study into psychical phenomena, the parameters of which were to include a systematic review of the "vast occultistic [sic] litera-ture," as well as a field trip to visit "the Pythia in Berlin" (Frau Seidler). Freud not only engaged enthusiastically with this proposal by offering to expedite its publication but also proposed a title – "The Ucs. and Thought Transference," adducing – quite reasonably – that "The term induction is not well enough known by the public." For good or ill, this work never materialised, not least because the "induction experiments" with Frau Seidler proved to be a "complete fail-ure" (Brabant et al., 1993, pp. 379–380). Yet, despite these not inconsiderable

---

17 In the first paragraph, Freud begins with the disclaimer: "You will learn nothing from this paper of mine about the enigma of telepathy; indeed, you will not even gather whether I believe in the exist-ence of 'telepathy' or not," an assertion that mirrors the rhetorical aporia of his concluding sentence, "I have no opinion; I know nothing about it" (Freud, 1922, pp. 69, 86).

setbacks, Ferenczi's belief in the potential significance of occult phenomena for psychoanalysis persisted:

> On examining Ferenczi's accounts on his occult experiences, it is clear that his primary aim was to find a rational, scientific explanation for the supposed supernatural phenomena . . . it seems that Ferenczi was much more involved in spiritistic practices than his letters to Freud or his published papers reveal.
>
> (Gyimesi, 2016b, p. 374)

The comparative neglect thus far of the contribution made by Ferenczi to the theories of his analysand, Melanie Klein (1882–1960), is something that has been remarked upon (Hernandez-Halton, 2015). While their views notably differed with regard to their respective emphases on the role played by external trauma in the genesis of psychopathology, Ferenczi's influence can nonetheless be discerned in Klein's ideas concerning the role of primitive phantasies in early infantile experience, as well as in the importance that she attributes to pre-Oedipal processes and the primacy of the mother (Reiner, 2017, p. 134).

The significance of projective identification as a "psychoanalytic imaginary" that manages simultaneously to function as a "stop concept" is something that is worth pausing to reflect upon at this point (Soreanu, 2018, p. 440, n. 4; Brottman, 2011, p. 107). The idea of "stop concepts" (*concepts butoirs*) is derived from the work of the French sociologist of psychical research and animal magnetism Bernard Méheust: "notions which, no doubt possessing an incontestable heuristic power, have at the same time a strategic function, that of limiting, by tacit convention, an obscure domain of experience, thus stopping the flight of thought into the unknown" (Méheust, cited in Kripal, 2010, p. 221). More dramatically, they have also been likened to "defence mechanisms invoked by the internal logic of a social system in a cognitive or metaphysical emergency" (Kripal, 2010, p. 222). While subsequent developments in the concept of projective identification were indebted to the legacies of Ferenczi and Balint, its pre-Kleinian origins have been traced to the work of the Italian analyst Eduardo Weiss, who corresponded with Freud on their shared interest in telepathy and the unconscious transmission of thoughts (Steiner, 1999; Grotstein, 2009a, p. 271; Haynal, 2017, p. 94). The persistence of purportedly "uncanny" phenomena continues to haunt the peripheries of contemporary conceptualisations of projective identification (Brottman, 2011).

Two contemporary commentators have concluded that the significance of the occult themes explored in the Freud–Ferenczi correspondence lies predominantly in their potential importance as harbingers for future developments in psychoanalytic theories of intersubjective communication (Rabeyron & Evrard, 2012). It is true that Freud and Ferenczi's nascent comprehension of such processes was necessarily constrained by the inherently limited theoretical vistas that were available to them at the time of their original formulation. However, there are at least two caveats that should be attached to such a reading. The first is to emphasise the importance of eschewing an unduly "progressive" approach to intellectual history, in which more recent theoretical developments are thereby assumed to be inherently superior to their conceptual predecessors. Second, it is important to engage with the possibility that concepts can also be defensively appropriated, thereby resulting in the formation of "stop concepts" functioning as cultural defence mechanisms intended to discourage speculation outside of the pre-existing parameters of a tacitly shared cultural and intellectual milieu (Kripal, 2010, p. 199).

For example, the diachronic discourses structurally aligned to divergent terminologies such as "telepathy" (nineteenth-century psychical research), "projective identification" (Kleinian psychoanalysis) and "unconscious intersubjective communication" (contemporary relational psychoanalysis) are in many respects virtually interchangeable when viewed from a phenomenological or clinical perspective; yet they remain as mutually exclusive as regards their discrete conceptual alignments as signifiers denoting membership of particular theoretical and professional groupings. In tandem with their demarcatory functions, these competing descriptive frameworks also serve to place limits upon what might be thought in terms of the culturally permissible *episteme* (Foucault, 1997). In this respect, they share some of the characteristics of those "ontology-making practices" associated with the psychological "sciences" more generally (Shamdasani, 2006). Notably, all three of these discourses share as a common denominator the absence of a robust *explanatory* framework capable of maintaining their existence outside of the conceptual framework engendered and sustained by their respective semiotic networks. In order to more clearly illustrate the extent of their semiotic instability, we can creatively revise an observation originally made by Maria Torok on the topic of telepathy so as to arrive at the following *varifocal* redescription of the phenomenon (Okropiridze, 2021):

> Telepathy [or projective identification, or unconscious intersubjective communication] would be the name [s] of an ongoing and groping research that – at the moment of [their] emergence and in the area of [their] relevance – had not yet grasped either the true scope of [their] own inquiry or the conceptual rigour necessary for [their] elaboration.
> (Abraham & Torok, 1986, p. 86 [additions to the original text are in brackets])

Having briefly outlined the significance of the "occult" in the Freud–Ferenczi correspondence for the development of their respective ideas, we can now embark on a consideration of Ferenczi's mature views on this topic as described in his posthumously published *Clinical Diary*. As we shall see, his speculations concerning the role of trauma acting as a catalyst for engendering anomalous modes of experience were to be radically influenced by his involvement with his most controversial and theoretically important patient – the so-called "evil genius," Elizabeth Severn (Rachman, 2018).

4.4   From metapsychology to magnetic gnosis

It has been proposed that the essential themes encountered in Ferenczi's *Clinical Diary* centre around three major preoccupations or axes:

1. a theoretical axis that concerns trauma and its metapsychological status in pathologies at the limits of classical analysis;
2. a technical axis, closely linked to his conceptions of trauma, which leads him to establish and experiment with "mutual analysis";
3. lastly, a personal axis, which concerns the crux of his relations with Sigmund Freud and the analysis of their disagreement, as well as his attempt to elaborate on it.

(Bokanowski, 2018, p. 65)

To these three axes, I would like to propose a fourth, namely an esoteric axis, to denote a persistent preoccupation with occult themes in psychoanalysis that was shared to a marked degree both by Ferenczi and by Severn.[18] However, before we can evaluate the evidence that might be adduced in support of this contention, it is important to begin with a frank acknowledgement of the various challenges associated with embarking upon such an exegetical reading of Ferenczi's *Clinical Diary*, not the least of which relates to its intertextual imbrication with a series of other closely related writings, including the Freud–Ferenczi correspondence, Freud's "Analysis Terminable and Interminable" (1937) and most especially Severn's book, *The Discovery of the Self: A Study in Psychological Cure* (1933).[19] To further complicate matters of perspective and of authorship, we find that in Severn's *The Discovery of the Self*, there exists not only a disguised account of her own analysis with Ferenczi but also an anonymised case study of Ferenczi himself, both of these studies presumably being based upon their controversial explorations in undertaking a "mutual analysis." Moreover, Severn's *The Discovery of the Self* has itself been construed as a "mutual publication," the contents of which reportedly received

---

18 See, for example, the following entry taken from Ferenczi's *Clinical Diary*:

> I do not exclude the possibility that delusional productions contain more objective reality than we have assumed until now. From the very beginning I was inclined to think that the hallucinations of the insane, or at least a part of them, are not imaginings but real perceptions, stemming from the environment and from the psyches of other human beings, which are accessible to them – precisely because of their psychologically motivated hypersensitivity – whereas normal people, focusing only upon immediate matters of direct concern to them, remain unaffected. What comes to mind in this connection is the so-called occult powers of certain people, and the close relationship and easy transition between the two states: paranoia and superperformance.
>
> (Ferenczi, 1995 [1932], p. 58)

19 On the role of the Freud–Ferenczi correspondence as an adjunct to reading the *Clinical Diary*, as well as some remarks on Freud's thinly anonymised commentary on his relationship with Ferenczi as depicted in his 1937 paper, see the "Introduction" by Judith Dupont (Ferenczi, 1995 [1932], pp. xi–xvii & xxv–xxvi).

Ferenczi's blessing prior to his death (Rudnytsky, in Severn, 2017 [1933], pp. 10, 96–97, 107–110; Bonomi, 2018, p. 203; Rachman, 2018, p. 28; Rudnytsky, 2022, p. 8). One commentator has gone so far as to describe it as "an indispensable companion volume to the *Clinical Diary*" (Rudnytsky, in Severn, 2017 [1933], p. 2).

The relationship between Ferenczi and Severn was complex and multifaceted, with Ferenczi referring to Severn on various occasions as occupying a spectrum of roles, including those of "main patient," "colleague" and "teacher" (Bonomi, 2018, p. 202). Consequently, it seems appropriate to contextualise her wider importance to psychoanalysis by situating her within the lineage of female patients, beginning with "Anna O" (Bertha Pappenheim), who were themselves significant contributors to the development of psychoanalytic theory (Harris & Aron, in Severn, 2017 [1933], p. xv). Moreover, there is reason to suppose that Severn herself inhabited, at times, a liminal space located somewhere between that of "medium" and "analysand," thereby conjoining her psychoanalytic lineage to that of her similarly liminal precursors who inhabited an analogous interstitial "lineage" located somewhere between the psychological and the esoteric, figures such as Friederike Hauffe (1801–1829), Hélène Smith (1861–1929), Elfriede Hirschfeld (1873–?) and Hélène Preiswerk (1881–1911), the collective importance of whom for the encryption of the esoteric within psychoanalytic theory has thus far only been partially explored (Flournoy, 1994 [1899]; Hanegraaff, 2001; Falzeder, 2015, pp. 19–48; Shamdasani, 2015b).

It was only retrospectively that Severn was able to conclude that "an omnipotent" part of her "intelligence," to which she assigned the title "Orpha" had "scoured the universe" in order to find the one, unique individual "who owing to his special personal fate could and would make amends for the injury that had been done to her" (Ferenczi, 1995 [1932], p. 121). It was on the basis of such experiences that Severn eventually arrived at "a remarkably prescient position, to which Ferenczi would catch up only in his final period," thereby enabling them to collaborate in the creation of an innovative theory of trauma structured around dissociative phenomena and the splitting of the ego (Rudnytsky, 2022, p. 15).

There are reasons to suppose that Severn had a catalysing effect upon Ferenczi's already quite considerable interest in the relationship between psychoanalysis and the occult. Her influence can be deeply felt throughout Ferenczi's work on the "dialogue of the unconscious," a clinical idea whose attributes are in many ways analogous to those of the phenomenologically contiguous concept of telepathy (Rachman, 2019, pp. 279–280; Luckhurst, 2002). In the light of such comparisons, it might not be too much of an exaggeration to describe Severn as Ferenczi's "esoteric muse."[20] Severn was herself a student of esoteric spiritualities, including

---

20

Certainly, in [Severn's] espousal in *The Discovery of the Self* of "*psychognosis*" . . . she was more attuned than either Thompson or de Forest to his mystical tendencies or what Groddeck, in a letter to Gizella Ferenczi after Sándor's death, termed his "ascent to the stars."

Rudnytsky, in Severn (2017 [1933], p. 6)

gnosticism, transcendentalism, theosophy and the fourth way, the respective tenets of which could collectively be grouped under the rubric of *New Age Religion* (Hanegraaff, 1998).[21] In Rachman's estimation, she "was part of the development of secularizing mysticism" (Rachman, 2019, p. 261). Severn was critical of the naïve materialism of psychoanalysis and sought to reassert what she conceived to be its transcendental potentialities via a series of portmanteau neologisms, such as *psychognosis* and *psychosophy*, for which she drew inspiration from a diverse range of figures that included Plotinus, Ouspensky and William James (Severn, 2017 [1933], pp. 56, 148–149).[22] Although Severn's writings have been criticised for being "pious, mystical, unprofessional and unscholarly," some of her more trenchant criticisms and proposed revisions to classical Freudian approaches have been given a revisionist gloss as untimely interventions prefiguring developments in contemporary relational psychoanalysis and transpersonal psychology.[23] One commentator has even described her as a "forerunner of the Independent tradition in psychoanalysis" (Rudnytsky, 2022, p. 56). Moreover, she could be equally trenchant in her criticism of concepts such as telepathy that were commonly employed within psychical research:

> It has been my experience many times, for instance, so to enter into the mind of a person whom I wished to help that the *identity* between him and me became practically complete for the time being. The word "telepathy" is quite inadequate to express this kind of connection. Nothing is communicated because this implies distance and there is no distance. . . . One must have, I suppose, great *permeability* to accomplish this psychic transfusion and identification.
>
> (Severn, 2017 [1933], p. 149)

In some respects, Severn's mature writings can be thought of as inhabiting an ambiguous territory contiguous both to psychoanalysis and to the "somnambulist"

---

21 In order to longitudinally contextualise the esoteric aspects of Severn's *The Discovery of the Self* (1933), it is important to note that her first book, *Psychotherapy: its Doctrine and Practice* (1913), addressed the topic of "telepathic healing," while, in 1914, she published an article on alchemy in the *Journal of the Alchemical Society* (a society of which she was also a member). Her second book, *The Psychology of Behaviour* (1917), similarly engaged with themes of an explicitly "metaphysical" nature (Fortune, 1993, p. 437).

22 In Vida's estimation, " 'Orpha' ought to be regarded more as Severn's construct than Ferenczi's: it belonged to *her* experience, and the quotation marks accompanying it in the diary are suggestive that the *name itself* came from Severn" (Vida, 2005, p. 8). Given Severn's acknowledged role as Ferenczi's "teacher," I consider it reasonable to apply a similar line of reasoning to Ferenczi's introduction of the portmanteau neologism "psychognostic" in his "Notes and Fragments" (Ferenczi, 2018 [1932], p. 263). Moreover, Severn's deployment of the neologism *psychognosis* situates her own work within the esoteric "lineage" of ancient Gnosticism, which sought to heal the primal traumas of existence by means of "ecstatic ascents into the transcendental realms" – Severn (2017 [1933], p. 148); DeConick (2016, p. 192).

23 Jeffrey Masson, cited in Smith (1998, p. 241). However, Smith concludes that Severn's writings do in fact prefigure many developments in contemporary psychoanalysis – Smith, 1998, p. 245.

tradition of nineteenth-century psychiatry, which drew heavily upon ideas of dissociation stemming back via Janet to Mesmer, the descendants of which were subsequently to be found within the Jungian and transpersonal schools of psychology.[24]
While the extent of Severn's significance for subsequent generations of psychoanalysts is a matter for ongoing debate and reappraisal, her influence can be discerned,
for example, in the work of Nandor Fodor (1895–1964), a hitherto well-known but
subsequently neglected pioneer of "psychoanalytic parapsychology" who, somewhat enigmatically, referred to himself as being a metaphorical "son" of Elizabeth
Severn.[25]

The transition of the mythologem from Oedipus to Orpha has been conceptualised as possessing a "paradigmatic" significance for psychoanalysis, marking a
shift in its therapeutic focus "from unravelling the unconscious drives to the revival
of dead parts" (Gurevich, 2016, p. 329). Indeed, this shift in mythological registers
has been interpreted as providing "a metapsychologically plausible account of a
particular kind of clairvoyance" entailing "an enduring modification of the ego,
that can be imagined as a new kind of psychic agency, neither (conscious) ego
nor superego" (Soreanu, 2018, p. 438). Since the figure of "Orpha" is presented
throughout the *Clinical Diary* in a notably obscure and fragmentary fashion, it
will be useful at this point to briefly revisit these references, alongside those of its
proximate analogue, "astra" (Ferenczi, 1995 [1932], pp. 206–207). As we shall see,
two of the more intriguing implications arising from this line of enquiry include
its problematisation of attempts to clearly demarcate the "psychoanalytic" from
the "occult," in tandem with an ensuing genealogical entanglement of the "occult"

---

24 On the notion of a "somnambulist" tradition within psychology, see Kerslake (2007, pp. 58–61).
For a helpful overview of the progression of themes in Severn's three published books, see Smith
(1998). Notably, the themes explored in the seventh and final chapter of Severn's last book, *The
Discovery of the Self* (1933), constitute an exemplary instance of the "sacralization of psychology"
as described by Hanegraaff (1998, pp. 224–229).

25

> It was from Elizabeth Severn, Sandor Ferenczi's pupil, that I learned the elementaries [sic] of a
> psychoanalytic approach to mediums. It was a standard joke between us that I was her illegitimate
> son, until one day she told me, now you can consider yourself legitimate.
>
> (Fodor, 1968, p. 105)

Severn was a member of the International Institute for Psychical Research from 1934 onwards,
acting both as Fodor's "analyst" and as "consultant" during the course of his investigation into the
notorious Thornton Heath poltergeist case. Fodor was a member of the NPAP/American Psychological Association and the editorial board for the *Psychoanalytic Review*, and his own publications
clearly indicate that he practised as a psychoanalytically informed clinician (Rudnytsky [e-mail
correspondence, 22/01/21]; Summerscale (2020, pp. 107–108, 243–245, 304). That both Severn and
Fodor acquired general recognition as "psychoanalysts" during their respective lifetimes hints at the
possibility of a psychoanalytic "transmission of knowledge" occurring outside of IPA-accredited
institutional frameworks. It is worth remarking in this context that Ferenczi considered Severn to
be a "capable psychologist" and regarded her as being in a training analysis with him (Hristeva,
2019, p. 518; Ferenczi, 2018 [1931]), p. 133). The significance of Fodor's work for "psychoanalytic
parapsychology" is discussed in the concluding part of this chapter.

with the "metapsychological" via the tertium quid of *magnetic gnosis* (a term which signifies a particular "mystical" variant of trance phenomena originating within the mesmeric traditions, the attributes of which are explored in more detail later in this chapter). Moreover, this tertium quid is accessed via the "initiatory" role played by extreme (or "sacred") trauma acting as the catalyst for transcendent modes of experience – "In the moment of the trauma some sort of omniscience about the world . . . makes the person in question . . . more or less clairvoyant" (Ferenczi, 2018 ["Note and Fragments, 2.4.1931"], p. 243).[26]

By February 1932, we find Ferenczi speculating on the potential links that could exist between the experience of trauma and the manifestation of "occult powers":

> To what extent do those who have "gone mad" from pain, that is, those who have departed from the usual egocentric point of view, become able through their special situation to experience a part of that immaterial reality which remains inaccessible to us materialists? And here the direction of research must become involved with the so-called occult. Cases of thought transference during the analysis of suffering people are extraordinarily frequent. One sometimes has the impression that the reality of such processes encounters strong emotional resistance in us materialists. . . . It is possible that here we are facing a fourth "narcissistic wound," namely that even the intelligence of which we are so proud, though analysts, is not our property but must be replaced or regenerated through the rhythmic outpouring of the ego into the universe, which alone is all knowing and therefore intelligent.
>
> (Ferenczi, 1995 [1932], p. 33)

While Ferenczi does not explicitly refer to Severn ("R.N.") in this entry, it is hard not to surmise from this that his expressed views may have been influenced by their exchanges on these topics. Notably in this regard, both Myers and his colleague William James subscribed to a theory of mind in which the respective pathways leading to psychopathology and transcendent alterations in consciousness could in practice prove difficult to disentangle due to their propensity to utilise the same channels for obtaining access to conscious awareness (Taylor, 1996, p. 81). Thurschwell has observed that

> For Ferenczi, occult powers are aligned with psychosis; paranormal hypersensitivity and psychic illness issue from the same causes . . . Ferenczi's theory of trauma suggests that the psychosis caused by a childhood sexual attack results

---

26

    We might thus speak here of sacred trauma, that is, of extremely positive religious events characterised by dissociative or "split" states of consciousness, which themselves encode histories of extreme forms of human suffering. In effect, something really bad catalyses/causes something really good.

                                                                            (Kripal, 2024 [2nd ed.], p. 226)

in a collapsing of the body and mind which can initiate clairvoyant or telepathic hypersensitivity.

(Thurschwell, 2001, p. 146)

Having highlighted the role of trauma acting as a potential catalyst to transcendence, we can now move on to consider the role of "Orpha" – and its equally enigmatic analogue, "astra" – as the exemplars of a shift in register from the domain of the metapsychological to the realm of magnetic *gnosis*. We can surmise from this transposition that both "Orpha" and "astra" exist within the parameters of the *paraconceptual,* an isomorphic "space" within which the psychological, the psychical and the occult co-exist in a tensional state of reciprocal superimposition.[27]

Ferenczi's references to Orpha occur on only a few occasions in his *Clinical Diary* (12 January, 17 January, 1 May, and 12 June). His first reference to Orpha is as follows and relates to his analysis of Severn ("R.N."):

The enormity of suffering, plus helplessness and despair of any outside help, propels her towards death; but as conscious thought is lost, or abandoned, the organizing life instincts ("Orpha") awaken, and in place of death allow insanity to intervene. (The same "Orphic" powers appear to have been already present at the time of the first shock [i.e. childhood sexual abuse aged eighteen months].) The consequence of the second shock [i.e. childhood sexual abuse aged five years] is a further "fragmentation" of the individuality. The person now consists of the following fragments: (1) A being suffering purely psychically in his unconscious, the actual child, of whom the awakened ego knows absolutely nothing. This fragment is accessible only in deep sleep, or in deep trance, following extreme exertion or exhaustion, that is, in a neurotic (hysterical) crisis situation. . . . (2) A singular being, for whom the preservation of life is of "coûte que coûte" significance. (Orpha.) This fragment plays the role of the guardian angel; it produces wish-fulfilling hallucinations, consolation fantasies; it anesthetizes the consciousness and sensitivity against sensations as they become unbearable.

(Ferenczi, 1995 [1932], pp. 8–9)

While neither Ferenczi nor Severn made any explicit allusions in their writings to the etymological or mythological background to Orpha, the term itself has obvious resonances with the myth of Orpheus and Eurydice – most notably with the theme of a "fragmented" yet "enshrined" "Orphic intelligence," brought into existence as a response to devastating experiences of trauma and loss (Smith, 1998, p. 242, n.

---

27 As we saw in Chapter 1, the term *paraconceptual* is taken from the work of the conceptual artist Susan Hiller (1940–2019). My introduction of this term in the present context constitutes an extension to the seminal work on demarcation in psychoanalysis and the occult undertaken by Gyimesi (2009).

2). Orpheus was one of the few Greek mythological heroes who managed both to descend to the underworld and to return again (Rachman, 2018, p. 265). However, it is also possible that the rubric of Orpha may have harkened back to the figure of a goddess who was at one time a part of the ancient Orphic cult, thereby constituting a "feminine" variant of the Orpheus myth (Gurevich, 2016, p. 329). As we have seen, the term itself appears to have originated with Severn, and there is evidence that it was even used by her, on occasion, as a kind of *nom de plume* (Gurevich, 2016, p. 327; Rudnytsky, 2022, pp. 129–130). Nonetheless, in the estimation of at least one commentator, "Orpha . . . is the hallmark, leitmotif and backbone of his [Ferenczi's] work prefigured there even before he met Severn. . . . From the very beginning he has had an Orphic mind" (Hristeva, 2019, p. 518). According to Rachman,

> The Orpha fragment was Severn's guardian angel, providing her with a positive functioning part of her personality which could cope with trauma by anesthetizing the self from unbearable sensations. It also produces fantasies, hallucinations that allowed Severn to restore her emotional equilibrium. At moments of severe trauma, when Severn felt she was on the verge of suicide or insanity from which she could not return, the Orpha function of her personality split itself off from the traumatised self with a fragment as a life-enhancing mechanism.
>
> (Rachman, 2018, p. 265)

Ferenczi's clinical work with Severn often required him to focus upon those forms of pathological fragmentation that entailed either a regression to infantile states or a precocious progression embarked upon for defensive purposes. Notably, Ferenczi credited his indebtedness to Severn for assisting him in his discoveries concerning psychotic splitting and dissociation (Fortune, 1993). In an addendum in his *Clinical Diary*, Ferenczi briefly alluded to a further, enigmatic fragmentation, which he termed "astra" (the Latin word for "stars"), in which the destructive consequences of trauma effectively function as a catalyst for accessing transcendent alterations in consciousness so that:

> the soul passes through a hole in the head into the universe and shines far off in the distance like a star (this would be clairvoyance, which goes beyond understanding the aggressor and understands the whole universe, so to speak, in order to be able to grasp the genesis of even such a monstrous thing).
>
> (Ferenczi, 1995 [1932], pp. 206–207)

The frequent appearance of trance phenomena constitutes a striking feature of Ferenczi's later writings.[28] The combined use of relaxation, regression and trance

---

28 See Ferenczi, "Child analysis in the analysis of adults" (1931) as well as the numerous references made to trance states in the *Clinical Diary*.

states featured prominently in Ferenczi's work with Severn, and it is evident that Severn's extensive prior experience in the use of trance states actively contributed to Ferenczi's development of therapeutic regression (Fortune, 1993, p. 438; Rachman, 2018, pp. 246–249; Rudnytsky, 2022, p. 84). Notably, access to "Orphic frenzy" was traditionally associated with trance states and alterations in consciousness (Uždavinys, 2011, p. 30; Ustinova, 2018, pp. 115–117). Moreover, the *mythos* of Orpheus is one that looms large across the multiple historical trajectories of Western esotericism, up to and including the various European fin de siècle magical orders, the teachings of which it seems reasonable to surmise that Severn might at least have had some passing acquaintance with (Goodrick-Clarke, 2008; Burns, 2015; Stein, 2016; Rudnytsky, 2022, p. 34).[29] Consequently, while the conceptual coordinates of Ferenczi's work with Severn may have originated from within the ambit provided by Freudian metapsychology, the ensuing trajectory of their combined discoveries subsequently became imbricated not only with the alternate consciousness paradigm associated with figures such as William James and F. W. H. Myers but was also imbued with traces of a more explicitly esoteric provenance (Taylor, 1983; Crabtree, 1993; Myers, 2001 [1903–4]; Raia, 2019).

As a point of comparison, James (who drew extensively upon the pioneering work of his friend and colleague Myers) held that psychic fragments possessed the potential to develop into "seemingly independent personalities" with the potential to access "permanently superior dimensions not normally accessible to waking awareness" (Taylor, 1983, p. 6). Moreover, he construed psychotherapy, mental healing and psychical phenomena to be closely contiguous to each other. James avowed a personal belief in "supernormal" forms of healing and cognition even while admitting that he possessed "no vestige of a theory" as to what lay behind such occurrences. His theory of mind embraced a "polypsychism" entailing "a confederation of psychic entities," within which "mediumship" was viewed as a non-pathological state of "alternating personality" that had the potential to access transcendent states of mind (Taylor, 1983, pp. 12, 35, 74). James surmised that "if there are supernormal powers, it is through the cracked and fragmented self that they enter" (Taylor, 1983, p. 110). While he did not view hypnosis as being directly causative of paranormal events, he nonetheless believed that trance states were favourable for the appearance of phenomena such as telepathy and clairvoyance (Taylor, 1983, p. 92).

In an analogous vein, Kalsched has drawn our attention to some striking parallels that exist between Jung and Ferenczi's ideas concerning trauma that emphasise their shared sense of its potential contiguity with the realms of the "supra-personal":

in both Ferenczi and Jung . . . we find not only primitive, infantile material, but something "progressed," uncanny, and of a "higher" order than primitive

---

29 For a helpful overview of Orphic themes in nineteenth- to twentieth-century culture, see von Stuck-rad (2022, pp. 28ff).

narcissism . . . Ferenczi found himself staring through the violent ruptures of trauma into an alternative world of extraordinary, "mythopoetic" inner presences – from Orphic guardians to wise babies . . . Ferenczi's research with his severely traumatized patients points in the same direction as Jung's – towards an implicate order of "supra-personal" powers co-mingled with the mundane ordinary realities of ego-development in the body.

(Kalsched, 2003, pp. 484–486)

While notable efforts have been made to situate Orpha within its historical and literary contexts (Gurevich, 2016; Rachman, 2018; Hristeva, 2019), I would like to propose that these accounts can be usefully augmented by aligning Orpha with its mesmeric and somnambulistic precursors located within Romantic psychology, and, more particularly, to an esoteric variant of these traditions referred to in the literature as *mystical magnetism* or *magnetic gnosis* initially alluded to in Chapter two (Gauld, 1992, pp. 141–178; Crabtree, 1993, pp. 171–212; Ellenberger, 1994 [1970], pp. 57–120; Hanegraaff, 2010). Moreover, while the phenomenon of mesmerism is commonly misconstrued as a distant historical artefact, there are reasons for supposing that its demise is more frequently presumed than proven (Harrington, 2004). In order to briefly illustrate what might be understood by these essentially synonymous terms, we can refer to Carl Alexander Ferdinand Kluge's textbook on animal magnetism (1811), in which the author distinguished six discrete levels of magnetic somnambulism, culminating in a final stage entailing "universal clarity," through which the percipient purportedly transcended time and space and attained a state of clairvoyance (Ellenberger, 1994 [1970], p. 78).

Having set out the proximate and distal "origins" to what I have described as an *Orphic trajectory* within psychoanalysis, we shall now conclude this chapter with a brief account of the work of the protégé and only psychoanalytic "heir" to Elizabeth Severn, the "psychoanalytic parapsychologist" Nandor Fodor (Coleman, 1964, p. 155; Rudnytsky, 2022, pp. 145, 148). As we shall see, Fodor's attempt to forge a rapprochement between Freudian and Jungian conceptualisations of the unconscious can be construed as an untimely intervention prefiguring future developments in post-Bionian psychoanalysis.

4.5 "The Haunted Mind" – the psychoanalytic parapsychology of Nandor Fodor

It is an understandable – if unfortunate – state of affairs that the Hungarian psychoanalyst, parapsychologist and journalist Nandor Fodor has been relegated to the footnotes of psychoanalytic history.[30] Despite his numerous publications in the

---

30 For an entertaining account of Fodor's life, see Summerscale (2020, pp. 29ff). See also Rudnytsky (2022, pp. 141–148) for a more scholarly account of Fodor's psychoanalytic affiliations and his relations with Severn.

fields of psychoanalysis and psychical research, his work has largely been consigned to the peripheries of both disciplines due to the inherently liminal nature of his investigations. More specifically, his preoccupation with sexuality was frequently frowned upon within the more conservative circles of psychical research, while his "occult" interests (as well as his openness to Jungian analytical psychology) placed him on the periphery of the established norms of the psychoanalytic establishment.[31] Fodor was under no illusions as to the significance of his work – as well as its associated costs – observing that "to be a pioneer – as I have been – is an ungrateful task. It means simply that many people will brand you as crazy" (Spraggett, 1969, p. 135). The ensuing neglect of his work is undeserved, insofar as he made important – albeit frequently unacknowledged – contributions in a number of areas, including those of psychoanalytic parapsychology, the psychoanalysis of pre-birth states, dream analysis and the development of a framework for understanding the transgenerational transmission of trauma.[32] Notably, his book *New Approaches to Dream Interpretation* (1962) was deemed by one commentator to constitute a "landmark" in the development of dream psychology, while his posthumously published *Freud, Jung, and Occultism* (1971) was described by one of its reviewers as "an indispensable guide to all practitioners who seek a deeper understanding of their patients and are interested in the theory of the mind and the modus operandi of psi. It is a jumping-off point to myriad future discoveries." This same reviewer goes on to describe Fodor as "a master dream analyst."[33] Moreover, Marie Coleman Nelson assessed Fodor's contributions to psychoanalysis to be in the same category as major psychoanalytic "dissidents" such as Jung, Ferenczi, Reich and Stekel (Nelson, 1969, pp. 5–6). Notably, Fodor's approach to the treatment of trauma was ahead of its time and was indebted to the ideas of Ferenczi and Severn (Summerscale, 2020, p. 311). Nonetheless, due to his comparative obscurity, it will be helpful to begin with a brief biographical outline before embarking upon a tightly focused exposition of two of the key findings arising from his research into "psychoanalytic parapsychology."[34]

---

31 "Within the Establishment ostracism of colleagues who take parapsychology seriously continues to prevail" Marie C. Nelson (1969, p. 4). See also Timms (2012) for a helpful overview of Fodor's life and work. On the significance of Jung for Fodor, see Fodor (1964, pp. 74–78). Fodor argued that Freud's findings had to be augmented with those of Jung and Groddeck if an adequate conceptualisation of the unconscious was to be arrived at – see Fodor (1949, p. 326).

32 See the following: Schwarz (1973–1974), pp. 636–638; Feldman (1960, pp. 111–113); Nelson (1964, pp. 155–157); Fodor (1949); Fodor (1951). According to one commentator, Fodor "elaborated Rank's 'birth trauma' into a theory of prenatal traumata based on telepathic contact between the mother and her unborn child" (Spraggett, 1969, p. 128).

33 See Spraggett (1969, p. 131); Schwarz (1973–1974, p. 637). The following texts are referenced in these remarks: Fodor (1951); Fodor (1971).

34 My use of the term "psychoanalytic parapsychology" is taken from Nelson (1964, p. 155). Hewitt (2020, pp. 94–95) has more recently coined the term *parapsychoanalysis* to denote the theories of those "contemporary mystical psychoanalytic writers" who seek to "blend psychoanalysis and paranormal research."

Nandor Fodor (previously Friedlander) was the 16th of 18 siblings born in the Hungarian town of Beregszász on 13 May 1895. After obtaining a doctorate in law from the Royal Hungarian University of Science, Fodor emigrated to the United States of America in 1921 to pursue a career as a journalist. He married Amaria Iren in 1922, with whom he had one daughter, Andrea. Fodor's chance discovery of Hereward Carrington's Modern *Psychic Phenomena* (1919) had a profound effect upon him and led to both parties developing a lifelong friendship. While Fodor did not consider himself to be "psychic," this did not prevent him from seeking tutelage in "occult" breathing and automatic writing techniques from the "spiritualist" writer Marjorie Livingston. In 1926, Fodor had an opportunity to interview Sándor Ferenczi, who provided him with a model for his subsequent efforts to combine psychoanalysis with psychical research. In 1929, Fodor left the United States for England after being offered the post of personal secretary to the millionaire newspaper magnate Lord Rothmere, a position which also gave him the opportunity to pursue a journalistic career on Fleet Street while deepening his knowledge of psychical research and psychoanalysis through his contact with figures such as Elizabeth Severn, who not only acted as Fodor's analyst but also took on the role of "consultant" during the course of his investigations into the case of Alma Fielding. From 1934 to 1938, Fodor was employed as the research officer for The International Institute for Psychical Research, during which time he participated in a series of increasingly psychoanalytically informed investigations into supernatural phenomena, including the Thornton Heath poltergeist case (1938), his report into which Fodor considered to be his most significant contribution to psychical research. Fodor's work on this investigation was subsequently lauded by Freud, while costing him his post as research officer due to the controversy that arose in the wake of his identification of early sexual trauma as constituting the main aetiological context for the purported "manifestations" associated with this case.[35] In Freud's estimation, Fodor's:

> turning away from interest in whether the observed phenomena were genuine or fraudulent, your turning towards the psychological study of the medium and the uncovering of her previous history seem to me to be the important steps which will lead to the elucidation of the phenomena under review.[36]

However, while his book-length publications and journalistic writings did much to popularise the application of psychoanalytic ideas as an explanatory schema for understanding alleged psychical phenomena, his persistent attempts to develop a

---

35 This brief account of Fodor's life is indebted to the following sources: Summerscale (2020); Fodor (1959); Fodor (1968); Timms (2012); Anonymous, "Nandor Fodor": http://survivalafterdeath.info/researchers/fodor.htm (downloaded 20/04/2020).

36 Correspondence from Sigmund Freud to Nandor Fodor (1938), cited in Nelson (1964, pp. 155–156). For the full text of this letter, see Fodor (1959, pp. 8–9).

rapprochement between both disciplines tended to alienate the more ideologically committed of both camps. In Fodor's estimation:

> For sixty years, psychical research has gone round in a vicious circle . . . it has failed to give due consideration to the essentially psychological nature of mediumistic phenomena. I am convinced that the exploration of the unconscious minds of mediums by the means provided in psychoanalysis would solve many mysteries and would lead to discoveries of considerable importance both to psychology and psychical research.[37]

Towards the end of his life during an interview in which he reflected on the course of his life and career, Fodor made a series of forthright observations on the topics of psychoanalysis and psychical research, during which he remarked that "Freud was practically a mystic [who was] kept under restraint by his own followers," before going on to observe that "we do not have to understand something to know that it is" (Spraggett, 1969, pp. 131–132). Although Fodor concluded that "[p]sychic phenomena do exist," he was nonetheless highly parsimonious in his judgements, asserting that over the course of a lifetime of research spanning a period of some 40 years, he had encountered only three cases that he considered to possess evidential value for post-mortem survival. In the estimation of one of his psychoanalytic peers, Fodor's approach to such questions was adjudged to be one that combined "healthy scepticism with an open-minded research approach that deserves emulation" (Fodor, 1959, 1968; Nelson, 1969, p. 8). The former of these traits is evidenced in his publications, as can be seen, for example, in a series of "reductive" interpretations regarding Swedenborg's *Dream Diary,* as well as "mystical participation," astral travel, theosophy, reincarnation and automatic writing (Fodor, 1949, pp. 67, 173, 207–208).[38] It could be legitimately argued that Fodor possessed a more comprehensive knowledge of occult, esoteric and parapsychological topics compared to that small number of his psychoanalytic peers who pursued a similar interest in such matters, and his contributions correspondingly reflect the diversity of his interests.[39] Fodor's importance as a theoretician and researcher

37 Nandor Fodor (1945), cited in Timms (2012, p. 12).
38 On Fodor's views regarding the "unreliability" of automatic writing, see Fodor (1968, p. 45).
39 Fodor published the well-received *Encyclopaedia of Psychic Science* (1933) and was friendly with a wide range of individuals involved with psychical research and the translation of "esoteric" literature (including G.R.S. Mead, a notable translator of "Gnostic" and hermetic texts). Moreover, his writings contain numerous references to a wide range of "esoteric" and "occult" figures, such as John Dee (1527–1608), Emanuel Swedenborg (1688–1772), Justinus Kerner (1786–1862), F.W.H. Myers (1843–1901), Théodore Flournoy (1854–1920) and Hélène Smith (1861–1929) – see Fodor (1951, pp. 130, 163, 1959, p. 262, 1968, p. 220). Fodor supported the work of figures such as Jules Eisenbud (1908–1998), a psychoanalyst and pioneering investigator into the paranormal. Eisenbud was a major contributor to research into the role of paranormal phenomena (especially telepathy and precognition) in psychoanalysis – for a helpful overview and appraisal of Eisenbud's work, see Reichbart (2019, pp. 6–7, 50–57, 100–102). For details concerning some of Fodor's

into "psychoanalytic parapsychology" can be illustrated by briefly summarising his work on the role of telepathy in psychoanalysis and his investigations into an obscure phenomenon for which he coined the term "poltergeist psychosis."

Fodor came to the study of telepathic dreams through the discovery of uncanny parallels arising between the contents of his own dreams and those of his wife and daughter (Fodor, 1951, p. 164). Early on in his book-length study of dream interpretation, Fodor observed that "the unconscious has its own channels of awareness. What we call 'telepathy' appears to be one such channel" (Fodor, 1951, p. 15). While Fodor frankly acknowledged in an earlier study into prenatal states that he had no special insights into the actual mechanisms that facilitated telepathy, he nonetheless speculated that it could entail an "archaic method of communication antedating the development of speech" (Fodor, 1949, p. 328).[40] In Fodor's estimation, the chief contribution of Freud's 1933 paper on telepathy lay in its deployment of dream interpretation as a means for unearthing those latent telepathic communications that would not otherwise be recognisable as such. However, Fodor's research also led him to elaborate upon Freud's original findings:

> The telepathic dream, regardless of its stimulating role, reflects like a mirror the contents of the unconscious mind of the agent, paralleling it by similar contents in the recipient's mind which are shaped into a personal dream. The similarity of parallelism of psychic content may be the predisposing factor rendering telepathy a possibility. . . . In other words, telepathic communications can only be received because there exists in the dreamer's unconscious a psychic content which, in its latent meaning, corresponds to the manifest content of the message.
>
> (Fodor, 1951, p. 164)

Moreover, when Fodor alludes in passing to the notion of "Displacement of affect by way of telepathy," it is difficult not to construe this idea as being phenomenologically contiguous to evolving ideas concerning "communicative" forms of counter-transference translated into the idiom of psychical research (Fodor, 1951, p. 15). While Fodor was parsimonious regarding the claims that he made concerning "the hypothetical but by no means impossible telepathic interaction between mother and child," he nonetheless considered the potential for further research into this area to be a matter of particular importance (Fodor, 1951, pp. 327, 339). In Fodor's estimation, "unrecognised telepathy" played a significant – albeit unacknowledged – role in the "emotional interchange between analyst and patient," the obscure dynamics of which are more frequently encountered in the clinical literature under the rubric of psychoanalytic "intuition" (Fodor, 1951, p. 204). Moreover,

---

peers in "psychoanalytic parapsychology," see Fodor (1959, p. 13). See also the authors collected in Devereux (ed.) (1974 [1953]).

40 Fodor (1949, p. 328). Fodor's knowledge of the associated literature is extensive, as can be inferred from his citing no less than 12 papers (including two of his own) in support of his argument.

he considered the role of "unrecognised telepathy" in the "analytic transference" to be a topic worthy of further research (Fodor, 1951, p. 205). However, it is in the area of dream interpretation that the clinical implications of Fodor's research into telepathy become most apparent:

> It may be objected that in the author's technique of dream interpretation considerable play is allowed for analytic intuition. The answer is that once telepathic associations are admitted, what appears to be intuition may turn out to be only the unconscious perception of a content in the patient's mind which the analyst himself brings into consciousness.[41]

Fodor subscribed to the views of Dr J. N. Rosen, who proposed that "everybody's unconscious perfectly understands everybody else's unconscious." As a consequence, Fodor's view of telepathy was essentially that of a faculty which operated predominantly on an unconscious level that tended to be most active between individuals among whom there already existed a strong emotional bond (Fodor, 1951, pp. 204–205).

In Fodor's estimation, it was his concept of "Poltergeist Psychosis" that constituted his most important contribution to psychoanalytic parapsychology (Fodor, 1948, 1968, p. 112). Fodor freely acknowledged that his deployment of this term was essentially descriptive, since the mechanisms of this "psycho-biological disorder" were essentially unknown, although he did consider it to be "an episodic mental disturbance of schizophrenic character" frequently associated with the temporary occurrence of amnesiac and dissociative states of mind (Fodor, 1959, p. 71). However, Gyimesi has proposed that it was through the research of figures such as Fodor that:

> the idea of hysterical conversion . . . gained its true parapsychological significance: if it is possible to produce physical symptoms within the body, then it might also be possible to produce them outside the body as well. In this sense, parapsychological phenomena were identified as symptoms of the sufferer.
>
> (Gyimesi, 2016a, p. 50)

While Fodor did not rule out the possibility of psychokinesis as an associated phenomenon, he nonetheless observed that

> psychoanalytic inquiry may disclose motives of revenge, spite, or self-castigation behind the phenomena, all of which raise the question: Are we facing in the poltergeist a psychosomatic dissociation, a mental split conjoined with an abnormal employment of extra-physical organismic energies?
>
> (Fodor, 1959, p. 72)

---

41 Fodor, 1951, pp. xii–xiii. Fodor's speculations on these topics arguably prefigure some of the theoretical developments encountered in post-Bionian theories of *reverie* discussed in Chapters 5 and 6.

Fodor's most famous (and controversial) investigation into "poltergeist psychosis" took place in the context of his report into the Thornton Heath case alluded to earlier (see Fodor, 1959, pp. 5–9). As we have seen, it was this case that brought Fodor's work to Freud's attention, in the form of a supportive letter in which the correctness of Fodor's approach to psychoanalytic parapsychology was emphasised by Freud.

However, as Fodor subsequently observed, during the time when his correspondence with Freud originally took place, Fodor himself possessed no particular insight into the deeply personal significance that poltergeist phenomena originally held for Freud. Fodor subsequently wrote on this topic, focusing upon the deteriorating relations between Freud and Jung as exemplified by their respective reactions to an anomalous occurrence involving a bookcase that took place on 25 March 1909, which was initially described by Freud as a "poltergeist phenomenon" and subsequently by Fodor as a "telekinetic phenomenon" (Fodor, 1963). Fodor trenchantly described the attempts made by Freud in his correspondence to Jung on 16 April 1909 to downplay the impact that this incident had upon him as "pathetic." He also speculated on Jung's own conflicts arising from a possible desire to disguise from Freud the "tainted heredity" associated with his maternal family's mediumistic abilities.

While the controversy surrounding the Thornton Heath case initially disillusioned Fodor in his attempts to develop a "psychoanalytic parapsychology," he eventually arrived at the following position, which he maintained throughout the remainder of his career:[42]

> Sifting out the real from the delusional, psychology will have to come to grips with unsuspected powers of the unconscious. . . . The addition of the psychoanalytic method of approach promises a greater understanding of psychic manifestations than the exclusive utilization of objective methods of research, as used in parapsychology and psychical research. These disciplines must work hand-in-hand, lest the conquest of great mental realms be postponed to future generations.
>
> (Fodor, 1959, p. 311)

While Fodor's personal hopes in this regard were to remain as largely unrealised in his own lifetime, his vision of a "psychoanalytic parapsychology" can nonetheless be construed as constituting a largely neglected contribution towards the development of an *Orphic trajectory* within psychoanalysis. Moreover, some of Fodor's ideas concerning dreams and the nature of prenatal existence are suggestive of a tacit and untimely apprehension of the numinous and infinite unconscious

---

42 Remarking on the impact of Freud's supporting correspondence previously alluded to, Fodor observed that "This had the immediate effect of silencing my opponents and of confirming me in my decision to forsake parapsychology as a professional pursuit" (Fodor, 1963, p. 119).

postulated by Bionian and post-Bionian psychoanalysis, the distinctive attributes of which will be explored further in the next two chapters. Keeping these perspectives in mind, it is to the seminal contributions made by W.R. Bion (1897–1979) towards the formation of an *Orphic trajectory* within psychoanalysis that our attention shall now turn.

Acknowledgement

Part of this chapter first appeared in the article 'From Metapsychology to Magnetic Gnosis: An Esoteric Context for interpreting Traumatic Modes of Transcendence in Sándor Ferenczi's *Clinical Diary* and Elizabeth Severn's *The Discovery of the Self,' Psychoanalysis and History*, Volume 23, number 3 (2021). I acknowledge the use of these materials in this chapter.

Chapter 5

From mystical gnosis to esoteric *technē*[1]

5.1 Introduction

I can understand someone saying that they had an experience like thought-reading. . . . It might be compatible with the idea that there is some mental phenomenon which is not bounded by what I can see and what I can hear, what I can smell touch and feel. Although you and I are in different places not known to each other there may . . . be some over-lapping. I could not prove it . . . I suspect it is one of those things called "extrasensory perception," but that is probably too crude. As our intuition continues to develop we get nearer to a situation where we seem to be aware that the boundaries of our mind are not our physical boundaries, nor yet the boundaries which are imposed by our central nervous system. That is more like a guess, or a "hunch," than anything one could call evidence or fact. But it may be a fact one day.

W. R. Bion, 1974, Rio de Janeiro[2]

---

1 Copyright © 2023 the Johns Hopkins University Press. Part of this chapter first appeared in the article "Mystical *Gnosis* and Esoteric *Technē* in the Writings of W.R. Bion" published in *American Imago*, Volume 80, Number 2, 2023. Published with permission by the Johns Hopkins University Press.
2 Chris Mawson (editor); Francesca Bion (consultant editor) *The Complete Works of W. R. Bion, Vols. I to XVI* (London: Karnac, 2014), Vol. 7, p. 90. Reprinted with permission. For ease of reference, the *Complete Works* will subsequently be referred to as CWB, followed by the volume (in Roman numerals) and the page number. For reasons of brevity, the Los Angeles seminars (which were published after CWB) under the auspices of Joseph Aguayo and Barnet Marin (eds.), *Wilfred Bion: Los Angeles Seminars and Supervision* (London: Routledge, 2018) will be referenced as LASS. For comparison with the extract cited in the epigraph to this chapter, see CWB X: 24 ("The Grid," 1971), where Bion writes, "I do not feel the need to postulate 'extra-sensory' perception" immediately subsequent to having stated that "I think we need to keep an open mind." By the time we get to *A Memoir of the Future* (1975), we encounter the following enigmatic addendum to these speculations: "Now, the Mind . . . you just try it. Just attach it to your sensory perceptions! How do I know it won't just turn into extrasensory perceptions – s.p→e.s.p.?" (CWB XII: 62). By 1976, we find Bion observing that " we don't know what the mind really is capable of perceiving" (CWB X: 156). There are grounds to suppose that Bion's speculations on ESP arose out of his experience of working with the phenomenon of projective identification in his clinical practice (CWB VII: 68; LASS, p. 100), in addition to discussions he had with clinicians in his seminars (CWB IX: 155–158). See also the following: "one suspects that there is a relationship in analysis which extends beyond the analytic spectrum. It belongs, as it were, to the analytic ultraviolet, or the analytic infrared" (LASS, p. 97) [c.f. Jung (1947/1954), para. 384, 414]. Notably, both Bion and Jung's respective deployments of the idea of a

DOI: 10.4324/9781003476733-5

Bion could be notably reticent when it came to the matter of explicitly acknowledging the contributions made by those authors whose ideas he tacitly drew upon during the course of developing his own innovations in psychoanalytic theory and practice.[3] This is a matter of some importance, given that in the estimation of the Symingtons, Bion is adjudged to be "the deepest thinker within psychoanalysis – and this statement does not exclude Freud" (Symington & Symington, 1996, p. 12). As we shall see, this state of affairs can be at least partially attributed to Bion's own very particular understanding of the relations that pertain between a writer and the purported sources of their clinical and theoretical creativity. Bion's most innovative period as a theorist corresponded with his decision to move from London to California in 1968. One associated consequence that arose out of this move concerned the vehemence with which some of the London Kleinians, in particular, began to question the value of his later writings, even going so far as to question the sanity of their author (Symington & Symington, 1996, p. 10). While we do not know the precise reasons that led to this *caesura* in Bion's life and work, there is nonetheless good reason to suppose that for some time prior to this, Bion had become increasingly dissatisfied with the lack of professional freedom he experienced in England in the context of his work as a leading Kleinian analyst (Vermote, 2019, pp. 12–13; Abel-Hirsch, 2019, pp. 406–411). In a manner of speaking, he became (for some of his previous colleagues at least) the "repository . . . of a heretic and subversive legacy that was unconsciously passed on to him at the Tavistock" (Mancia, 2018, p. 66). The intensity of the feelings engendered by these disputes concerning the putative value that should be ascribed to Bion's work during his later, so-called mystical phase has proven sufficiently powerful as to continue to reverberate in contemporary debates concerning the reception of his writings (Grotstein, 2007, pp. 20–21; Blass, 2011).

Gérard Bléandonu (1994) has proposed that Bion's writings can be thought of as inhabiting several phases, which he categorised under the following rubrics: the group period; understanding psychosis; the epistemological period – the ideal of a scientific psychoanalysis, the epistemological period – the quest for ultimate truth and the final period. This chapter sets out to provide an overview of the evidence that can be adduced for the existence of an *esoteric matrix* active within the latter phases of Bion's work, the ensuing effects of which it is argued came to play a

---

psychic "spectrum" bear comparison with Frederic Myers' metaphoric usage of the electromagnetic spectrum as "one of the central organizing principles of his theorizing and poetics" (Kripal, 2010, p. 60; see also Shamdasani, 2003, p. 261). It is from within the mesh of tensions conjoining these various positionings (separated as they are from each other by a period of some eight years) that the arguments set out in this chapter are situated.

3 See, for example, Culbert-Koehn (1997, p. 16), in which Grotstein remarks that "Bion . . . was not a scholar who would cite other people's works." See also Borgogno and Merciai (2000, p. 59). It is a matter of great regret that the untimely demise of Bion's daughter Parthenope prevented her from bringing to fruition her envisaged project on "Bion and his Books – Pathways to the World of Bion," the brief surviving notes from which can be found in Hinshelwood and Torres (2013, pp. xiv–xvii). For a useful (but not exhaustive) summary of the texts known to exist in Bion's personal library, see Sandler (2006).

significant role with regard to the associated theoretical innovations that arose out of the later "mystical" phase of his work.[4] However, before we can set out the wider context of these developments, it is necessary to begin with an overview of the oblique yet pervasive influence exerted by the ideas of C. G. Jung (1875–1961) in the development of Bion's later thinking.[5]

Having set the stage by means of outlining the contribution made by Jung in the formation of a specifically Bionian approach to psychoanalysis, this chapter moves on to engage with a series of esoterically inflected "techniques" (*technē/ technai*)[6] that it is argued became prominent in Bion's later writings, whose provenance owes much to esoteric modes of discourse and thinking (mysticism, Neoplatonism, "O,"[7] "without memory or desire," "a beam of intense darkness" and "reverie"). As we shall see subsequently, Bion's revisioning of a "mystical" psychoanalysis entailed the concomitant development of an *apophatic* discourse,

---

4 My use of the term *matrix* in this context echoes that of Bion's concept of the *protomental matrix* (CWB IV; 177), in addition to that of the *hallucinatory matrix* accessed during states of deep regression (Vermote, 2019, p. 63). Notably, Matte-Blanco has referred in his own writings to a

> basic matrix . . . in which symmetrisation exerts a major influence on representation and is in the region of the deeper unconscious. . . . The result is that when we begin to explore this stratum and think that something belongs to what we call the inside, but find that it may equally correctly be said to belong to what we call the outside, we tend to solve this difficulty by saying that this is something that has been projected outwards.
>
> (Matte-Blanco, 1998, pp. 193–194)

What is striking is the extent to which both of these conceptualisations of "matrices" overlap with Jung's idea of the *psychoid,* at least to the degree to which their shared convergence – tending towards a dual-aspect monism – indirectly draws upon Bergson's *panpsychism* as a common resource – see Addison (2016, p. 574) for more on this. For an account of Bion's indebtedness to Bergson, see Torres (2013a, pp. 20–34). For a reading of both Bion and Bergson as tending towards a position of panpsychism, see Torres (2013b, pp. 56–67). While my argument does not extend in the present context to include "Eastern" sources, it should not be inferred from this that such elements do not have a significant role to play in the later Bion's writings. For an exemplary instance of recent work in this area, see Zhang (2019).

5 For a helpful summary of the extensive role played by esotericism in Jung's work, see Wehr (2016).

6

> Aristotle distinguishes three kinds of knowledge: episteme, techne and phronesis. They don't have exact equivalents in English, but they can be explained without too much difficulty. Episteme is abstract, context-independent, invariant and general. It is based on analytical reasoning . . . it represents the left hemisphere [of the brain] in action. Techne is the skill of the craftsman: practical, embodied, flexible and dependent on context. Phronesis is a kind of pragmatic wisdom, which involves the appreciation of values, is more reflective, but is also flexible, tacit, intuitive and context-sensitive like techne, to which it is closer than it is to episteme. Both phronesis and techne show signs of being more right hemisphere-dependent. Aristotle also distinguishes nous (intuition) and sophia (another kind of wisdom).
>
> (McGilchrist, 2021, p. 698)

7 While the term "O" as employed by Bion is one that has come to acquire an increasingly baroque penumbra of meanings as elaborated within the secondary literature, perhaps its most lucid and lapidary exposition is the one given by Bion himself in his 1973 São Paulo seminars: "When I use the letter, O, I mean it to indicate noumenon, the thing itself of which nobody can know anything" (CWB VII: 69).

operative as a *technē* for disarticulating the ineffable modes of experiencing, thereby engendered between analyst and analysand during the course of their combined efforts to arrive at a state of "at-one-ment" with *O*. It is further proposed that the synergistic rapprochement between theory and *praxis* thereby arrived at in Bion's late writings can be conceptualised as constituting a contemporary iteration of the dialectic conjoining mystical *gnosis* to esoteric *technai* in a manner that is – in some respects at least – analogous to the theurgical practices encountered in Late Antiquity:

> Understanding esotericism leads us back to mysticism, as the fundamental theoretical groundwork for esoteric currents . . . esotericism is virtually unintelligible without an appreciation for its roots in mystic *gnosis*. And it can be plausibly argued that *gnosis* leads to esoteric *technē*. . . . Thus we frequently find mystics of all types engaged in esoteric practices.
>
> (Magee, 2016, p. xxxi)

This dialectic can be construed as an ouroboric, textually mediated process that is itself the performative enactment of a "visionary" quest for "mystical" modes of self-transformation, the essential features of which Jeffrey Kripal has theorised under the rubric of *academic esotericism* (Kripal, 2001, p. 25), a hermeneutic stratagem reminiscent in many respects with the idea of *defensive esotericism*, whose essential tenets are explored further below.

From a textual viewpoint, a particularly striking aspect of this dialectical interplay pertains to the linguistic and conceptual difficulties commonly experienced both by neophyte and by more experienced readers during the course of their encounter with Bion's *oeuvre*. Bion was aware of these difficulties and sought on occasion to address some of the concerns raised by his critics:

> It may seem that I am mis-using words with an established meaning, as in my use of the terms "function" and "factors." A critic has pointed out to me that the terms are used ambiguously and the sophisticated reader may be misled by the association of both words with mathematics and philosophy. I have deliberately used them because of the association, and I wish the ambiguity to remain. I want the reader to be reminded of mathematics, philosophy and common usage, because a characteristic of the human mind I am discussing may develop in such a way that it is seen at a later stage to be classifiable under those headings – and others.
>
> (CWB IV: 264)

At the literal level, the reader has to contend with a series of increasingly complex, recondite and opaque modes of discourse, whose range of reference not only spans the more usual topics commonly encountered in psychoanalytic theory, whose purview is further extended so as to include subjects as disparate and diverse as astronomy, quantum theory, higher mathematics, ancient history, mysticism, ideographs and hieroglyphs, and the *sui generis* construct known as "the grid," not to mention detours into some of the more obscure byways of philosophical speculation. Moreover, Bion's own attitude towards the communicative possibilities of language undergoes a series of complex transformations over time, during the course of which his preferred modes of discourse shift from the neopositivistic towards a *bricolage* of the literary, the apophatic and the mystical. This can be illustrated by means of an extract, which is taken from his *magnum opus, A Memoir of the Future* (1975):[8]

> BION If you think the problems that we have to solve can be solved in a framework where "things" happen in time and space, with ideas taken from the vocabulary and grammar invented for the senses, we shall fail. . . . You cannot resolve the apparent conflict of wave mechanics with the theories of quanta without supposing a domain suitable for harbouring the theory which has to be entertained. This theory has been formulated by Melanie Klein as operative in a psychoanalytic domain expanded to contain it. It is analogous to expanding the domain of arithmetic to contain irrational numbers, negative numbers, compound conjugate numbers. The domain which is adequate for the operation of natural numbers cannot contain these numbers.
>
> (CWB XII: 174–175)

As the textual recipients of such a conceptual and terminological barrage of psychoanalytic, quantum mechanical and mathematical discourses, it comes as something of a relief for the reader to find the character of Rosemary (with whose responses the overwhelmed reader is likely to identify) reply to the character Bion's speculations with a simple "I don't understand" (the state of "unknowing" itself constituting the necessary precondition for attaining the state of *apophasis* advocated as an integral element of the late Bion's epistemological *technē*). Moreover, there are reasons to suppose that Bion may have on occasion utilised a mode of discourse known as *defensive esotericism* as a rhetorical stratagem enabling him to articulate a "mystical" approach to psychoanalysis while simultaneously guarding himself against the attempts made by the psychoanalytic "establishment" to undermine the dissemination of some of his more provocative and controversial ideas.[9] As we

---

8 At least it was deemed to be such by Francesca Bion (Lopez-Corvo, 2018, pp. 14 and 173) as well as by Bion himself – see Vermote (2019, p. 11). On the rather more mixed reception this text received from its first readers, see Vermote (2019, pp. 177–178).

9 For more on the idea of *defensive esotericism,* see Melzer (2014, pp. 90–91, 127–159). While Melzer's argument requires the book-length exposition that he devotes to these topics (defensive, protective, pedagogical and political esotericism), the central tenets of his work can nonetheless be aptly summarised in the words of the Abbé Galiani (1728–1787) to a friend: You tell me . . . that after the reading of my book, you are hardly any further along concerning the heart of the question. How, by the devil! . . . do you not read the white [spaces] of works? Certainly, those who read only the black of a writing will not have seen anything decisive in my book; but you, read the white, read what I did not write and what is there nonetheless; and then you will find it. (cited in Melzer, 2014, p. 287) In view of Bion's proclivity to deploy paradoxical metaphors to encode his meaning (as might be seen, for example, in his recurrent references to the ostensibly Freudian metaphor of "a beam of intense darkness" explored later in this chapter), the adoption of this advice as given by Galiani to his interlocutor

shall see, some of these developments were obliquely indebted to the inspiration that he received from his engagement with the psychoanalytically heterodox ideas of C.G. Jung.

5.2   The spectral encryption of Jung in the late writings of Bion

An attempt to argue that Bion might have drawn upon the ideas of Jung during the course of arriving at his own thoughts may appear at first sight to be mis-guided. In his correspondence with John Rickman, Bion was disparaging not only regarding Jung's idea of a "collective unconscious" but was also even more dismissive when it came to the matter of Jungian scholarship more generally (Vonofakos & Hinshelwood, 2012, pp. 67–68; see also n. 9, 15/03/1940). Yet, despite this seemingly unpromising start, various arguments have been put for-ward by a range of scholars in support of the contention that a number of Bion's concepts are either to some degree indebted to Jungian ideas (whether directly, indirectly or via more obscure processes such as cryptomnesia) or at least bear some similarity to their proximate Jungian analogues.[10] The range of compara-ble ideas is considerable and includes the following (not exhaustive) list of con-cepts: projective identification and container/contained (Maier, 2016),[11] analytic "intuition" (Williams, 2006), reversible perspective (synchronicity) (Williams, 2006, p. 92), the protomental matrix (psychoid) (Addison, 2019, pp. 52–68), primordial mind (archetypes), gnostic mysticism, preconceptions (archetypes) (Winborn, 2018), myths, transformations, the numinous (Culbert-Koehn, 1997), "O" (Sullivan, 2010), reverie (amplification), constant conjunction (synchronic-ity) (Mancia, 2018) and *A Memoir of the Future* (*Liber Novus*).[12] Yet, despite these confluences, on the few occasions when Bion explicitly discusses Jung's work, his acknowledgement of any parallels or potential influences tends to

---

might conceivably constitute a "model" approach for reading the later Bion in particular. Notably in this regard, Grotstein has queried "*may not Bion have learned early on to think and speak in code like his forebear, Spinoza?*" (Grotstein, 2007, p. 14), a figure whom Meltzer cites in his work as belonging to his genealogy of "esoteric" philosophers. See especially chapter 7 of *Attention and Interpretation* (1970), in which Bion's reflections concerning the nature of the tensions existing between the "mystic" and the "group" can arguably be read as a thinly disguised commentary on the circumstances leading up to his departure to California in 1968 (CWB VI: 287).

10 See Aguayo (2025, p. 101, n. 4) for a helpful overview of the secondary literature on this topic.

11 Jung referred to "the problem of the container and the contained" in his paper "Marriage as a psy-chological relationship" (1925 [English trans. 1931]). Notably, Maier (2016, p. 144) identifies "a chain of authors of projective identification – Weiss, Jung, Rosenfeld, Melanie Klein, Bion," thereby complicating, in a fruitful fashion, the conceptual lineage of this ostensibly "Kleinian" idea.

12 Mancia (2018, pp. 67–77). However, cf. with Jung (1960, p. 514, para. 963), where, in the context of an explanatory diagram, Jung describes synchronicity as constituting "Inconstant Connection through Contingency, Equivalence, or 'Meaning.'"

be somewhat ambivalent or "minimalist" with regard to its nature.[13] The only explicit acknowledgement of Jung's writings referenced in the *Collected Works* pertains to Jung's 1925 paper, "Marriage as a psychological relationship" (CWB XVI: 10). Yet we also know that an annotated copy of Jung's *Memories, Dreams, Reflections* (1965) exists in Bion's library (Aguayo, 2025; Winborn, 2018, p. 89).[14] Furthermore, in the estimation of James Grotstein, the parallels that can be drawn between their respective ideas are "uncanny" to the extent whereby he deemed Bion to be a "closet Jungian." Grotstein concludes, "It remains a mystery why Bion, who obviously appreciated Jung's thinking, never really acknowledged Jung" (Grotstein, 2006, p. xiii). However, it is worth remarking at this point that, for Bion, attempts to establish a proprietorial ownership of ideas were deemed by him to be a fundamentally misguided exercise.[15] When questioned in a seminar regarding the parallels that might be adduced between his own ideas and those of Jung, Bion remarked as follows:

> The relationship of one idea to another is quite a difficult problem because ideas are not so clearly defined as words – and that is bad enough. For purposes of verbal communication you can do a lot with dictionary definitions and the rules of grammar, but when it comes to ideas themselves – the real thing, whatever that is – I think it is extremely optimistic to imagine that they also conform to the ways in which we think or even express our thoughts or ideas.
>
> (CWB IX: 68)

In order to illustrate more fully the complexities that can arise when attempting to unravel the labyrinthine pathways conjoining Jung's ideas to those of Bion, it will be useful at this point to provide a brief illustrative outline concerning the only face-to-face encounter between Jung and Bion known to have occurred. This took place in 1935 when Bion (who, for the third lecture, was accompanied by his patient, the writer Samuel Beckett) attended the first three out of a series of five lectures given by Jung at the Tavistock Clinic between 30 September and 4 October (Hinshelwood, 2023, p. 24). Christian Maier has put forward a cogent case

---

13 For example, in *A Memoir of the Future*, Bion describes the "postulate of a collective unconscious . . . to be unnecessary" (CWB XIII: 188); yet, in *Four Discussions* (1976), he seems to be quite comfortable adducing parallels between his own ideas concerning a "primordial mind" and "Jung's archetypes" (CWB X: 62).

14 According to Joseph Aguayo (2025) – who has had direct access to Bion's annotated copy of Jung's *Memories, Dreams, Reflections* – "Bion privately evinced a selective interest in Jung's direct psychological experiences, especially in the areas of clinical intuition, dreams and spiritual experiences" (p. 108).

15

> I think that with Freud, Stekel and Jung there was an attempt to apportion out the areas that would be occupied by those three particular forces, but I can't say that I find the struggle for possession of some particular sphere at all enthralling.
>
> (CWB IX: 69 [The Tavistock Seminars, Seminar 6, 5 July 1978])

for surmising that Bion's recollection of the content of Jung's Tavistock lectures may have been subject to a process of cryptomnesia, resulting in a state of affairs whereby the ideas of one's predecessors are initially "forgotten," only to reappear as one's own "discovery" at a later date.[16] Bion devised his own theory with its associated nomenclature for such episodes of "forgetfulness," to which he assigned the rubric of "wild thoughts":

> If a thought without a thinker comes along, it may be what is a "stray thought," or it could be a thought with the owner's name and address upon it, or it could be a "wild thought." . . . What I am concerned with at the moment is the wild thoughts that turn up and for which there is no possibility of being able to trace immediately any kind of ownership, or even any sort of way of being aware of the genealogy of that particular thought.
>
> (CWB X: 175)

Regardless of what we might choose to adduce from such lapses in recall, it is evident that Bion's attendance at Jung's Tavistock lectures had a dramatic impact upon him (Maier, 2016; Vermote, 2019). Moreover, as the first-ever psychoanalytic training candidate to resist pressure to discontinue working at the Tavistock during his candidature, Bion would have had ample opportunity to encounter the ideas of Jung within the eclectic milieu promoted by the Tavistock (Hinshelwood, 2013). Indeed, there are grounds for supposing that Bion's complex and evolving ideas concerning the use of psychoanalytic "intuition" (Sandler, 2005, pp. 348–360; Civitarese, 2024) as a means for making "contact with an unknowable reality" (Vermote, 2019, p. 30) may own more to his receptivity to Jungian ideas than is commonly supposed.[17]

During the discussion at the end of the second lecture, Bion questioned Jung concerning the relations between mind and brain, with Jung responding at length to Bion's queries. As we shall see subsequently, ensuing attempts to arrive at an ever more adequate articulation of this central problem were to constitute a recurrent feature of Bion's *oeuvre*. Maier has highlighted the importance of the themes adumbrated by Jung in lectures II and V of the Tavistock series for Bion's future work, noting how Jung's approach to transferential and projective phenomena as outlined in lecture II bears comparison with Bion's later ideas concerning a "communicative" form of projective identification, the dynamics of which entail a process of psychic "contagion." Furthermore, in his fifth and

16 As Maier (2016, p. 144) astutely observes, "cryptomnesias occur in psychoanalysis with remarkable frequency." The following account of Jung's Tavistock lectures is heavily indebted to Maier's paper, although I've additionally drawn upon details provided by Vermote (2019, pp. 66–67).
17 See, for example, the following, which is taken from Jung's first Tavistock lecture: "For instance, anticipatory dreams, telepathic phenomena, and all that kind of thing are intuitions. I have seen plenty of them, and I am convinced that they do exist" (Jung, 2014 [1935], p. 11). See also Aguayo (2025) for a nuanced and judicious account of the impact that Jung's ideas concerning intuition may have had upon Bion.

final lecture, Jung elaborates a theory of psychic "containment," the features of which bear comparison with Bion's later development of the concept of container/contained (Maier, 2016, pp. 135–138). Moreover, Jung's account of a girl who "had never been born entirely" resonated sufficiently with Bion (and even more so with his guest and patient, Samuel Beckett, for whom this remark of Jung's became a recurrent motif throughout his later writings) as to make a reappearance in his inaugural psychoanalytic paper, "The Imaginary Twin" (1950), under the guise of "not-being-born" (Maier, 2016, pp. 139–142; Vermote, 2019, pp. 66–69; Knowlson, 1996, p. 616).

As Andrew Samuels has remarked, "Many of the central issues and features of contemporary psychoanalysis are reminiscent of positions taken by Jung in earlier years" – a contention that can easily be supported via the notable increase of interest arising in the status of the "psycho-spiritual" within psychoanalysis, entailing a resurgence of interest in the idea of a "creative" or "generative" unconscious (Winborn, 2018, p. 86). Consequently, in the light of the theoretical convergence that has more recently become prominent across Jungian and psychoanalytic conceptualisations of the unconscious, the role played by the later Bion's writings can be construed as providing a significant conduit for the covert dissemination of Jungian ideas across the wider field of contemporary psychoanalytic theorising more generally (Brown, 2018).

5.3   Mystical gnosis and esoteric *technē* in the late writings of Bion

It has been proposed that Bion's approach to the phenomenon of "mysticism" in his later writings constitutes "a psychoanalytic model of mysticism, not a mystical model of psychoanalysis" (Caper, 1998, p. 420). Moreover, Bion himself explicitly denied having any first-hand experience of this phenomenon, stating that his own "knowledge of mysticism is through hearsay" (CWB VII: 68). However, while it could be inferred from such remarks that Bion's own outlook on mysticism was essentially etic in terms of its orientation and instrumental with regard to its nature, some commentators have sought to contest such a reductive reading of his involvement with this phenomenon. For example, Michael Eigen has proposed that "Bion uses many images and expressions from religious and mystical life to portray psychoanalytic processes. But he does more. He filters mysticism through psychoanalysis and psychoanalysis through mysticism" (Eigen, 1998, p. 16). Consequently, I would like to propose there are grounds for supposing that Bion's knowledge of mysticism not only extended into the realm of the emic but that he also developed within the main body of his later work a series of psychoanalytically grounded, esoteric *technai* ("thoughts without a thinker," "without memory or desire," "O" and "reverie"), the practice of which effectively served to facilitate alterations in consciousness within both analyst and analysand in a manner that can be construed to be analogous to those given in the accounts of "mystical" states described in the emic literature.[18] James Grotstein has defined the idea of a "psychoanalytic mystic" in the following terms:

> What is a psychoanalytic mystic? It is one who eschews the known cant of a body of knowledge, *turned dogma* – along with its three-dimensional, linear outlook (i.e., transference, resistance, psychic apparatus, etc.) – for a mystical outlook, one that deals with emptiness, contemplation, infinity, chaos, unpredictability, spirituality, and immanence.
>
> (Grotstein, 1994, p. xi)

While the adoption of such terms within psychoanalysis may at first sight appear to entail a radical reorientation of traditional psychoanalytic assumptions, their deployment in this context can perhaps more accurately be understood as an act of historical retrieval.[19] Moreover, there are grounds to suppose that Bion's revisioning of the ultimate aim of psychoanalysis as entailing a state of "at-one-ment" with "O" means that attempts to perpetuate a clear distinction between a "psychoanalytic model of mysticism" and "a mystical model of psychoanalysis" exemplify a form of binary demarcation that can no longer be meaningfully sustained, at least within a specifically Bionian understanding of their mutual interdependency for arriving at a state of "at-one-ment" with O:

> O stands for the absolute truth in and of any object; it is assumed that this cannot be known by any human being; it can be known about, its presence can be recognized and felt, but it cannot be known. It is possible to be one with it. . . . No psychoanalytic discovery is possible without recognition of its existence, at-one-ment with it and evolution. The religious mystics have probably approximated most closely to expression of experience of it.
>
> (CWB VI: 245)

In the estimation of James Grotstein, "the concept of O transforms all existing psychoanalytic theories . . . into veritable psychoanalytic manic defences against

---

18 It is possible to speculate that the psychological ideas of William James could have played a tacit role in the formation of Bion's dictum, concerning 'Thoughts without a thinker' (CWB VI: 202; CWB VIII: 283, 285, 326; CWB IX: 142 ff.): '*If the passing thought be the directly verifiable existent which no school has hitherto doubted it to be, then that thought is itself the thinker,* and psychology need not look beyond. The only pathway that I can discover for bringing in a more transcendental thinker would be to *deny* that we have any *direct* knowledge of the thought as such. The latter's existence would then be reduced to a postulate, an assertion that there *must* be a knower correlative to all this *known;* and the problem *who that knower is* would have become a metaphysical problem. With the question once stated in these terms, the spiritualist and transcendentalist solutions must be considered as *prima facie* on a par with our own psychological one, and discussed impartially. But that carries us beyond the psychological or naturalistic point of view' (James, 1950 [1890], p. 401).
19 "impressive analogues . . . exist between traditional Christian mystical phenomena and the research findings of early French psychiatry and Freud's psychoanalysis on psychosis, hysteria, and other altered states of consciousness" Kripal (2001, p. 10).

the unknown" (Grotstein, 2007, p. 121). The perspective on psychoanalysis thereby arrived at is congruent with an idea of psychoanalysis more generally as providing "a contemporary site for *apophasis*" (Henderson, 2018, p. 200). In the case of Bion, this can be evidenced most clearly through his repeated references to an extract which he took from the correspondence between Freud and Lou Andreas-Salomé – the details of which are explored further below – in conjunction with his adoption of the writings of John of the Cross (1542–1591) as a resource in his later work. As we shall see, Bion's deployment of "mystical" and "esoteric" sources is further augmented by his use of the Kabbalah to provide a "framework" for psychoanalysis. This confluence of sources provides the wider context for a reading of the literary effects of *apophasis*, the outworkings of which are at least partially attributable to the invocation of a performative "meaning event," in which the language of *apophasis* is mimetically enacted so as to evoke within its intended recipient a state of mind "structurally analogous to the event of mystical union" (Sells, 1994, p. 10). However, before we embark upon a more detailed account of how these processes are encoded in Bion's writings, it will be useful to begin with a brief definition of the term "mysticism," following which we will be in a better position to explore how cognate terms such as esotericism, *apophasis*, *gnosis* and *technē* are conceptually encoded in the later Bion's writings. With respect to the concept of "mysticism" as it is construed within the contemporary academy, Kripal has observed that

> Mysticism is a modern comparative category that has been used in a wide variety of ways to locate, describe, and evaluate individuals' experiences of communion, union, or identity with the sacred . . . [it entails] a radical relationship to language expressed through forms of poetic and philosophic writing that subvert or deconstruct the grammatical stabilities and metaphysical substances of normative doctrine and practice; the attainment of supernormal or psychic powers . . . the ritual transformation of consciousness, visionary phenomena.
>
> (Kripal, 2008, p. 321)

By way of contrast, Bion's own adoption of the rubric of "mysticism" is notably more idiosyncratic with regard to its associated connotations and is explicitly moulded to suit the specific needs of its author:

> The "exceptional individual" may be variously described as a genius, a messiah, a mystic. . . . For convenience, I shall use the term "mystic" to describe these exceptional individuals. I include scientists, and Newton is the outstanding example of such a man; his mystical and religious preoccupations have been dismissed as an aberration when they should be considered as the matrix from which his mathematical formulations evolved.
>
> (CWB VI: 274–275)

Faced with the multivalent hermeneutical possibilities arising out of such conceptual fluidities, it is perhaps not surprising to find at least one contemporary psychoanalytic theorist strategically sidestepping such definitional questions by deploying a heuristic approach – already tending towards the apophatic – wherein gestures made towards the definitional are deconstructed prior to being reconstituted in the very act of their formation:

> I have not defined mystical feeling because I am unable to. My hope is, if I speak around it, or from it, well enough, something of value will get communicated to the reader and myself. Discussions of mystical awareness tend to undo themselves because of the paradoxical nature of the experiencing involved.
>
> (Eigen, 1998, p. 31)

Bion's development of the technical terminology of O, F (faith) and K (knowledge) is indebted to a wide range of philosophical, literary, theological and mystical resources (not all of which are explicitly acknowledged by him in his writings), including those of Plato, the Neoplatonists, Eckhart, John of the Cross and Kant (White, 2011; Pickering, 2019). One commentator has gone so far as to assert that "Bion . . . was a Neoplatonist . . . [who] tailored psychoanalysis to suit his Neoplatonism" (Merkur, 2010, p. 227). While such a viewpoint may at first glance appear to be somewhat perplexing, it is nonetheless one that is congruent with a close reading of Bion's later texts in particular. For example, when situated within an explicitly Neoplatonic frame of reference, beta elements become "mental representations of Platonic forms that a psychotic possesses but does not comprehend" (Merkur, 2010, p. 229). Moreover, while mystical experience is understood by Bion to constitute a form of "regression," this latter term – if interpreted Neoplatonically – comes to denote "an *epistrophe,* a 'reversion' of the decline of the one into the many through an ascension of the many to the one" (op cit., p. 245). Such a perspectival shift requires a revolutionary reconceptualisation of psychoanalysis as entailing "a pursuit of mystical experience on the part of both analyst and patient. By means of reverie and alpha-function, the analyst achieves transformations in O for himself, and facilitates a parallel transformation in the patient" (Merkur, 2010, p. 246). The efforts made by analysts such as Bion to transpose such ineffable processes into the language of psychoanalysis led Merkur to conclude that

> Psychoanalytic mystics have repeatedly detected evidence of the existence of a higher mental function, or group of functions, that have escaped conventional ways of thinking about the unconscious. The topic awaits further research.
>
> (Merkur, 2010, p. 256)

While it is impossible in the present context to provide a comprehensive account of the role of *apophasis* in mysticism, an initial orientation to this highly complex topic might very briefly be outlined as follows. The term *apophatic* derives from the Greek *apophasis,* whose meaning can be deduced via a nexus of associated terms such as "unsaying," "negation," but also "revelation." It is contrasted with the "affirmative" strands within the mystical traditions, both of which are deemed to be interdependent, insofar as one cannot "unsay" except by means of "saying" (Pickering, 2019,

p. 10). Although elements of apophasis existed earlier, it is generally acknowledged that the Western apophatic tradition began with Plotinus (204/5-270) and attained its classic exposition in the sixth century CE in the "mystical theology" of the Pseudo-Dionysus. Its subsequent exemplars spanned the European, Jewish and Islamic cultures and included figures such as Ibn al-'Arabi (1165–1240), Meister Eckhart (1260–1328), Isaac Luria (1534–1572), John of the Cross (1542–1591) and Jacob Böhme (1575–1624) (Sells, 1994, p. 5). According to Michael Sells:

> Classical Western apophasis shares three key features: (1) the metaphor of overflowing or "emanation" which is often in creative tension with the language of intentional, demiurgic creation; (2) dis-ontological discursive effort to avoid reifying the transcendent as an "entity" or "being" or "thing"; (3) a distinctive dialectic of transcendence and immanence in which the utterly transcendent is revealed as the utterly immanent.
>
> (Sells, 1994, p. 6)

The underlying principles of apophatic discourse are not easily summarised but can briefly be itemised under the following seven rubrics: the aporia of transcendence; a language of ephemeral, double propositions; a dialectic of transcendence and immanence; a dis-ontological and non-substantialist deity; the use of metaphors of emanation, procession and return; semantic transformations; and the meaning event. This latter rubric denotes the literary re-enactment of these prior principles so as to linguistically mirror "the fusion of self and other within mystical union" (ibid., pp. 207–209). Notably within the present context, Bion's own use of language has been described as recalling "mystical unsaying in the way it exposes and overcomes subject-object dichotomies" (Webb & Sells, 1995, p. 208). Hence, we find in his late writings apophatically inflected utterances, such as the following:

> I shall use the sign O to denote that which is the ultimate reality represented by terms such as ultimate reality, absolute truth, the god-head, the infinite, the thing-in-itself. O does not fall in the domain of knowledge or learning save incidentally; it can be "become," but it cannot be "known." It is darkness and formlessness but it enters the domain K when it has evolved to a point where it can be known, through knowledge gained by experience: its existence is conjectured phenomenologically.
>
> (CWB VI: 242)

Perhaps somewhat surprisingly, Bion's initiation into the way of apophasis appears to have arisen out of his acquaintance with the correspondence between Freud and Lou Andreas-Salomé, in which we find Freud describing his own deployment of a de facto apophatic *technē* transposed into a psychoanalytic register:

> I know that in writing I have to blind myself artificially in order to focus all the light on one dark spot, renouncing cohesion, harmony, rhetoric and everything which you call symbolic, frightened as I am by the experience that any such

claim or expectation involves the danger of distorting the matter under investigation, even though it may embellish it.

(Freud to Lou Andreas-Salomé, 25th May 1916, in Pfeiffer, 1972)

This letter was not only referenced by Bion on a number of occasions throughout his own writings but also even cited by Bion to Grotstein during the course of the latter's analysis (with Bion providing on one occasion an impromptu translation into English from his copy of the German edition of this correspondence).[20] In *Attention and Interpretation* (1970), we find the following allusion to this apophatic *technē*, the practice of which is closely associated by Bion with the abandonment of the faculties of memory and desire:

> Freud, in a letter to Lou Andreas-Salome, suggested his method of achieving a state of mind which would give advantages that would compensate for obscurity when the object investigated was particularly obscure. He speaks of blinding himself artificially. As a method of achieving this artificial blinding I have indicated the importance of eschewing memory and desire. Continuing and extending this process, I include understanding and sense perception with the properties to be eschewed . . . the psychoanalyst is seeking something that differs from what is normally known as reality . . . for the purpose of achieving contact with psychic reality, namely, the evolved characteristics of "O."
>
> (CWB VI: 257)[21]

There are grounds to surmise that this letter from Freud to Lou Andreas-Salomé constituted an *ur-text* for Bion, the key tenets of which were to provide a recurrent object for meditation that inspired further theoretical elaboration throughout the course of Bion's later writings. Having made explicit reference to this text, Bion provided an additional gloss with regard to its contents during the course of his 1973 São Paulo lectures:

> Instead of trying to bring a brilliant, intelligent, knowledgeable light to bear on obscure problems, I suggest we bring to bear a diminution of the "light" – a penetrating beam of darkness: a reciprocal of the searchlight. The peculiarity of

20 According to Grotstein (2007, p. 1), Bion's idiosyncratic translation of this passage (which he took notes on immediately thereafter) was as follows: "When conducting an analysis, one must cast a *beam of intense darkness* so that something which has hitherto been obscured by the glare of the illumination can glitter all the more in the darkness."

21 Cf. the following:

So clear is it of intelligible forms, which are the adequate objects of understanding, that the understanding is not conscious of its presence. Sometimes, indeed – when it is most pure – it creates darkness, because it withdraws the understanding from its accustomed lights, forms, and fantasies, and then the darkness becomes palpable and visible. St John of the Cross, *The Ascent of Mount Carmel*, trans. By David Lewis

(London: Thomas Baker, 1922), p. 127

this penetrating ray is that it would be directed towards the object of our curiosity, and this object would absorb whatever light already existed, leaving the area of examination exhausted of any light that it possessed. The darkness would be so absolute that it would achieve a luminous, absolute vacuum. So that, if any object existed, however faint, it would show up very clearly. Thus, a very faint light would become visible in maximum conditions of darkness.

(CWB VII: 25)[22]

While Judith Pickering has argued that Freud's letter to Lou Andreas-Salomé explicitly "places Freud in the tradition of Dionysius," she otherwise acknowledges that Freud "did not apply such a principle to a spiritual end" (Pickering, 2019, p. 12). The same caveat could not be applied to Bion, however. In Pickering's estimation, Bion's ostensible indebtedness to Freud as the source for this metaphoric "paradox" constituted a "diversion" to distract attention from his underlying "borrowing" from Dionysius' *The Mystical Theology* (Pickering, 2019, pp. 218–219). If Pickering is correct in her surmise, then there are grounds to suppose that Bion himself was a covert exponent of the practice of "defensive esotericism" alluded to earlier. It is notable in this regard that Pickering not only goes on to establish a strong evidential basis to support her contention that "[t]he apophatic mystics were a major inspiration for Bion" but also further illustrates in fine detail the extent to which Bion's writings on the abandonment of memory and desire were deeply indebted to the writings of John of the Cross in particular (Pickering, 2019, pp. 11, 216–217, 221ff.). It is notable in this regard that Bion's personal copy of *The Ascent of Mount Carmel* is marked in his own hand (CWB VI: 5–6). Moreover, for Bion, the *technē* of *apophasis* is central to the relinquishment of memory and desire, thereby constituting in their totality an imbricated series of esoteric *technai,* reciprocally orientated towards the achievement of a state of "at-one-ment" integral for the attainment of O (Grotstein, 2000, p. 687):

What I am suggesting, then, is that an effort is required which is an actual discipline, difficult to achieve . . . it is a matter of trying to get out of the habit of remembering things, and trying to get out of the habit of desiring or wanting anything *while you are predominantly engaged on your work.* I am not expressing views about this as a philosophy of life or anything; it is simply an attempt to promulgate an actual rule – as if one could make rules for psychoanalytic training. This is the kind of rule that I would like to make. . . . The consequences of this . . . are peculiar . . . in order to see clearly one really needs to be pretty well blind – metaphorically and literally. It is really a sort of positive lack of anything in one's mind . . . the darker the spot that you wish to illuminate, the darker you have to be – you have to shut out all light in order to be able to see it. Only in that way is it possible to get the conditions in which a real object – but one which

---

22 For a brief account of the Purkyně shift, the effects of which constitute the physiological context to Bion's remarks on this topic, see CWB VI: 5 n.1.

is formless and not in any way appreciable to what we ordinarily regard as the senses – emerges, evolves, and becomes possible for us to be aware of.

(CWB VI: 12–13)

According to Francesca Bion, this "technique . . . was central to Bion's own psychoanalytic method" (CWB XV: 107):

> Every session must have no history and no future – the only point of importance in any session is the unknown . . . Bion knew that it was extremely difficult to achieve and can at first arouse fear and anxiety in the analyst, but he also knew from experience and perseverance that it make [sic] possible what he called "at-one-ment" with the patient.
>
> (CWB VI: 12–13)

The application of this Bionian *technē* within the analytic session not only serves to increase the receptivity of the analyst to the patient's projective transidentificatory communications but also promotes the integration of right- and left-hemispheric brain functioning, thereby enhancing the analysis (Grotstein, 2000, p. 692, 2007, pp. 168–189). However, before the analyst can embark upon this process of arriving at a state of "at-one-ment" with the analysand, he or she must first learn how to therapeutically navigate the associated alterations in consciousness commonly referred to in the Bionian lexicon as entailing access to a state of *reverie*.[23] Moreover, in Grotstein's estimation, it was during such altered states that "Bion *dreamed* his utterances and his writings . . . he spoke and wrote in a transformational state of reverie (wakeful sleep)" (Grotstein, 2007, p. 15):

> According to Bion, the analyst, in response to and in resonance with the emotional outpourings from the analysand, must allow himself, in a state of reverie, to become induced into a trance-like state in which his (the analyst's) own, native internal reservoir of emotions and repertoire of buried experiences can become selectively recruited to match those he is experiencing resonantly from the analysand's inductions – and then *become* them (transformations *in* O) . . . . Then the analyst ponders over his experience, thinks about it, and then interprets it (T O→K).
>
> (Grotstein, 2007, p. 54)

Although Bion's concept of reverie bears some comparison with Freud's notion of "free floating attention," it may perhaps be more accurately construed as an example

---

23 For some helpful background on how this term was originally developed by Bion, see Lopez-Corvo (2018 [2003]), pp. 167–168; Sandler (2005, pp. 643–646); Vermote (2019, p. 76). According to André Green, "The capacity for reverie is merely the visible aspect of a largely unconscious form of thought" ("Review of *Cogitations*," cited in CWB XI: 355). For an influential post-Bionian elaboration of the concept of reverie, see Ogden (1999).

of the way in which Bion sought to adapt "classical concepts in a new way and within a different framework" (Wieland, 2013, p. 117). Moreover, the concept itself has become the locus for a complex ecosystem of associated ideas that includes not only unconscious perception and communication, empathy and intersubjectivity but also whose clinical applications were retrospectively prefigured in the experiments undertaken by Sándor Ferenczi and Elizabeth Severn into the phenomenon of "inter-subjective dream-work" (Bandeira, 2017, pp. 265–266; Rudnytsky, 2022). Furthermore, the meditative states arising out of the esoteric *technai* of *reverie* and *a beam of intense darkness* are intriguingly reminiscent of the alterations in consciousness induced in research subjects during the course of administering the *ganzfeld procedure* that is commonly employed by experimenters conducting research into modes of anomalous information transfer such as telepathy.[24] The utility of the ganzfeld procedure as an empirical research technique is premised on the idea that

> anomalous cognition might best be characterized as a set of weak perceptual signals that ordinarily went unnoticed, drowned out by the noise of everyday life. . . . The idea behind the ganzfeld technique was to deprive subjects of as much outside sensory stimuli as possible. . . . The goal of the ganzfeld state was to create an unchanging sensory field. In the absence of new input, the nervous system gradually became responsive to faint, barely noticeable perceptions that were normally overwhelmed by the constant stimulation of perpetually shifting perceptual environments.
>
> (Mayer, 2007, pp. 193–194)

The phenomenological parallels thereby adduced as existing between parapsychological research methodologies such as the ganzfeld procedure and post-Bionian clinical techniques such as reverie are explicitly conceptualised by James Grotstein in his account of Bion's "transformations in O" as constituting the theoretical backdrop to a communicative "spectrum that ranges from telepathy or ESP . . . or even prescience, to subtle bodily evoked communications" (Grotstein, 2009a, p. 270).

It is in the light of such phenomenological isomorphisms aligning parapsychological research methodologies to post-Bionian clinical techniques that we can begin to see how Grotstein came to associate Bion's idea of "transformations in O" with a communicative "spectrum that ranges from telepathy or ESP . . . or even

---

24 For comparisons between meditation and reverie, see Cooper (2014, pp. 795–813) and Pelled (2007, pp. 1507–1526). The term *ganzfeld* is taken from the German for "total field" and was originally developed as a research technique during the 1930s. For useful accounts of the ganzfeld procedure, see Baruš (2020, pp. 15–17); Beloff (1993, pp. 165–167); and Mayer (2007, pp. 194–211). Notably, Mayer recounts a first-hand experience of undergoing the ganzfeld procedure, during which she relates what arguably appears to be an instance of anomalous information transfer that occurred at an unconscious level of perceptual awareness (Mayer, 2007, pp. 205–211). However, Hewitt (2020, p. 162, n. 2) believes that Mayer's account of her experience was inadvertently distorted by "active promptings" provided by the researchers.

prescience, to subtle bodily evoked communications" (Grotstein, 2009a, p. 270). Having briefly outlined a series of esoteric *technai* actively employed by Bion in his later writings, we can now move on to consider his use of the Jewish Kabbalah to provide a "framework" for psychoanalysis.

5.4   Bion and the Kabbalah

[There] was a spontaneous interchange I had with Wilfred R. Bion in 1978, the year before he died . . . out of the blue he asked, "Do you know the Kabbalah, the Zohar?" As far as I was aware, there was no preparation for this remark. He just said it. I was a bit taken aback and said, "Well, I know it, but I don't really *know* it." . . . He quickly said, "I don't either, really know it," modestly reassuring me. It was established that neither of us were scholars, experts, "knowers," but had awareness, acquaintance. There was a pause. Then he looked at me and said, "I use the Kabbalah as a framework for psychoanalysis."

(Eigen, 2012, pp. ix–x)[25]

The above meeting proved to be a momentous encounter for Michael Eigen, insofar as it provided the inspiration for a "trilogy" of books that he authored some three decades later, in which he sought to explicate at length the Kabbalistic themes and influences that he discerned to be active within the Bionian *corpus* (Eigen, 2012, 2014a, 2014b).

One notable consequence that ensued from these exegetical efforts is that Eigen came to be identified by at least one major contemporary Kabbalistic scholar as "the most prominent psychological thinker to be significantly influenced by Kabbalistic and other Jewish texts" (Garb, 2015, p. 10).[26] This assessment is perhaps not so surprising when we consider the extensive nature of Eigen's studies into the Kabbalah, which have included meetings with figures such as R. Menachem Mendel Schneerson, the last rebbe of Habad Hasidism (Garb, 2015, p. 10).[27] However, it is evident from Eigen's own account that the initial impetus for his Kabbalistic studies originated from his seminal encounter with Bion in 1978, as a consequence of which he has – among many other achievements – arguably become the pre-eminent interpreter and exemplar of the role played by the Kabbalah in post-Bionian psychoanalysis.[28] For Eigen, the Kabbalah denotes "a loose term that covers an archipelago

---

25 See also Grotstein (2007, p. 117), in which he refers to a personal exchange he had with Bion in 1976, in which the latter alluded to his deep interest in the Kabbalah. As a gloss to these verbal exchanges, see the following: "I use the term 'esoteric' to denote that which cannot be communicated fully in writing and which should be only alluded to partially in written form and transmitted orally" (Wolfson 1994, p. 189).

26 See also Berke and Schneider (2008), in which the role of the Kabbalah in the writings of Bion is discussed at some length.

27 For a more detailed account of Eigen's studies on the Kabbalah, see Eigen (2012, pp. 3–4, 129–131).

28 In the estimation of Berke and Schneider (2008, p. 6), the Kabbalah itself is one of the "principle sources" for psychoanalysis.

of possibilities," whose historical, geographical and authorial pluralism eludes the provision of simple definitions or the reduction of complexity to an easily communicable, systematised teaching (Eigen, 2012, p. xi). With regard to making the case for its significance within psychoanalysis (or "at least the psychoanalysis I am interested in"), Eigen identifies seventeen "intersections" between psychoanalysis and Kabbalah – a figure which he otherwise treats as an approximation that serves to illustrate its pervasive influence throughout psychoanalytic theory more generally (Eigen, 2012, pp. 40ff.). Although the figures of Freud and Klein are integral to Eigen's overall project, it is to the writings of Bion that he most frequently turns in his attempts to foreground and articulate the theoretic possibilities of the Kabbalah as a "framework" for psychoanalysis – efforts which he nonetheless brackets with the apophatically inflected disclaimer, "everything I say is hypothetical, fantasy, attempts to express the inexpressible" (ibid., p. 79). Such caveats notwithstanding, by the time we reach the third book in Eigen's Kabbalistic "trilogy," we encounter the following unambiguously worded evaluation: "Once one begins to look at the interplay of Bion and Kabbalah, interweaving themes become obvious" (Eigen, 2014b, p. x).

Eigen devised the striking neologism "O-gram" to denote his Kabbalistically inflected interpretation of two enigmatic "genograms" that Bion included in his *Cogitations* (1958–1979) (CWB XI: 310, 312). Moreover, he extends his exegesis of these Kabbalistic parallels to include within their ambit the enigmatic psychoanalytic "cartography" developed by Bion under the aegis of his (in) famous "grid."[29] Eigen goes on to describe these parallels in a language notable for its powers of poetic evocation:

> Let me sum up some of the overlapping themes in Bion and Kabbalah: catastrophe, faith, intensity of affect, shatter and transformation. Bion's grid and O-grams are like inversions of the *sephirot*. . . . The grid as a whole can be taken to portray growth of thought, experience and feeling. I propose that it explores growth of sensation as well. The forest can easily be lost in the trees, so before I get bogged down in details, let me say that the whole grid quivers, trembles, is aglow. It shakes like a jelly, ripples, and, like the *sephirot*, any part can link with any other and all parts are contained in each other. All parts of the grid, like the *sephirot*, express transformations.
>
> (Eigen, 2012, pp. 26, 109)

There is evidence that Bion consulted at least two works by the founder of modern Kabbalistic scholarship, Gershom Scholem (1897–1982). Scholem's *Major Trends in Jewish Mysticism* (1955) is cited by Bion in his bibliography for *Attention and Interpretation* (1970), while a copy of Scholem's *On the Kabbalah and*

---

29 See CWB X: 7–32; Lopez-Corvo (2018, pp. 115–124) for more detailed accounts of Bion's development and use of the grid.

its Symbolism (1965) is known to exist in Bion's personal library (Sandler, 2006, p. 181 [table 1]). In the absence of a published account of any annotations that Bion may have made in his original copies of these texts, one can only speculate as to their potential significance for the development of his ideas. However, we can nonetheless discern the presence of some thematic contiguities and parallels, the details of which it will be worthwhile alluding to briefly, albeit with the proviso that nothing of a definitive nature can thereby be adduced regarding Bion's use of these particular texts. As we saw earlier, such reticence with regard to identifying his indebtedness to third-party sources constitutes a distinctive feature of Bion's use of sources more generally. However, it is worth highlighting in the present context that during the course of reading Jung's *Memories, Dreams, Reflections* (1965), Bion would have encountered Jung's description of undergoing a series of Kabbalistic "visions" that he experienced over a period of some three weeks following a heart attack which he suffered in 1944. As Jung subsequently remarked, "It is impossible to convey the beauty and intensity of emotion during those visions. They were the most tremendous things I have ever experienced" (Jung, 1995 [1963], p. 326).[30]

Although Bion averred that his knowledge of mysticism came only via "hearsay," it is nonetheless possible to surmise that his reticence on such matters may have been at least partially motivated by the exigencies arising out of a strategy of "defensive" esotericism alluded to earlier. Moreover, according to Scholem, the practice of reticence with regard to the disclosure of first-hand "mystical" experience was congruent with the tenets of traditional Kabbalistic teaching.[31] Scholem himself drew attention to the significant parallels he adduced to exist between the practice of "free association" in psychoanalysis and the Kabbalist Abraham Abulafia's (1240–1291?) meditative method of "jumping" and "skipping" (*dillug* and *kefitsah*) (Scholem, 1995 [1946], pp. 135–136). Furthermore, it is possible to deduce from Scholem's commentary on Abulafia's doctrine a distinctively Kabbalistic context for construing Bion's use of esoteric *technai* as a means for accessing "O" within a psychoanalytic setting:

> There is a dam which keeps the soul confined within the natural and normal borders of human existence and protects it against the flood of the divine stream . . . the same dam, however, also prevents the soul from taking cognizance of the divine. . . . As the mind perceives all kinds of gross natural objects and admits their images into its consciousness, it creates for itself, out of this natural function, a certain mode of existence which bears the stamp of finiteness. The normal life of the soul . . . is kept within the limits determined by our sensory perceptions and emotions, and so long as it is full of these, it finds it extremely difficult to perceive the existence of spiritual forms and things divine. The problem is,

30 For a helpful commentary on Jung's Kabbalistic visions, see Drob (2010, pp. 207–227).
31 "Jewish mystics are inclined to be reticent about the hidden regions of the religious mind" (Scholem 1995 [1946], p. 121).

therefore, to find a way of helping the soul to perceive more than the forms of nature, without it becoming blinded and overwhelmed by the divine light.

(Scholem, 1995 [1946], pp. 131–132)[32]

It is possible that Bion may have drawn at least some of his inspiration for chapters six and seven of *Attention and Interpretation* (1970) (CWB VI; 273–290) from Scholem's *On the Kabbalah and its Symbolism*. For the purposes of comparison, we might note, for example, the following:

> The mystic may declare himself as revolutionary or he may claim that his function is to fulfil the laws, conventions, and destiny of his group. It would be surprising if any true mystic were not regarded by the group as a mystical nihilist at some stage of his career and by a greater or less proportion of the group. It would be equally surprising if he were not in fact nihilistic to some group if for no other reason than that the nature of his contribution is certain to be destructive of the laws, conventions, culture, and therefore coherence, of a group within the group, if not the whole group. . . . The disruptive force of the mystical nihilist, or of the mystic whose impact on a particular group is of a disruptive or nihilistic character, extends to and depends on the Language of Achievement, be it expressed in action, speech, writing or aesthetic.
>
> (CWB VI: 275)

In Scholem's *On the Kabbalah and Its Symbolism*, we encounter the following remarks, the details of which could arguably be construed as providing an exegetical backdrop to those remarks by Bion just alluded to:

> The mystic who lends new symbolic meaning to his holy texts, to the doctrine and ritual of his religion . . . discovers a new dimension, a new depth in his own tradition. . . . He bows to no authority in pious veneration, but this does not prevent him from transforming it, sometimes radically. He uses old symbols and lends them new meaning, he may even use new symbols and give them an old meaning – in either case we find dialectical interrelationship between the conservative aspects and the novel, productive aspects of mysticism.
>
> (Scholem, 1996 [1965], pp. 22–23)

Notably, we find in the pages immediately prior to this extract the following apposite remarks made by Scholem concerning the Kabbalist Isaac Luria (1534–1572). Bion not only alluded to the figure of Luria on a number of occasions throughout

---

32 Later in the same text, Scholem provides an intriguing account of a book written by an anonymous disciple of Abulafia's, in which the author described an encounter with some "Moslem ascetics," who "employ all manner of devices to shut out from their souls all 'natural forms.' . . . This removal of all natural forms and images from the soul is called with them *Effacement.*" Cited in Scholem (1995 [1946], p. 147).

the course of his own writings but also seemed in some respects to have drawn upon Luria's approach to reinvigorating the Jewish Kabbalistic tradition as a source of inspiration for guiding his own comparable innovations in psychoanalysis.[33] More-over, Luria – much like Bion himself – was reticent with regard to the sources that he drew upon for his inspiration (Scholem, 1996 [1965], p. 21). Indeed, there are grounds to suppose that in many respects, the approach that each of these two fig-ures took with regard to managing the tensions between conservatism and innova-tion as manifested within their respective spheres of activity bore striking parallels with each other:

> Luria represents both aspects of mysticism in their fullest development. His whole attitude was decidedly conservative. He fully accepted the established religious authority, which indeed he undertook to reinforce by enhancing its stature and giving it deeper meaning. Nevertheless, the ideas he employed in this seemingly conservative task were utterly new and seem doubly daring in their conservative context. And yet, for all their glaring novelty, they were not regarded as a break with traditional authority. . . . But though defined in tradi-tional categories, this new authority, once accepted, brought about profound changes in Judaism, even when its advocates claimed to be doing nothing of the sort.
>
> (Scholem, 1996 [1965], p. 21)

Bion himself was explicit in the comparisons that he sought to adduce between the history of psychoanalysis and the history of mysticism:

> My object is to show that certain elements in the development of psycho-analysis are not new or peculiar to analysis, but have in fact a history that suggests that they transcend barriers of race, time, and discipline, and are inherent in the rela-tionship of the mystic and the group.
>
> (CWB VI: 284)

While it is necessarily a matter of speculation to construe Bion's writings on "the mystic" and "the group" as providing, in places, a kind of veiled "autobiography," there are nonetheless grounds for supposing that this may (at times) have been the case. For example, when we read in Chapter 7 of *Attention and Interpretation* of an "individual" (whose activities vis-à-vis the "group" also appear to place him in the role of "mystic") is imagined in his "epitaph" as someone who was "loaded with

---

33 See, for example, the following: The problem posed by the relationship between the mystic and the institution has an emotional pattern that repeats itself in history and in a variety of forms. The pattern may appear in the relationship of new phenomena to the formulation that has to present it . . . [such as] . . . the relationship of the rabbinical directorate of the Kabbalah to revolutionary mystics such as Isaac Luria. (CWB VI: 284)

honours and sank without a trace" (CWB VI: 287), we can discern in the rhetorical irony of this remark the echoes of a covert autobiographical allusion.[34] If we were to extend this reading further, it would arguably not be too much of a leap to interpret Bion's remarks concerning the tensions between the "mystic" and the "group," as providing a thinly disguised commentary on how he had come to perceive his own role as a leading London Kleinian psychoanalyst immediately prior to his departure for California in 1968.

Having outlined selected aspects of the Kabbalistic "framework" active within the late Bionian *corpus*, I would like to put forward a case for conceptualising the confluence of Platonic and Kabbalistic influences in Bion's writings as constituting a de facto modern-day reconfiguration of late antique theurgy translated into a contemporary psychoanalytic register.

The term *theurgy* has been described as "notoriously difficult to define, partly because ancient philosophers conceived of theurgy as *a way of life* or, strictly speaking, as *a way of being,* as well as a nexus of ritual practices" (Addey, 2019, p. 24). This caveat notwithstanding, theurgy has been defined as "a set of ritual practices coupled with a way of life based on ethical and intellectual practices. The aim of theurgy was contact with, assimilation to and, ultimately, union with, the divine" (Addey, 2019, p. 3). While attempts have been made to derive theurgy from hermetic and ancient Egyptian sources, its formation as a series of ritual-noetic practices is commonly dated from the mid- to late second century AD in the wake of the composition of the fragmentary series of documents known as the *Chaldean Oracles* (Fowden, 1986; Uždavinys, 2010; Majercik, 1989). The purposes of theurgic ritual included the purification of the soul in preparation for embarking upon a hyper-noetic ascent of the divine hierarchy, a process that entailed the adoption of an inner attitude of spiritual "receptivity" towards the "gods" that was explicitly intended to differentiate the activities of the theurgist from those of the more wilful and instrumentalising approaches employed by the *magoi* (Johnson, 2019; Hanegraaff, 2022). In its essentials, the cosmology of theurgy entailed the adoption of a "locative" world-view in which the divine order was construed as permeating all aspects of reality via a process of natural *sympatheia*, the actions of which have been likened to "a sort of theologized science" (Addey, 2019, pp. 28–29).

Theurgy evolved out of Platonism and was further developed by later Platonists such as Plotinus, Porphyry, Iamblichus, Proclus and Damascius (Johnson, 2019, p. 696). While the practice of theurgy entailed the induction of trance states employed in conjunction with the use of *telestika*, the "Iynx-Wheel" and "symbola," it has been suggested that its rituals "could also be interpreted as stages of an

---

34 See, for example, the following: "When once asked why he [Bion] moved to Los Angeles from London, he humorously answered that 'I was so loaded with honors, I nearly sank without a trace!'" (Grotstein, 1981, p. 5). See also LAS, p. 52, where this same remark is referenced by Bion in the context of a seminar (14 April 1967).

inner process without any exterior physical action" (Johnson, 1990, pp. 82, 87 ff.; Tanaseanu-Döbler, 2013, pp. 30, 33). Zeke Mazur coined the term "inner ritual" to express this notion of ritual operative as a noetic act (Mazur, 2004). This specific understanding of "theurgy" is of particular importance if we seek to discern the genealogical trajectory of its "traces" as remaining active within the ambit of a post-Bionian psychoanalysis.

By the Byzantine and Renaissance periods, theurgic ideas had already become deeply embedded within Christian theology via the writings of the Pseudo-Dionysius. In tandem with this development, we find that theurgy had also become "one of the main defining components of the medieval Kabbalah" (Tanaseanu-Döbler, 2013, pp. 13, 15, n. 30). Between the sixteenth and nineteenth centuries, the polysemous derivatives of "theurgy" proliferated under a disparate network of terms, only some of which bore a tenuous relationship to its originally intended meaning (Johnson, 2019, p. 699). However, by the mid-twentieth century, the concept of "theurgy" had recovered a degree of academic respectability via its adoption by Gershom Scholem as a technical term for describing "ascent-centred mysticism as a category" within Kabbalah (Johnson, 2019, p. 700; Fanger, 2012, pp. 25–26). As we saw previously, Scholem's *Major Trends in Jewish Mysticism* is cited by Bion in his bibliography for *Attention and Interpretation* (1970), while a copy of Scholem's *On the Kabbalah and its Symbolism* is known to exist in Bion's personal library (Sandler, 2006, p. 181). Throughout the course of Bion's collected works, explicit reference is made to Scholem on three occasions, to John of the Cross on 12 occasions and to Plato on 38 occasions (CWB XVI [index]). Notably, both theurgy and psychotherapy require the proper maintenance of "ritual space" as a constitutive feature of their respective practices (Davies, 2009, pp. 81–83; Henderson, 2014, pp. 49–50, 147–150).

Consequently, it is possible that a synergistic rapprochement between psychoanalysis and the noetic idioms of theurgic "inner ritual" may have assisted Bion in the development of a revolutionary psychoanalysis entailing the attainment of a state of radical "at-one-ment" with O reminiscent of Jungian intuitions concerning the existence of a numinous "higher" Self.[35] Such parallels are reminiscent of Matte-Blanco's depiction of a psychoanalytic subject who "may be dwelling psychically in higher dimensions and be able, thanks to bi-logical operations, to experience an object – or self – in a lesser dimension (n-1)" (Grotstein, 1996, p. 1058). In the light of these contiguities, it is to a comparison between Matte-Blanco's and Bion's speculations concerning an "infinite" unconscious that our attention shall now turn.

---

35 See Samuels et al. (1986, pp. 135–137) for a helpful overview of the Jungian concept of the self that emphasises its numinous qualities. It is notable that Jung, too, utilised the term "at-one-ment," which he deployed as follows: "Individuation is an at-one-ment with oneself and at the same time with humanity, since oneself is a part of humanity" (S. 227) (Jung, 2014, 2nd ed. [1954]).

5.5   Jung, Bion and Matte-Blanco – towards a genealogy for an Orphic unconscious

In the estimation of Ignacio Matte-Blanco (1908–1995), "Many analysts have not taken seriously enough the idea that the mind works within a framework of time-lessness and spacelessness" (Matte-Blanco, 1998 [1988]), p. 5). In this respect at least, his life's work can be thought of as an extended attempt to rectify this over-sight by providing a "glimpse of the corporal-non-corporal nature of man, seen as a spacelessness-timelessness immersed in a spatio-temporality" (Matte-Blanco, 1998 [1975], p. 462). Although Matte-Blanco and Bion trained as psychoanalysts in London at approximately the same time, both men only became acquainted with each other shortly before the latter's death (Mondrzak, 2004, p. 602).[36] While Bion referred to Matte-Blanco's ideas on only a few occasions within his own writings, he nonetheless told his daughter Parthenope that Matte-Blanco's work constituted the best starting point for comprehending his own ideas. Parthenope subsequently undertook a doctoral thesis comparing their respective approaches to mathemati-cal logic in a psychoanalytic context (Mondrzak, 2004, p. 602).[37] In a memorial volume dedicated to the work of Bion, Matte-Blanco published a lengthy paper, which he concluded by comparing Bion's influence upon him to that of an "elder brother" or "father" (Matte-Blanco, 1983, p. 528). He also alluded to Bion's ideas on a number of occasions in his two major works, *The Unconscious as Infinite Sets: An Essay in Bi-Logic* (1975) and *Thinking, Feeling and Being: Clinical reflec-tions on the fundamental antinomy of human beings and world* (1998). In a manner reminiscent of the comparisons drawn between the ideas of Bion and the quantum physicist David Bohm, analogous parallels between the theories of Matte-Blanco and Bohm have also been proposed, suggestive of the presence of a "quantum" convergence active within the sensibilities of both authors (Lombardi, 2019). Although Matte-Blanco was a lifelong practising Roman Catholic, he nonetheless endeavoured to keep his writings within the boundaries of what he conceived to be psychoanalytic "science,"[38] although this act of demarcation did not prevent him from hinting that if the findings of Freud were to be reformulated in the light of his own ideas, then "immanent notions about God, interpreted as bi-logical expe-riences, lead to interesting perspectives" (Lombardi, 2019, p. xxvi).[39] In order to

---

36 For helpful accounts of Matte-Blanco's life, see Rayner (1995, pp. 1–7) and Jordan-Moore (1995, pp. 1035–1041).

37 The existence of a "logical tradition" within psychoanalysis that included figures such as Freud, Ferenczi, Bion and Matte-Blanco is something that has been remarked upon – see Skelton (1995).

38 However, Matte-Blanco was careful to clarify that *"The philosophy of science which is valid for physical phenomena cannot be applied to psychoanalytic research. New formulations are required for the latter,"* Matte-Blanco (1998 [1975], p. 153).

39 For references to Matte-Blanco's Catholicism, see Jordan-Moore (1995, p. 1036) and Bomford (1999, p. 24). The latter text constitutes an in-depth application of Matte-Blanco's ideas to some of the central teachings of Christian theology. It is perhaps worth remarking that a case could be made for construing "traditional" Catholicism as meeting the criteria for being a de facto "esoteric"

illustrate what Matte-Blanco may have meant by his reference to such "perspectives," we can turn to the frontispiece of *The Unconscious as Infinite Sets*, where we find, under the representation of an archangel taken from a Byzantine mosaic in the Khora Museum, Istanbul, the following evocative "bi-logical" gloss in which the reader is asked to consider how:

> the artist intuitively conceived the archangel as a being submitted to laws which are beyond those of Aristotelian logic or of three-dimensional space but which could be "translated" or "unfolded" into these laws.
>
> (Matte-Blanco, 1998 [1975], frontispiece)

The difficulties encountered in the course of attempting to unpack the implications arising from such perspectives are further compounded when we consider that "*the principle of symmetry is an external logical way of describing something which in itself is completely alien to logic*" (Matte-Blanco, 1998 [1975], p. 148). The existence of a specifically *clinical* convergence between Bion and Matte-Blanco has been elaborated upon at some length by Lombardi (2016). While it is impossible in the present context to provide a comprehensive overview of Matte-Blanco's highly innovative theory of the unconscious, it will nonetheless be useful at this juncture to provide a brief outline of its essential characteristics as the prelude to embarking upon a brief account of his indebtedness to a range of esoteric sources whose ideas he utilised to augment his more explicit adoption of the conceptual models provided by Freud and Klein.[40]

According to Matte-Blanco, rather than conceptualising the fundamental antinomy of the psyche as consisting in the demarcation between conscious and unconscious, it is more accurate to speak in terms of two modes of being that can be distinguished by the respective characteristics of *symmetry* and *asymmetry*:

> The *asymmetrical mode of being* is characterised by its capacity to use asymmetrical relations which are the basis of Aristotelian logic. Things are divided, individuated and separated. Time, space and causality are felt to exist. . . . The *symmetrical mode of being,* on the other hand . . . experiences the world as undivided, infinite and at the same time spaceless/timeless *and* multidimensional. Part and whole are seen as equal, and normal laws of logic do not appear to exist.
>
> (Alava, 2010, p. 23)

---

religion if Antoine Faivre's esoteric typology – as outlined in Chapter 1 – were to be applied to its teachings and practices.

40 Notably, at least one recent study has sought to contextualise Matte-Blanco's ideas by situating his theory of mind within the ambit of the "filter" theory of consciousness proposed by figures such as William James, Frederic Myers and Henri Bergson – see Corbett (2020, p. 674).

Active within this ontological antinomy, Matte-Blanco posits the existence of three coexisting modalities of "logic," namely symmetrical, asymmetrical and bi-logic, the latter of which is composed of the various logical dialectics that are created from the interplay arising between the logics of symmetry and asymmetry. Matte-Blanco extends this account to include a series of five strata, through which he seeks both to demarcate and to delineate the complex range of logics operative between the homogeneous and heterogeneous strata of the psyche (Carvalho, 2010). The specific features of these discrete "bi-logics" are denoted by means of the introduction of a range of distinctive neologisms that include *Alassi* (alternating asymmetrical/ symmetrical), *Simassi* (simultaneously asymmetrical/symmetrical) and *Tridum* (tri-dimensionalised bi-logical structure). Matte-Blanco augments this account with the inclusion of an additional concept, which he terms the *epistemological see-saw,* a term which serves "to designate a curious alternation of manifestations of both modes, which has some similarity to both the Alassi and the Simassi types of bi-logical structures, without, however, being either of them" (Matte-Blanco, 1998 [1988], p. 49).[41] One is left with the impression that this proliferating bi-logical typology could be infinitely extended until such times as a state of absolute symmetry is achieved.[42] The notion of infinity is fundamental for Bion's and Matte-Blanco's respective theories concerning the attainment of mystical states.[43] One of the corollaries arising from this process of bi-logical stratification is that different modalities of discourse need to be utilised depending upon the proportion of asymmetry to symmetry present in the particular speech act articulated.[44]

Having briefly outlined the essential features of Matte-Blanco's conceptualisation of an "infinite" unconscious, we can now conclude this chapter by drawing attention to its contiguity with a Jungian–Bionian model of a numinous unconscious.

It is worth emphasising that this understanding of the unconscious is inherently synchronistic due to its possession of "acausal" properties. Matte-Blanco published a paper on Jung's theory of synchronicity as early as 1962, synchronicity being a phenomenon which he considered as constituting a manifestation of symmetrical

---

41 Notably, Matte-Blanco goes on to illustrate this concept by citing an example taken from Bion's *A Memoir of the Future* (1975).

42

> There are two types of infinitization in bi-logic. Firstly, an individual can become to represent a (unbounded) set which extends infinitely. Secondly, any individual can become to represent a (bounded or limited) set with infinite elements. Matte-Blanco calls these two types of infinitization extensive and intensive infinite sets. These correspond loosely to increasable infinities and infinitesimals respectively.
>
> (Alava, 2010, p. 41)

43 "Bion and Matte-Blanco agree in considering the experience of infinity to be possible at some very special moments of insight, in artistic displays and in mystical states" (Mondrzak, 2004, p. 604).

44 Bomford (writing with specific reference to theology) identifies five discrete levels of discourse spanning the asymmetrical–symmetrical "continuum," which he distinguishes as follows: empirical discourse, devotional discourse, mythical discourse, doctrinal discourse and mystical discourse – see Bomford (2004, p. 16).

logic (Matte-Blanco, 1962, 1998 [1975], pp. 11–12). It has been observed that while Matte-Blanco emphasised his indebtedness to Freud, his work was in fact "highly subversive" to many aspects of orthodox Freudian theory and was in many respects more closely aligned to Jungian modes of thinking, through which he was to arrive at a model of the unconscious that is "essentially affective, interpersonal and synchronistic" (Carvalho, 2014, pp. 367, 381). This can be attributed to the fact that by the time we descend to the level of the *basic matrix,* "time and space between objects and events are obliterated" (Carvalho, 2014, p. 387).[45] Jung's theory of synchronicity has been described as a "sophisticated restatement" of the more ancient theory of *correspondences,* which proposed that "reality consists of multiple 'levels' which in some manner mirror one another" (Brach & Hanegraaff, 2006, pp. 275, 278).[46] Echoes of this ancient doctrine can be discerned within Matte-Blanco's writings, the component elements of which he initially derives from a "subjective" source, prior to moving towards a position in which he conjectures not only "*that each stratum* [of the psyche] *is present in a mysterious way in every one of the strata which are nearer to the surface*" but also "that there is some sort of morphism between the psychical structure of humanity and the structure of nature" in a manner that is arguably reminiscent of the *Naturphilosophie* of German Romanticism (Matte-Blanco, 1998 [1988], pp. 55, 65; Faivre, 2006a). At the deepest, most symmetrical levels of the unconscious, the territory of the mystic and that of the psychotic converge upon' each other in a manner reminiscent to those states of mind described by William James in his 1896 Lowell lectures alluded to Chapter four:[47]

> It might be said that symmetrical relations reveal obscure aspects of being, those where the individual merges into the others (through disappearance of contiguity relations or space) and into the infinite (through the disappearance of both space and time or relations of succession).
>
> (Matte-Blanco, 1998 [1975], p. 265)

With regard to a possible convergence between the ideas of Matte-Blanco and those of Bion, it is striking that both authors were similarly drawn to apophatic modes of

---

45 On the notion of a *basic matrix,* see the following:

> The region of the basic matrix is that in which symmetrisation exerts a major influence on representation and is the region of the deeper unconscious . . . the "region" of the basic matrix is a pure manifestation of being with no happening, where outside and inside do not exist.
>
> (Matte-Blanco, 1998 [1988], pp. 193–195)

> As Matte-Blanco goes on to discuss in some detail in this same text, his idea of a *basic matrix* has major implications with regard to how we conceptualise fundamental psychoanalytic ideas such as "introjection," "projection" and especially "projective identification."

46 The authors attribute this doctrine to a "spontaneous tendency of the human mind," the neurobiological origins of which they propose might ultimately "lie in the way the human brain uses 'topographical maps' to organize data into functional hierarchies" (Matte-Blanco, 1998 [1988], pp. 193–195). See also Main (2013 [2004], pp. 168–169).

47 See also Corbett (2020, p. 679).

discourse in which notions of "light" and "dark" are paradoxically "reversed" via a "coincidence of opposites," the teachings regarding which Matte-Blanco appears to have encountered in his study of the writings of Nicholas of Cusa (1401–1464).[48] It is this "duplex" account of the human subject as consisting of a *coincidentia oppositorum*[49] that lies at the heart of Matte-Blanco's revisioning of psychoanalysis:

> Therefore, it can be affirmed that there is in the very structure of humans a fundamental antinomy resulting from the co-presence of the two modes of being which are incompatible with one another and, in spite of this, exist and appear together in the same subject.
>
> (Matte-Blanco, 1998 [1988], p. 70)

In the final chapter, we shall consider how the "Orphic trajectory" within psychoanalysis manifested in James Grotstein's account of the "numinous and immanent psychoanalytic subject," whose attributes he set out to explore in his book, *Who is the Dreamer Who Dreams the Dream? A Study of Psychic Presences* (2000).

---

48 "It is my hope that they [Matte-Blanco's ideas] may have contributed something to illuminating this dazzling light which is at the same time a complete darkness, depending on the angle from which it is looked at" (Matte-Blanco, 1998 [1975], p. 288). See also Alava (2010), p. 24. For an account of Matte-Blanco's interest in the writings of Nicholas of Cusa, see Bomford (2004, p. 5). Matte-Blanco specifically refers to "the identity of opposites" in his discussion concerning the four antinomies of the death instinct – see Matte-Blanco (2005, p. 1469). For a helpful overview of Nicholas of Cusa's teachings, see Counet (2006, pp. 293–296).

49 For an illuminating account of the *coincidentia oppositorum*, see McGilchrist (2021, pp. 813–841).

Chapter 6

Conclusion

Who Is the Dreamer Who Dreams the Dream?[1]

When I was a second year medical student I had a dream the night before the final examination in pharmacology which I remember across the years as follows:

> the setting was a bleak piece of moorland in the Scottish Highlands engulfed by a dense fog. A small portion of the fog slowly cleared and an angel appeared surrealistically asking, "Where is James Grotstein?" The voice was solemn and litanical. The fog slowly re-enveloped her form as if she had never existed or spoken. Then, as if part of a prearranged pageant, the fog cleared again but now some distance away, at a higher promontory where a rocky crag appeared from the cloud bank revealing another angel who, in response to the first angel's question, answered as follows: "He is aloft, contemplating the dosage of sorrow upon the Earth." (p. 111)
>
> (Grotstein, J. S. (1979) Who Is the Dreamer Who Dreams the Dream and Who is the Dreamer Who Understands It—A Psychoanalytic Inquiry Into the Ultimate Nature of Being. *Contemporary Psychoanalysis* 15:110–169)[2]

6.1 Introduction

This book has argued for the presence of an *Orphic trajectory* within psychoanalysis, the distinguishing features of which it has traced from its prehistory, through to its inception, and beyond. It has proposed that the *hieroglyphs* encoded in this trajectory

---

2 C.f. The following: The setting is a bleak piece of moorland in the Scottish Highlands, engulfed by a dense fog. A small portion of the fog slowly clears, and an angel appears surrealistically, asking, "Where is James Grotstein?" The voice is solemn and awesome, almost eerie. The fog slowly reenvelops her form, as if she had never existed or spoken. Then, as if part of a prearranged pageant, the fog clears again; but now some distance away, on a higher promontory where a rocky crag appears from the cloud bank, another angel is revealed, who, in response to the first angel's question, answers, "He is aloft, contemplating the dosage of sorrow upon the earth." (Grotstein, 2000a, p. 5). Grotstein's long-standing preoccupation with the meaning and significance of this dream gives some indication as to its importance with regards to his formation as a psychoanalyst.

DOI: 10.4324/9781003476733-6

were transmitted to later generations of psychoanalysts in the guise of enigmatic signifiers encrypted in theory. In the concluding chapter of this book, a case is made for discerning the persistence of this trajectory in the writings of James Grotstein and the "oneiric" school of post-Bionian psychoanalysis. However, before we embark upon this itinerary, it will be helpful to provide a recap of the argument set out thus far.

Chapter 1 provided an overview of the historical and conceptual scope of the Orphic trajectory, as well as an outline of the methodology adopted to undertake the task of its exposition. It also summarised the motives of the author for embarking upon this task. Theories originally developed within the academic study of Western esotericism were introduced to facilitate an enhanced understanding of the role played by the "occult" in the formation of psychoanalytic theory and technique. These ideas were elaborated upon to develop a distinctive theoretical framework for conceptualising how esoteric "traces" came to be *encrypted* via processes of *enigmatic signification* to form semiotic *hieroglyphs* whose presence can be discerned throughout the course of psychoanalytic history and concept formation. Chapter 2 located the "dark precursors" to psychoanalysis within the various mesmeric, somnambulistic and hypnotic "currents" arising out of the Christian theosophical, German philosophical and Romantic "traditions." It explored how these sources contributed to the development of an occluded conceptual matrix that conjoined mesmerism, animal magnetism, artificial somnambulism and hypnotism to the formation of a nascent psychoanalytic unconscious. Chapter 3 explored the complex web of relations linking Freudian psychoanalysis to telepathy, fin de siècle occultism, psychical research and the Kabbalah. Chapter 4 focused on the pioneering investigations into anomalous psychic phenomena undertaken by the Hungarian school of psychoanalysis as exemplified in the writings of Sándor Ferenczi, Elizabeth Severn and Nandor Fodor. It also highlighted the persistence of somnambulistic currents active within Hungarian developments in trauma theory. Chapter 5 examined the evidential basis for construing the later writings of W.R. Bion as displaying distinctive apophatic, Kabbalistic and theurgic elements, the distinguishing features of which were conjectured as integral to late Bionian theory and technique. It also hypothesised phenomenological parallels as existing between the Bionian technique of *reverie* and the parapsychological research technique known as the *ganzfeld procedure*.[3] This final chapter illustrates the persistence of the Orphic trajectory in contemporary psychoanalysis as exemplified in the work of James Grotstein (1925–2015)

---

3 It has been observed that

> These states of mind [i.e. those alterations in consciousness correlated with psi phenomena], not surprisingly, pose challenges to being studied through conventional scientific methods because asking someone to "produce" them at will runs counter to their very "spontaneous" and "uncontrolled" nature. That challenge has sometimes been overcome in Ganzfeld experiments, where the participant is exposed to homogeneous and unpatterned sensory stimulation that induces a similar state . . . this state of mind and its attending challenges is probably one quite familiar to the psychoanalytic clinician, as it is none other but the state of "reverie" from which we listen for our patients' unconscious communication.
>
> (Ivan, 2009, p. 109)

and the "oneiric" school of post-Bionian psychoanalysis. It also identifies these representatives of the Orphic trajectory as constituting a potential source of inspiration for future developments in psychoanalytic theory and technique.

It is important to emphasise that the Orphic trajectory constitutes only one of a potential number of esoteric "currents" that have contributed to the formation of a contemporary pluralistic psychoanalysis.[4] Its diachronic influence has nonetheless played a distinctive role in fashioning a conceptual and clinical recalibration resulting in a revisioning of psychoanalysis as "a *mystical science,* an *emotional science, a non-linear, intuitionistic science*" (Grotstein, 2007, p. 104). This "recalibration" is located within the ambit of an "after" science that includes the sublation of its "before," entailing an acknowledgement that "the 'occult' was always a part of our scientific and intellectual heritage" (Sommer, 2016, p. 109). Moreover, it proposes that its hermeneutic possibilities have the potential to provide a fertile source of inspiration for future developments in psychoanalytic theory and practice. As Susan Rowland has remarked:

> Relatively recent forms of academic study, such as psychology, were constructed by dividing a heritage along lines of "respectable" proto-scientific ideas and magical practices better forgotten and left in the dark. Unfortunately, these lost magical arts took with them ways of relating to symbols, images and words that are arguably too valuable to discard.
>
> (Rowland, 2017, p. 91)

In order to illustrate the persistence of the *Orphic trajectory* into the present day, we shall consider how these "lost magical arts" underwent a resurgence in the guise of a particular version of post-Bionian psychoanalysis, the distinctive attributes of which are exemplified for my current purposes by James Grotstein's book *Who is the Dreamer Who Dreams the Dream: A Study of Psychic Presences* (2000a). Grotstein's work is subsequently aligned with developments in the "oneiric" school of post-Bionian psychoanalysis, the distinguishing features of which it is proposed tacitly identify it as constituting a significant manifestation of an *encrypted* "psychoanalytic parapsychology."

6.2   Who Is the Dreamer Who Dreams the Dream?

James Grotstein was one of a small group of American analysts who extended an invitation to a number of major London Kleinian analysts – including Hanna Segal, Herbert Rosenfeld, Donald Meltzer and Wilfred Bion – to visit Los Angeles during the early 1960s (Aguayo, 2017, pp. 4–5).[5] Grotstein coined the rubric of "The Four Horsemen of the Apocalypse" to describe the study group that grew out of these

---

4 See, for example, Hewitt (2020) for an exemplary account that focuses upon the significance of the work of F.W.H. Myers and William James as conduits for the "occult" in psychoanalysis.

5 For a helpful overview of Grotstein's early life and career, see Franey and Grotstein (2008).

meetings, thereby giving apt and witty expression to the marked degree of ideo-logical turbulence – referred to by its protagonists as "The Time of Troubles" – that subsequently gripped the Los Angeles psychoanalytic community in response to the appearance of these novel and "heterodox" psychoanalytic teachings. Grotstein him-self underwent an unusually wide psychoanalytic education that included personal analyses with the classical Freudian, Robert Jokl; the Fairbairnian Ivan McGuire; a third analysis with Wilfred Bion that lasted for some six years before ending pre-maturely due to the latter's poor health; and a fourth and final analysis with the British Kleinian, Albert Mason (Aguayo, 2017, pp. 4–5). However, in Grotstein's estimation, it was his analysis with Bion that "taught me to revere my own imagina-tion" (Franey & Grotstein, 2008, p. 101). Notably, it was during the latter stages of his analysis with Bion that Grotstein's first publications began to appear.[6] Although Grotstein never made any explicit allusion in his own writings to the figure of Orpheus, he was certainly acquainted with the Orphic mythology, having discussed its psychological meaning with Judith Pickering during the course of a visit that she made to his home in Los Angeles.[7] Although Grotstein did not encounter Ferenczi's concept of "astra" until shortly before his death, his analysis with Bion – coupled with the extensive contributions that he made towards innovative developments within post-Bionian theory and technique – nonetheless locates his work within the ambit of the Orphic trajectory within psychoanalysis (Reiner, 2017, pp. 131–132).

The publication of *Who is the Dreamer Who Dreams the Dream?* initially met with something of a mixed reception. While some early reviewers lauded it as a "tour de force" whose "attempts to theorise at and beyond the mental perimeters of the knowable are as striking as they are clinically invaluable," less positive com-mentators remarked that "Others with less tolerance for imagery and poetry in their consideration of internal worlds will have less patience with Grotstein's approach" (Gargiulo, 2001, p. 483; Malin, 2002, p. 304; Spielman, 2001, p. 1051). Despite such mixed evaluations, Grotstein considered this book to be the one he would most like to be remembered for (Franey & Grotstein, 2008, p. 105). Perhaps of more relevance in the present context is Kerry Gordon's evaluation of Grotstein's book (initially alluded to in chapter 1) as constituting "an elaborated Gnostic gos-pel of depth psychology" (Gordon, 2004, p. 18). However, before we can arrive at an assessment of Gordon's claims, we will need to begin with a brief overview of the main esoteric themes encountered in Grotstein's psychoanalytic "grimoire."

The text of *Who is the Dreamer Who Dreams the Dream* begins with a foreword by Thomas Ogden and a preface by James Grotstein – programmatically titled "Who Is the Unconscious?" – followed by ten chapters, all of which were previ-ously published by Grotstein as separate articles that were subsequently revised for the book, the earliest of which appeared in 1979. In his foreword, Ogden

---

6 Grotstein's analysis with Bion began in 1973, while his first publication on the psychoanalytic con-cept of schizophrenia occurred in 1977.
7 "We talked avidly about Bion, O, apophatic mysticism, about my analysis of the psychological mean-ing of the myth of Orpheus and Persephone" (Culbert-Koehn et al., 2015, p. 755).

emphasised, "Grotstein's ability to convey a sense of unlimited creative potential of the unconscious" before cautioning "that any attempt to paraphrase Grotstein is as doomed as an effort to paraphrase a poem" (Ogden, in Grotstein, 2000, p. vii). After introducing an idea of mental health entailing a "generative tension between the phenomenal subject and the Ineffable Subject of the unconscious," Ogden glosses Grotstein's conceptualisation of "rogue subjective objects" (chapter 6) by construing them as an elaboration and extension of Hans Loewald's "conception of analysis as a process of turning ghosts into ancestors" (Grotstein, 2000, pp. viii, x). In his preface, Grotstein defined the central task of his book as follows:

> I am seeking ways to rescue the id specifically and the unconscious generally from what I believe has been a prejudice – that it is primitive and impersonal, rather than subjective and ultra sophisticated . . . one of my aims is to revive the concept of the "alter ego" (second self) in order to restore the unconscious to its former conception before Freud, that of a mystical, preternatural, numinous second self – and then to reintegrate that older version with the more positivistic version that Freud gave us.
>
> (Grotstein, 2000a, p. xvi)[8]

In order to facilitate this project, Grotstein sets out to replace the secular and scientistic terminologies of "internal objects" with a more evocative and experiential lexicon populated by entities such as "angels," "demons," "ghosts" and "chimerae" (Grotstein, 2000a, p. 144). Grotstein's preface provides a road map for his book and introduces many of the central themes subsequently elaborated upon, at least some of which are avowedly Platonic with regard to their philosophical orientation.[9] References to a "sacred architecture of the psyche," aspects of which are deemed to be inherently "preternatural," are alluded to, as are themes derived from ancient Assyrian dream culture, unconscious capacities for prescience and premonition, as well as a conception of the analyst as a "practicing mystic" (Grotstein, 2000a, pp. xxii, xxvii, xxx.). It is no surprise to find in his later writings Grotstein advocating for a version of psychoanalysis in which access to trance states constitutes an acknowledged feature of psychoanalytic practice, while preternatural experiences – such as telepathy and prescience – are construed to possess the potential to be incorporated

---

8 In an earlier paper, Grotstein described Freud as a figure who

> imposed a catastrophic change on Western philosophy, epistemology, and culture, that was to represent the end of certain belief systems from all ages past and herald the new age of the inner mind. By his neurologising the Unconscious with the instinctual drives and assigning them causal priority for epistemology, affects and behaviour, he ultimately came to demonize the Unconscious and gradually lost sight of the value of its epistemological, existential, and numinous majesty and uniqueness.
>
> (Grotstein, 1996, p. 41)

9 The famous parable of the cave from Plato's *Republic* is explicitly deployed by Grotstein (2000) on pp. xvii–xviii as an "epistemological metaphor" to depict the manner in which "the religious, philosophical, and mystical . . . converge with the psychological and the psychoanalytic."

into a post-Bionian psychoanalysis (Grotstein, 2007, p. 32, 2009a, pp. 297–298). As we saw in chapter 5, Grotstein has explicitly alluded to encounters with telepathic phenomena in his own clinical practice, which he theoretically aligns with Bion's theory of transformations in O (Grotstein, 2007, p. 32, 2009a, pp. 297–298).

Chapter 1 begins with an "initiatory" dream that Grotstein "witnessed" as a second-year medical student, the oneiric effects arising from which were to constitute the experiential "core" and primary inspiration for many of his future ideas concerning the existence of a duplex "subject."[10] The numinous and uncanny elements of this dream provide the dramatic representation for many of his subsequent reflections concerning the phenomenal and noumenal aspects of a "preternatural" human subject, whose holographic attributes collectively constitute the "Supraordinate Subject of Being" (Grotstein, 2000a, p. 6). Chapter 2 begins with an epigraph taken from the Lurianic Kabbalah ("Keter Ayn Sof shrank and created the universe") as the preamble to Grotstein embarking upon a rationale for adopting – and creatively adapting – Ferenczi's (1932) concept of *autochthony* (Grotstein, 2000a, p. 40). While Ferenczi originally utilised this term to distinguish the internal from the external origins of paranoia arising out of trauma, Grotstein extends its theoretical dimensions to include "the unconscious phantasy of self-creation *and* of creation of the object" as the preamble to introducing its dialectical partner, "*alterity,* the awareness of the otherness of the object and cocreation by it and with it" (Grotstein, 2000a, p. 38; see also Merkur, 2010, pp. 273–274). Grotstein construes autochthony and *cosmogony* (i.e. "the creation of a world order") as principles belonging in the domain of the imagination that govern the process of personalising the random, chaotic data of internal and external experience. He subsequently defines both these terms as "faculties that constitute a prophylactic defence against the impact of trauma and Ananke (Necessity or Fate)" (Grotstein, 2000a, p. 51). In Chapters 3 and 4, Grotstein provides an extensive introduction to the ideas of Ignacio Matte-Blanco, during the course of which he compares Matte-Blanco's concept of an "infinite" unconscious with those of Freud and Klein. Notably, Grotstein seeks to draw out the mystical implications that are left implicit in Matte-Blanco's own writings, judiciously drawing upon Gnostic and Kabbalistic themes to illustrate the "mystical" dimensions he conjectures to exist enfolded within the bi-logical structures of Matte-Blanco's "infinite" unconscious (Grotstein, 2000a, p. 78, n. 4, p. 81).

Chapter 5 provides an innovative theory of the "psychoanalytic subject," the distinguishing features of which share a striking resemblance to ideas more usually encountered in gnostic and Neoplatonic texts. Since the arguments and phenomenological descriptions that it embarks upon arguably contain some of the most explicitly esoteric themes to be found in Grotstein's writings, a more substantive account of its contents will be elaborated upon in the next part of this chapter.

In Chapter 6, Grotstein charts an inner topography for the "demonic third forms" of the internal world, during the course of which he remarks upon the manner in

---

10 See the epigraph to this chapter for Grotstein's verbatim description of this dream. For an account of the impact that this dream had upon his subsequent theorising, see Grotstein (1996, p. 45).

which Freud's overshadowing of his German Romantic inheritance with the materialistic axioms of an "absolute science" contributed to the creation of "a lexicon of ontic, mechanistic, dehumanized entities such as 'drive' and 'object,' rather than 'homunculi,' 'chimera,' 'monsters,' 'demons,' 'angels,' 'ghosts,' or 'revenants'" (op cit., p. 144). Grotstein unfavourably contrasts Freud's reductive approach with the more expansive understanding of "psychic presences" exemplified by C. G. Jung and his followers and explicitly augments his account by including Kleinian and Bionian perspectives to act as correctives to these deficiencies (Grotstein, 2000a, p. 169).[11] Perhaps most strikingly for a psychoanalyst, Grotstein cites some of his own case material from this chapter as providing anecdotal evidence for Jung's theory of synchronicity (Grotstein, 2000a, p. 151, n. 4). During the course of his exposition, Grotstein introduces concepts such as "the magus object" and addresses a range of "preternatural" themes, including Hermetic angelology, the Devil and witchcraft.[12]

Chapter 7 provides a comparative account of Klein's archaic Oedipus complex and its hypothesised relationship to the ancient myth of the labyrinth, with particular emphasis being given to a clinical example in which extensive parallels are drawn between the myth of the labyrinth and the experience of the dream. In Chapters 8 and 9, Grotstein advocates for a judicious and nuanced use of the Christian *mythos* to creatively augment the insights provided by the Oedipus myth more usually encountered in psychoanalysis. Grotstein utilises these myths to develop clinical concepts, such as the *Pietà transference* and *transcendent position*, before launching upon an extended series of reflections on "exorcism," the role of suffering in analysis and the value of augmenting post-Kleinian theory with the introduction of a "transcendent position."[13] Grotstein takes particular care to highlight that his use of religious myth is motivated by psychoanalytic concerns while at the same time emphasising his indebtedness to his Jewish inheritance as the inspiration for certain ideas developed in these chapters. However, it is possible to speculate that Grotstein's emphasis upon the avowedly "psychoanalytic" nature of his interests may have been at least partially motivated by a variant of "defensive esotericism,"

---

11 Notably, earlier versions of chapters five, six and seven were originally published in *The Journal of Analytical Psychology*.

12 *The magus object*:

> The particular use I impute to them [i.e. the magus object] is their power as a superego-type internal object to ensorcell their subjects to play out scenarios seemingly belonging to them, the magi, but which they compel the subjects to enact, for their own good.

> (Grotstein, 2000a, p. 165)

13 It seems likely that Jungian sources (specifically, Jung's "The Psychology of the Transference" [1946]) may underlie Grotstein's formulation of the *Pietà transference* and his "claim that the analyst must take on the suffering of the patient" – see Brown (2020), p. 31. For a helpful account of Grotstein's indebtedness to Jung, see Culbert-Koehn (1997, pp. 30–31). In a later work, Grotstein describes how the patient "becomes more *evolved* as a finite→infinite self by receiving the legacy from his infinite, immortal, godly self. I call this state the attainment of the 'transcendent position'" (Grotstein, 2007, p. 107). The "theurgic" elements that are obliquely imbricated within Grotstein's definition of the "transcendent position" arguably constitute a part of his inheritance from Bion.

while the account that he gives of his Jewish inheritance reads like a deeply felt "confession" of the spiritual lineage that imbues his writings.[14] In Chapter 10, Grotstein revisits the idea of a "transcendent position," which he utilises as the basis for undertaking an intensely "mystical" reading of psychoanalysis, in which the ideas of Bion and Matte-Blanco are brought into creative rapprochement to form a model of the psyche in which gnostic, mystical and Kabbalistic themes are aligned into a state of synergistic convergence with his more explicitly psychoanalytic concerns.

Having adumbrated the esoteric themes encountered in *Who is the Dreamer Who Dreams the Dream? A Study of Psychic Presences*, we can now move on to elaborate a more substantive account of Grotstein's radical reconceptualisation of a numinous and immanent psychoanalytic subject.

6.3   The numinous and immanent nature of the psychoanalytic subject[15]

Grotstein begins this chapter by reminding his readers that

[a]n underlying theme of the entirety of this work is the idea of psychic presences. The idea of a psychic presence borrows heavily from the olden schools of vitalism and animism and yet seems to convey the emotional immediacy of the presence of the essence or being of something or someone.

(Grotstein, 2000a, p. 101)[16]

Grotstein proceeds to adduce parallels between psychoanalytic ideas of the "unconscious" and philosophical conceptualisations of the "subject" and "being," as a

---

14

I therefore wish to make clear that I am respectfully Jewish, became Bar Mitzva, am a grandson of a distinguished rabbi, and am a direct descendant of Rabbi Eliyahu ben Shelomo, Kalman, the Vilna Ga'on. Further, I see spiritual Christianity not only as an outgrowth of Judaism but also as a continuation of Judaism in a different guise.

(Grotstein, 2000a, p. 220)

15 See Grotstein (1998). This paper constitutes an earlier version of chapter five of *Who is the Dreamer Who Dreams the Dream? A Study of Psychic Presences*. Since this earlier paper elaborates upon some of the themes more concisely explored in the book chapter, selected extracts are cited in subsequent footnotes to provide an accompanying commentary. In his 1998 paper, Grotstein provides us with the following lapidary definition of the *Subject*, whose attributes he describes as follows: "It is my belief that the Subject, like the Unconscious itself, belongs to the domain of the ineffable, the inscrutable, the sacred, the always elusive, perhaps even to the part-divine aspects of ourselves" (Grotstein, 1998, p. 52).

16 See also the following:

the concept of the Subject is dealt with extensively but incognito in terms of the idea of God and man's spiritual connection to Him. Meister Eckhart, like the allegedly heretical Gnostics and Cathars, conceived of two gods, "God" and the Godhead, the former representing the human's personal experience with the immanent "God," and the latter the utterly ineffable and inscrutable One. In the Lurianic Kabbalah, there is mention of the ten Sephiroth that extend from the inner, most ineffable Godhead, "Keter Ayn Sof," to the most immanent one to mankind, "Malkuth."

Grotstein (1998, p. 46)

preamble to embarking upon a series of "highly speculative" musings concerning the parallels he adduces to exist between psychoanalysis and certain "mystic-religious" themes encountered in Meister Eckhart, the Gnostics and the Kabbalah, which he subsequently utilises both to extend and to enrich the conceptual ambit of his theory of the psychoanalytic subject (Grotstein, 2000a, pp. 101–102, 138). Grotstein begins his account with a summary of what he considers to be the main theories of subjectivity encountered in psychology and psychoanalysis, with particular reference to the work of a number of contemporary psychoanalytic theorists, notably Roger Kennedy, Jessica Benjamin, Frances Moran, Thomas Ogden and Ignacio Matte-Blanco. While drawing extensively upon the work of these authors, Grotstein goes on to propose a version of psychoanalysis that can – at times – seem to take on the attributes of a séance rather than a science: "Using my own terminology, I would say that the analysand's Ineffable Subject speaks to his Phenomenal Subject, who feels . . . reflexively through the analyst/container (Grotstein, 2000a, pp. 114–115)."[17] Grotstein posits a duplex subject, both holographically unitary *and* bi-logically multilayered, thereby lending itself to the creation of a virtually unlimited series of component subjectivities inhabiting a psychical continuum that extends from the conscious and preconscious layers of the ego through to the noumenal and ineffable reaches of the deep unconscious subject.[18] Grotstein observes that effective cooperation between the phenomenal and noumenal agencies can be sabotaged by "rogue, or renegade subjects," the defining features of which share many of the attributes of "pathological organizations" and "psychic retreats" encountered in post-Kleinian theory (Grotstein, 2000a, p. 124). Once such disruptions occur, the ensuing state of alienation manifested between these agencies can result in their taking on the form of symptoms (Grotstein, 2000a, p. 128).

Grotstein refers in his clinical vignettes to the active use of reverie as a technique for contacting the disowned or estranged aspects of his patients' unconscious subjectivity (Grotstein, 2000a, pp. 135–138).[19] Towards the end of the chapter, Grotstein embarks upon an extended series of speculations of an explicitly "mystic-religious" nature, whose provenance is based primarily (but not exclusively) upon inferences derived from direct clinical experience. Using Freud's Schreber case (1911) as the launch pad for his own theoretical speculations,

---

17 See also the following: "we might say that an analysand uses his analyst as his own personal mirror so that his inner subject, his soul, may find its reflection – and be contacted anew" (Grotstein 2000a, p. 130). It is notable that Grotstein employs the metaphor of the Ouija board on at least two occasions to describe the communicative dynamics of psychoanalysis (pp. 30, 137).

18
  Analogously to Bohm's [2002 (1980)] concept of "wholeness and the implicate order," the subject can be understood as being holistic as well as implicate, i.e., separate as a totalistic, all-encompassing unity and multiple, located in many transformations and disguises simultaneously.

  (Grotstein, 1998, p. 50)

19 It is possible that Grotstein may have acquired first-hand experience of this technique during the course of his own analysis with Bion – see Grotstein (2007, p. 32).

Grotstein draws upon a bricolage of esoteric and mystical themes that includes (but is not limited to) ideas derived from Platonism, Gnosticism and the Kabbalah, as a prelude to remarking that

> [i]t may very well be that the unconscious, while not really being the same as the Godhead, may be as close to God (the Demiurge that dwells within us as a direct descendent of the Godhead) as any mortal may ever be.
>
> (Grotstein, 2000a, p. 139)

In the final summation to this chapter, Grotstein recasts the ostensibly secular subject of psychoanalysis into an explicitly Neoplatonic register:

> Whereas the Ineffable Subject is numinous, the Phenomenal Subject is secular, manifest, incarnate, palpable. I consider these two subjectivities to be holographically and holistically part of an overall ultimately indivisible subjectivity – the Supraordinate Subject of Being and Agency – which is both holistic and divided. That is, although the Supraordinate Subject overarches the Ineffable Subject and the Phenomenal Subject and is inclusive of them, it can be understood in its own right to holographically include an ineffable as well as a secular (more tangible) aspect. I further hypothesise that this overall subjectivity, which is both ineffable and phenomenal, occurs in an infinite vertical layering of the psyche, thereby imparting structural and topographic complexity to the concept of the subject as well as to the concepts of agency and being.
>
> (Grotstein, 2000a, p. 141)[20]

There are elements of Grotstein's account of a numinous and immanent psychoanalytic subject that, in some respects at least, bear comparison with earlier ideas of a "transcendental subject," "subliminal self" or "creative unconscious" encountered in the work of figures such as Carl du Prel (1839–1899), William James (1842–1910), F.W.H. Myers (1843–1901), Theodore Flournoy (1854–1920) and – more recently – Jeffrey Kripal (1962-) in his theorisation of a *duplex* self:[21]

> I see transpersonal psychology as a modern expression of an ancient gnosis about the dual nature of human consciousness, a gnosis witnessed to in any number of

---

20 C.f. the following – 'There exists a more comprehensive consciousness, a profounder faculty, which for the most part remains potential only … but from which the consciousness and faculty of earth-life are mere selections … [N]o Self of which we can here have cognizance is in reality more than a fragment of a larger self, – revealed in a fashion at once shifting and limited through an organism not so framed as to afford it full manifestation' (F.W.H. Myers, *Human Personality* [1903], cited in Kelly et al.(2007), p. 73).

21 See du Prel, *The Philosophy of Mysticism Vol. 1* (2022 [1885]); Sommer (2009, pp. 59–68); Taylor (1996); Raia (2019, pp. 97–204); Kripal (2010, pp. 38 ff); Flournoy (1994 [1899]); Flournoy (2007 [1911]). In the estimation of Hewitt (2020, p. 79), Grotstein's approach to dreams in particular partially situates him within an American psychological tradition that extends back to William James.

Indic and Western traditions, and more recently in modern Mesmerism, animal magnetism, psychical research, and psychoanalysis. All these streams *put into conversation* constitute the true origins of my *homo duplex* speculations.

(Kripal, 2008, p. 277)

However, while the proximate source for Grotstein's theory of the psychoanalytic subject appears to have evolved out of a dialogue between eighteenth-century literary depictions of the *alter ego* and clinical accounts of a "dissociative" self,[22] its more distal origins can be traced back to ideas of a "divine double," whose textual antecedents span a range of ancient philosophical schools and heterodox spiritualities ranging from Platonism and Neoplatonism to theurgy and gnosticism.[23] Intimations of its activities can be found in nineteenth- and early twentieth-century depictions of the *doppelgänger*, most notably within psychoanalysis in the idea of the "double" as described by Freud in his 1919 paper on "The Uncanny" (see Stang, 2016, pp. 11–12).[24] In Stang's estimation, the Freudian conceptualisation of the double, in both its benign and more destructive aspects, constitutes the manifestation of "a developmental stage that ultimately supports his theory of repression and his explanation for the emergence of the superego" (Stang, 2016, 2016, p. 12). However, it was only after the publication of Henry Corbin's *The Man of Light in Iranian Sufism* (1971) that the idea of a "divine double" reappeared as a serious topic for study within academia (Stang, 2016, p. 6). Describing his approach to this topic as entailing "an innovation in philosophical anthropology" (Stang, 2016, p. 6), Corbin proposed that

To speak of the polar dimension as the transcendent dimension of the earthly individuality is to point out that it includes a counterpart, a heavenly "partner," and that its total structure is that of a bi-unity, a *unus ambo.*

(Corbin, 1994 [1971], p. 7)

Notably, one of the key determinants that Stang identifies as distinguishing modern from ancient conceptualisations of personhood is that, for the former, the inhabiting "powers" are felt to emerge from a psychologised "beneath," whereas for the ancients, these same "powers" were experienced as descending from a numinous "height" (Stang, 2016, pp. 250–251). It is the excesses of this imbalance that

---

22 In an earlier paper, after alluding to certain tropes found in eighteenth-century literature, Grotstein observes that

[t]here was a respectful recognition then of this "stranger within thee," a concept that was to help usher in the nineteenth century obsession with the alter ego or second self, not only in literary fiction but also in neurology and psychiatry in the form of autoscopy, animal magnetism, hypnosis, and the dissociation in hysteria, the latter of which became the provenance of psychoanalysis – but at the expense of the loss of the second self.

(Grotstein, 1998, p. 56)

23 In his allusions to the literary antecedents to the alter ego concept, Grotstein references Cox (1980).

24 In the estimation of Monk (2023, p. 61), the uncanny is itself a mode of "magical consciousness" that enables access to paranormal forms of cognition, such as "synchronicity, divination, and telepathy."

Grotstein sought to correct under the aegis of a numinous and immanent psycho-analytic subject. Stang describes how during late antiquity a dispute arose between Plotinian and Iamblichan accounts concerning whether the "descended intellect" was considered to be capable of maintaining contact with its "undescended" coun-terpart (Stang, 2016, pp. 231–232; see also Addey, 2019, pp. 147–157). Viewed through the lens provided by this much earlier debate, it is possible to align Grot-stein's account of the psychoanalytic subject as possessing an implicitly "theurgic" dimension with a version of post-Bionian psychoanalysis that potentiates the crea-tion of an ostensibly secularised "ritual," through which the self-alienated phenom-enal subject of the analysand can restore metaphysical contact with its noumenal "Other" via the "séance" of psychoanalysis.

The linguistic resonances active in Grotstein's writings possess the capacity to invoke within the engaged reader a state of mind in which "religious, philosophical, and mystical studies converge with the psychological and the psychoanalytic" (Grot-stein, 2000a, p. xvii). It is in this sense that the associated "meaning events" arising from Grotstein's combination of poetic and apophatic approaches to language con-verge with Kripal's "thesis that academic writing can also be a form of mystical writ-ing; that is, I want it to function as a kind of 'meaning event' in its own right" (Kripal, 2001, p. 28).[25] Much like Grotstein's own approach to psychoanalytic literary stylis-tics, Kripal's "approach to the scholar as mystic is unabashedly positive, poetic and romantic" (Kripal, 2001, p. 28). More recently, Wouter Hanegraaff has reconfigured Corbin's concept of the *imaginal* to suit the "radical agnosticism" embodied in his own approach to engaging with the hermeneutics of the encounter between the text and its reader (Hanegraaff, 2022, p. 367, n. 55, 2025, p. 260):

This paradoxical phenomenon of imaginal perception is not just central to Hermetic spirituality – it lies at the heart of the hermeneutic enterprise that I believe the humanities are all about. The *pharmakon* to which you have been exposed . . . was designed to change your consciousness, stimulate your imagi-nation, broaden your horizon, even open doors to noetic insight. I have delib-erately tried to draw your mind into profoundly ambiguous realms of human experience and practice, for although their very existence has seldom been rec-ognized in academic research, I see them as essential to human psychology and deserving of very serious attention.

(Hanegraaff, 2022, pp. 367–368)

It is precisely these "ambiguous realms" that analysts such as Wilfred Bion and James Grotstein have sought to bring under the purview of a more expansive understanding of the psychoanalytic subject. Some of the most intriguing devel-opments arising from the innovations of both theorists have occurred under the

---

25 "The meaning event is transreferential. Rather than pointing to an object, apophatic language attempts to evoke in the reader an event that is . . . structurally analogous to mystical union" (Sells (1994, p. 10).

auspices of the "oneiric" school of post-Bionian psychoanalysis – with Grotstein being described as one of its "principal authors" (Pietrantonio, 2018, p. 97). Hence, it is to an examination of these innovations developed within the *oneiric* school that our attention shall now turn.

6.4   The persistence of esoteric *traces* in the "oneiric" school of post-Bionian psychoanalysis

Since the oneiric model of post-Bionian psychoanalysis has its origins in contemporary psychoanalytic field theory, it will be helpful to provide some initial background by locating its distinctive features within its wider theoretical context.[26] The concept of the "field" ultimately derives from physics, where it is utilised to describe "the mutual interdependence and influences at a distance that occur between elements of a given system" (Civitarese, 2022, p. 7). While Donnel Stern has distinguished interpersonal/relational (primarily North American) and Bionian (South American/European) approaches to psychoanalytic field theory, S. Montana Katz has identified the *mythopoetic* (Baranger and Baranger), *plasmic* (North American) and *oneiric* (post-Bionian) models as constituting discrete "models" within contemporary psychoanalytic field theory. Clearly, there are some overlaps between these respective demarcations. However, while each of these orientations has subsequently embarked upon its own discrete theoretical trajectory, all of them share a debt to the social psychologist Kurt Lewin (1890–1947), whose work was to constitute a seminal influence in the development of "field theory."

Lewin's field theory entails a conceptualisation of the individual and their environment as existing in a state of mutual interdependency, giving rise to a "constellation" in which behaviour and development occur as functions of a "total situation," involving the creation of a dynamic field "in which the state of any part of the field depends upon every other part" (Katz, 2017, pp. 15–16). Lewin's ideas – alongside those of Gestalt psychology – played a significant role in the development of the psychoanalytic theory of the "bi-personal field" developed by Madeline and Willy Baranger. Their concept of unconscious phantasy was especially influenced by Bion's work on groups, as well as by Susan Isaacs' seminal 1948 paper on unconscious phantasy, resulting in a theory of phantasy in which it is no longer required to possess a source, an aim or an object, since its origins are attributed to feelings such as hope, fear and dread, rather than derived from the Freudian *mythos* of the *drive* (see Stern, 2013a, pp. 493–494). The Barangers gave particular emphasis to what they termed the *essential ambiguity* of the psychoanalytic situation, which entailed the mutual co-creation of the session from within a shared oneiric state of wakeful dreaming. They construed the essential ambiguity of the analytic process as arising out of its synchronous temporality – in which past, present and future spiral through each other simultaneously – thereby evoking within its participants the sense of

26 The following account of psychoanalytic field theory is indebted to the following sources: Civitarese (2022); Katz (2017); Stern (2013a, 2013b); Snell (2024).

inhabiting a *mythopoetic* realm of dream or fairy tale (Katz, 2017, pp. 30–31). Its evocation requires the analytic couple to inhabit a shared state of mind in which "each thing or event in the field be at the same time something else. If this essential ambiguity is lost, the analysis also disappears" (Baranger & Baranger, cited in Stern, 2013a, p. 493). In this regard, the "essential ambiguity" of the mythopoetic model parallels – in some of its aspects at least – the conceptual attributes and symbolic resonances of a psychologised theory of esoteric *correspondences*.

Proponents of the *plasmic* model have derived their ideas from a range of theoretical approaches, including interpersonal, intersubjective and motivational schools of thought, all of which share a common interest in language, human growth and the development of effective techniques for liberating the analysand from the constraints of distorting and imprisoning psychic structures. The adoption of the rubric *plasmic* (derived from the fourth state of matter, plasma) is intended to convey the idea of particles possessing a fundamentally interactive nature, with each plasma particle being reciprocally affected by the magnetic fields of its peers. One corollary of this approach is that it requires the adoption of a theory of brain/mind interaction in which the idea of mind is conceptualised as a field phenomenon. The notion of instinctual drives is therefore abandoned, with Jacob Arlow's work on unconscious fantasy being utilised to facilitate an enhanced understanding of fantasy as constituting a fundamental feature of waking and sleeping life. The plasmic model also supports an understanding of unconscious mental processes as possessing an inherently metaphorical quality (Katz, 2017, pp. 36 ff.).

The post-Bionian or "oneiric" model – otherwise known as Bionian field theory (BFT) – constitutes the most recent of these developments in psychoanalytic field theory and is centred around the work of a number of Italian analysts in particular, most notably Antonio Ferro and Giuseppe Civitarese. BFT's origins have been dated by Civitarese to 1989, due to the publication in that year of a paper by Bezoari and Ferro titled "Listening, Interpretations and Transformative Functions in the Analytical Dialogue" that definitively established for the first time a clear link between the contributions made by the Barangers and by Bion (Civitarese, 2022, p. 3; Snell, 2024, p. 26). A number of commentators have identified post-Bionian field theory as constituting one of "the main currents in contemporary psychoanalysis" (Civitarese, 2022, p. 4). While the proponents of this model are influenced by the work of the Barangers, they draw their primary source of inspiration from the ideas of Bion, making particular use of his theory of the *waking dream thought* to analyse the oneiric quality of sessions, the subjective dimension of which is accessed by means of *reverie* (Katz, 2017, p. 19; Snell, 2024, pp. 81–85). This adoption of a specifically qualitative approach to knowledge requiring a perceptual reliance upon the attainment of highly rarefied and subtle modes of subjectivity – such as those encountered while in a state of reverie – is reminiscent of ideas and themes more usually found in esoteric theories of epistemology (see Magee [ed.], 2016, pp. xxiii–xxix). Ferro draws inspiration for his writings from the ideas of the Barangers, Bion, Melanie Klein, Robert Langs and Thomas Ogden – among others – with his own theories being additionally formed by ideas taken from the discipline of narratology (Katz, 2017, p. 58; Snell, 2024, pp. 23–45). Ferro's distinctive approach accentuates the mythopoetic aspects of the Barangers' work, which he creatively integrates with Bion's notion of "waking dream thoughts" to arrive at a model of psychoanalysis "in which the oneiric quality of the sessions is essential and omni-present," this assumption being premised upon a clinical trajectory that assumes "[t]he goals of an analytic process are to increase the capacity of the analysand to symbolise, to dream and to feel" (Katz, 2017, pp. 58–59).

In 2008, Ferro published a subtle and insightful – as well as highly laudatory – review of Grotstein's *A Beam of Intense Darkness: Wilfred Bion's Legacy to Psychoanalysis* (2007) (Ferro, 2008). In this essay, Ferro hints at clinical encounters with quasi-telepathic phenomena, which he conceptualises by utilising ideas derived from post-Bionian field theory. Commenting on Grotstein's concept of projective transidentification, Ferro elaborates as follows:

> I believe the concept of projective transidentification allows us to clarify and enrich our understanding, but I also think that there is still a lot of work to be done on the theme of projective identifications. I think that many more things than we currently know and recognize actually occur between one mind and another. As far as the analytic session is concerned, I believe that emotional upsets really can pass from one mind to the other, especially if we consider that patient and analyst form a field of emotional forces which belong to both of them.
>
> (Ferro, 2008, p. 878)

In an earlier paper from 2002, Ferro related a clinical encounter with a female patient in which the patient's father's retinal vein thrombosis spontaneously "healed" subsequent to the patient's narrative of her father's illness being analysed as part of the wider oneiric field (Ferro, 2002, pp. 599–600; Katz, 2017, pp. 60–61). While Ferro did not explicitly allude in his case study to Jungian concepts such as "psychoid" and "synchronicity," it is nonetheless difficult for the reader not to employ these terms in order to make sense of the clinical material.[27] Certainly, the rather oblique

---

27

    Psychoid Unconscious: The idea of the psychoid unconscious was first put forward by Jung in 1946. His formulation has three aspects: (1) It refers to a level of, or in, the unconscious which is completely inaccessible to consciousness. (2) This most fundamental level of the unconscious has properties in common with the organic world; the psychological and the physiological worlds may be seen as two sides of a single coin. . . . (3) When Jung applied the notion of the archetype to the psychoid unconscious, the psychic/organic link was expressed in the form of a mind/body connection. . . . Synchronicity: Repeated experiences that indicated events do not always obey the rules of time, space and causality led Jung to search for what might lie beyond those rules. He developed the concept of synchronicity which he defined in several ways: (1) as an "acausal connecting principle"; (2) as referring to events meaningfully but not causally related (i.e. not coinciding in time and space); (3) as referring to events that coincide in time and space but can also be seen to have meaningful psychological connections; (4) as linking the psychic and material worlds.

                                                                (Samuels et al., 1986, pp. 122, 146)

   For in-depth accounts of these interrelated concepts, see Addison (2019) and Main (2013).

rhetoric adopted by Ferro in this case study (in which acausal relations, while never explicitly stated, are nonetheless implied) suggests the presence of a synchronistic process conjoining the "inner world" of the analysis to the "outer world" from which the story concerning the patient's father was initially taken prior to being "dreamt" by the analytic pair. Ferro's implicit "re-enchantment" of an ostensibly "disenchanted" analytic field exemplifies Robin Brown's contention that psychoanalysis has tacitly sought to remain "spiritually uncommitted while claiming sympathetic engagement with religion and spirituality. . . . This is expressed in a conception of the interpersonal field that accepts a disenchanted view of the world as normative" (Brown, 2020, p. 161). Hence, we find Civitarese asserting that to construe Bion as a "mystic" is to engage in a "gross misunderstanding," before concluding that "concepts like *faith, O, nameless dread, becoming, evolution*, etc., are by no means religious concepts" (Civitarese, 2022, pp. 98–99). As we have seen, while it is certainly true that it was a part of Bion's stated theoretical aims to extend his use of terms such as "mystic" and "religion" so as to enhance their resonance with his own very particular requirements as a theoretician, it is difficult to construe his later writings as unambiguously assuming a normative "disenchanted" world-view. As Civitarese himself has astutely observed,

> The most disingenuous thing there is, but which I suspect is quite widespread, is to think that analysts have a definite and clear concept of the unconscious. *They don't.* The theory, actually a plurality of theories, of psychoanalysis is always evolving. Even a theory is a dynamic field: if one theoretical element changes, all the others change. We can safely assume that we will never come to have a defined and stable concept of the unconscious.
>
> (Civitarese, 2022, p. 114)

Yet, despite these divergences of opinion, there are nonetheless reasons to suppose that deeper confluences might also be at work. Katz has remarked that "all psychoanalytic perspectives are converging towards the inclusion of a version of a field concept, at least implicitly" (Katz, 2017, p. 160). In the concluding section to this chapter, I will propose that one possible form this deeper convergence could potentially take would entail an increasing rapprochement between psychoanalysis, Jungian analytical psychology and research into the paranormal, leading to a de facto re-instantiation of "psychoanalytic parapsychology" entailing a dual-aspect monist theory of the subject that is sympathetic both to the psychoid and to the synchronistic dimensions of human experience.

6.5   Coda: post-Bionian psychoanalysis as *A Memoir of the Future*

As the historian Barbara Newman has astutely observed:

> any phenomenon that is widely and deeply studied becomes central to its field, while puzzling "fringe" phenomena may be ignored for so long that their very

existence is forgotten. Yet it is often those same phenomena, when somebody finally takes note of them, that force a paradigm shift.

(Newman, 2021, p. 274)

This book has foregrounded the persistence of esoteric "traces" in psychoanalysis in the hope that, by doing so, a more expansive theory of the human subject can at least begin to be envisaged, if not yet arrived at. The difficulties associated with embarking upon such a task are substantial. As George Makari has remarked,

> Modernity has answered many questions, but it has never found a way to fully reconcile the complex triumvirate of body, soul, and mind. Instead, it has left us haunted, divided, with competing histories, values, and rationales that have been at odds ever since . . .
> There is no accepted path from quantities to qualities, mechanics to creativity, facts to values, and brains to psyches.
> A vast attempted synthesis had failed and left behind modern men and women who now must navigate between competing notions of their own being.
> (Makari, 2015, pp. xvi, 511)[28]

However, it is also possible to situate Makari's sombre assessment of our current situation within the wider conceptual vistas provided by recent debates concerning the limits of contemporary critique, the search for more sophisticated post-critical alternatives, alongside proposals for an "apophatic anthropology" entailing a recognition of the *homo duplex* nature of the human subject (Kripal, 2021). Yet, despite these developments, it remains the case that many of the key questions arising from contemporary attempts to develop a coherent theory of the mind or psyche remain far from settled.[29] Indeed, the lack of consensus on these matters is of such a magnitude as to have led Iain McGilchrist to adopt the following striking metaphor to illustrate our current knowledge of mind/brain interaction:

> I believe it may be that consciousness does not depend upon a brain for its existence: just, in the absence of a brain, it is deprived of its expression as that particular mind. Another metaphor, far from original, but nonetheless useful, is

---

28 However, see also the following:

> We may think that our theories are shaped by observations, but it is as true that our observations are shaped by theories. . . . That a machine would be attractive as a model to science's help-mate, the left hemisphere, hardly needs . . . explaining. Machines are put together from parts and the left hemisphere's mode of operation is to break phenomena down into parts and then see how they can be put together again.
> (McGilchrist, 2021, p. 410)

29 For in-depth accounts of an innovative range of perspectives providing alternatives to the standard model of conceptualising mind as an epiphenomenon of the brain, see the following: Kelly et al. (eds.) (2007); Kelly et al. (eds.) (2015); Kelly and Marshall (eds.) (2021); McGilchrist (2021); Hart (2024).

that of the TV set. The TV set is proximally causative of the phenomena that appears on the screen: damage the electronic circuitry, and the picture's gone, or at any rate distorted – true enough. But the TV set is only mediative; it does not give rise to the programme you watch.

(McGilchrist, 2019, p. 465, n. 15)

Notably, in his most recent book, McGilchrist has argued for a *permissive* theory of consciousness, in which the phenomenon of consciousness is understood to be ontologically fundamental (McGilchrist, 2021, pp. 1043–1047).[30] It is from within the more expansive conceptual frameworks encountered in debates such as these that we can begin to reconstrue developments in post-Bionian psychoanalysis as constituting *A Memoir of the Future*, through which we can discern glimmers of the esoteric translated into the register of the psychoanalytic. Or, to revisit a remark made by Bion initially cited in the epigraph to chapter five of this book, this kind of "oneiric" approach to psychoanalytic theory formation can be thought of as "more like a guess or a 'hunch,' than anything one could call evidence or fact. But it may be a fact one day" (CWB: VIII, p. 90).

At its inception, psychoanalysis set itself the task of applying hermeneutics of suspicion to those realms of human experience that had previously been subject to religious, philosophical and spiritual modes of interpretation. This project – whose effects were to be simultaneously emancipatory, reductive and deconstructive in terms of their consequences – was given exemplary expression by Freud in his epigraph to *The Interpretation of Dreams* (1899): "If I cannot bend the Higher Powers, I will move the Infernal Regions" (Virgil, *Aeneid*). The history of psychoanalysis over the next century and beyond can be thought of as both a working out and a working through of the various implications and permutations arising from this hermeneutic trajectory.[31] However, there are reasons to suppose that these dynamics of descent have become subject in more recent times to a process of reversal, or *enantiodromia*, whereby some contemporary Jungians have been increasingly drawn to earth (in the form of the various Jungian developmental schools), while analysts such as Wilfred Bion, James Grotstein and Michael Eigen have, so to speak, been "ascending to heaven" (Ann Alvarez, cited in Culbert-Koehn [1998],

---

30

    When it comes to the brain, the intimate relation between brain activity and states of mind cannot in itself help distinguish between theories of emission, transmission, and permission as its basis. In other words, the same findings are equally compatible with the brain emitting consciousness, transmitting consciousness, or permitting consciousness . . . I am going to argue that it is the last of these possibilities – permission – that is the most convincing.

(McGilchrist, 2021, p. 1038)

31 For an illuminating account of the importance of katabatic metaphors in Freud's *The Interpretation of Dreams*, see Shann (2023). See especially the following: "Freud favours analepsis (psychoanalysis as katabatic recollection or anamnesis) while suppressing prophetic prolepsis (dreams as portents). This is the temporality of *après-coup*, not of precognition or prognosis" (p. 155).

p. 73).[32] As we have seen, Grotstein's writings, in particular, provide an exemplary instance of this Neoplatonic reversion to a psychoanalytic heavenly ascent.

This book has construed the presence of esoteric "traces" in psychoanalysis, which it has theorised in the form of an *Orphic trajectory* extending from its prehistory to the present.[33] These *traces* are posited as taking the form of trans-generationally transmitted *enigmatic signifiers*, the "encrypted" persistence of which can be inferred from the presence of a "decentred" psychoanalytic subject dialectically conjoined to its enigmatic (esoteric) *other*. The "destabilising" effects of these "traces" can be construed as the symptomatic expression of an underlying tension arising from the superimposition of esoteric and physicalist discourses into the conceptual scaffolding of psychoanalytic metapsychology. To the extent that this reconstruction – or perhaps retrieval – of an *Orphic trajectory* within psychoanalysis constitutes a disruption to the assumptions of a predominantly secular psychoanalytic ideology, these traces of the esoteric can be thought of as conceptual *hieroglyphs*, whose ongoing decipherment possesses the potential to contribute to future developments in psychoanalytic theory and practice. By way of bringing this book to a close, some of the ways in which these potentialities have already been given a more substantive form can be briefly adumbrated as follows.

Thomas Rabeyron has observed that "Psi studies are particularly interesting because whatever the reaction to the question 'does psi exist?' (Bem & Honorton, 1994), their results affect the whole of psychology" (Rabeyron, 2020, p. 7). Rabeyron's remarks equally apply to the potential significance of such findings for psychoanalysis. This has been explicitly acknowledged by Philip Bromberg, as can be seen in his claim that Elizabeth Mayer's *Extraordinary Knowing* (2007) "could well hold the future of psychoanalysis between its covers" (Bromberg, 2011, p. 137; Bromberg, 2012, pp. 11–13). In this work, Mayer argued that the future of psychoanalytic research into subtle modes of nonverbal communication would benefit from attention being given to the findings taken from rigorously conducted research into psi phenomena, a proposal that aligns her own explorations into "psychoanalytic parapsychology" with the work of figures such as Ferenczi (whose correspondence with Freud she cites in her book), Severn and Fodor. Such developments occupy a conceptual domain contiguous to that inhabited by Bion's research into the deployment of *reverie* as a clinical technique for facilitating access to unconscious intersubjective processes via the induction of the ganzfeld state within a psychoanalytic setting.

32
> Enantiodromia: [Jung] applied the term to the emergence of unconscious opposites in relation to the points of view held or expressed by consciousness. If an extreme, one-sided tendency dominates conscious life, in time an equally powerful counter-position is built up in the psyche.
>
> Samuels et al. (1986, p. 53)

33 Or, in the words of Mikkel Borch-Jacobsen: "What is important is to re-consider what Freud called the 'pre-history' of psychoanalysis, to return to it with the suspicion that this 'pre-history' belongs to a certain future of psychoanalysis rather than to a long-dead past" (Borch-Jacobsen, 1992, p. 44).

As we saw in Chapter four, an existential "compatibility" between psychoanalysis and gnostic modes of thought has been remarked upon by Sean McGrath (McGrath, 2012, p. 183). We can further extend the speculative reach of McGrath's observation by augmenting it with a hypothesis proposed by the scholar of Gnosticism, Ioan Couliano:

> It should be noticed from the beginning that *all* Gnostic systems, without exception, appear as transformations of one another and therefore can be said to be part of a larger "ideal object," whose possibilities are being explored by human minds at all times, regardless of time and space.
>
> (Couliano, 1992, pp. 62–63)

Such transformative potentials interrogate and destabilise the axioms of a received psychoanalytic historiography, replacing them instead with a more "heterodox" reading in which the various "schools" of psychoanalysis are conjectured to inhabit but one aspect of a more ancient, expansive and multivalent "ideal object," many of whose attributes remain in potentia within the ambit of a hauntological historiography. It is these ostensibly conflictual – and yet potentially creative – tensions conjoining Couliano's gnostic "ideal object" to the original "scientific" aspirations of classical Freudian psychoanalysis that the Orphic trajectory sets out to traverse.

Josephson-Storm has remarked that "most of what gets classified as contemporary esotericism or occultism came into being as an attempt to repair the rupture between religion and science" (Josephson-Storm, 2017, p. 15). Consequently, attempts to forge a tertium quid in the guise of a revitalised "psychoanalytic parapsychology" are to be expected. Thomas Rabeyron has been instrumental in establishing a "clinical service specialising in anomalous experiences" that not only undertakes innovative research into this obscure domain of therapeutic practice but also has additionally sought to develop pioneering clinical techniques for working with anomalous experiences within a psychotherapeutic setting (Rabeyron & Loose, 2015, p. 1). Elizabeth Mayer's depiction of the personal and professional costs suffered by both patients and professionals existing within a cultural milieu that fosters "occult disavowal" is heartfelt and has deep implications with regard to the future development of psychoanalysis (Mayer, 2007, pp. 25–38). As Adam Phillips astutely remarked during an interview with Mayer:

> But just consider it – the Oedipal taboo was nothing. Compared to the taboo invoked by this quality of connectedness – now *there's* a taboo. It suggests a capacity for connection that's far more fearful in implication than Oedipal love. It's far deeper, far more radical. Where are the boundaries? Where's Freud's concept of ego? It's overwhelming. Fascinating and full of promise but overwhelming.
>
> (Mayer, 2007, p. 270)

Jeffrey Kripal has described psychoanalysis as providing – among other things – a "spiritual map," a claim congruent with more recent accounts of a psychoanalytical mystical "tradition" possessing its own genealogical roster of "psychoanalytic mystics" (Kripal, 2001, p. 96; Merkur, 2010). Hence, we encounter a theoretical overlap between Kripal's investigations into the *supernormal* (a term originally coined by Frederic Myers in 1885) and Grotstein's theorisation of a post-Bionian psychoanalysis in which the effects arising from transformations in O have the capacity to potentiate preternatural effects. Both of these theorisations tend towards a view of reality that is inherently *paraconceptual* with regards to its destructuring and transformation of the subject–object relationship into a dual-aspect monism. The implications arising from such developments have led Kripal to propose a fundamental re-evaluation of the role of the humanities within the academy, entailing a revisioning of "the humanities as *the study of consciousness coded in culture*," a convergence of categories that resonates with the tertium quid propensities of the Orphic trajectory within psychoanalysis (Kripal, 2019, p. 45; Kripal, 2021, pp. 63–67).

The central features associated with the Orphic trajectory may include – but are not limited to – an interest in promoting dialogue between the various psychoanalytic and Jungian schools of thought; an openness to exploring "heterodox" theories of consciousness as a means of extending and enriching the ontological possibilities of the psychoanalytic "subject"; an interest in the use of dual-aspect monist perspectives to enhance our understanding of relations between the psyche and the world; and a commitment to investigating the "pre-history" of psychoanalysis as a source of potential inspiration for future developments in psychoanalytic theory and practice. Taken in the round, the cognitive and philosophical perspectives accessed through engagement with these synergised perspectives leads to a conceptualisation of the psychoanalytic "subject" whose ontological possibilities extend beyond the more circumscribed norms of interiority commonly associated with the "buffered self" and standardised psychological "subjects" encountered in modernity and post-modernity.[34]

While the scientific ambitions of classical psychoanalysis were to eventuate in what might more accurately be described as the *dream of a science,* their initial derailment and subsequent recalibration did not prevent the development – or perhaps better retrieval – of a psychoanalytic *scientia* of the subjective, the oneiric and the esoteric, the distinctive features of which this book has argued have been active within psychoanalysis since its inception (Shamdasani, 2006; Harrison, 2015, pp. 15–16, 42–43). Although the Orphic trajectory comprises but one facet of the wider psychoanalytic project, an acknowledgement of its importance in the formation of psychoanalysis constitutes one of the more intriguing and potentially creative disciplinary catalysts active within the contemporary psychoanalytic field.

34 For helpful accounts of the psychological and philosophical "subject" constructed under the aegis of modernity and post-modernity, see Danziger (1990) and Mansfield (2000). On the idea of the "buffered self" as an artefact of Post-Reformation modernity, see Taylor (2007).

Bibliography

Abel-Hirsch, Nicola, *Bion 365 Quotes* (New York: Routledge, 2019)

Abraham, Nicolas & Torok, Maria, *The Wolf Man's Magic Word: A Cryptonymy* [trans. Nicholas Rand with Foreword by Jacques Derrida] (Minneapolis: University of Minnesota, 1986)

Abraham, Nicolas & Torok, Maria, *The Shell and The Kernel* [ed., trans. & intro. Nicolas T. Rand] (London: University of Chicago Press, 1994)

Abrams, M. H., *Natural Supernaturalism: Tradition and Revolution in Romantic Literature* (New York: Norton, 1971)

Addey, Crystal, *Divination and Theurgy in Neoplatonism: Oracles of the Gods* (New York: Routledge, 2019)

Addison, Ann, 'Jung's Psychoid Concept and Bion's Proto-mental Concept: A Comparison,' *The Journal of Analytical Psychology* 61: 5 (2016) 567–587

Addison, Ann, *Jung's Psychoid Concept Contextualised* (New York: Routledge, 2019)

Aguayo, Joseph, 'The Early Psychoanalytic Work of James Grotstein (1966–1981): Turning a Kleinian/Bionian Tide Away from American Ego Psychology,' in: Annie Reiner (ed.), *Of Things Invisible to Mortal Sight: Celebrating the Work of James S. Grotstein* (London: Karnac, 2017) 1–18

Aguayo, Joseph, 'Conjoining Bion's Reading of C.G. Jung's *Memories, Dreams, Reflections* with His *Clinical Seminars in Rio de Janeiro* and *São Paulo*,' *Journal of Analytical Psychology* 70: 1 (2025) 93–113

Aguayo, Joseph & Malin, Barnet (eds.), *Wilfred Bion: Los Angeles Seminars and Supervision* (New York: Routledge, 2018)

Akhtar, Salman, *Comprehensive Dictionary of Psychoanalysis* (London: Karnac, 2009)

Alava, Pihla, *Infinite Emotion: Matte Blanco's Bi-Logic in Psychoanalytic Context* (Unpublished PhD thesis, University of Dublin, Trinity College, 2010)

Alisobhani, Afsaneh K. & Corstorphine, Glenda J. (eds.), *Explorations in Bion's 'O' Everything We Know Nothing about* (New York: Routledge, 2019)

Altman, Matthew C. & Coe, Cynthia D., *The Fractured Self in Freud and German Philosophy* (Basingstoke: Palgrave Macmillan, 2013)

Alvarado, A. S., 'On the Centenary of Frederic W. H. Myer's *Human Personality and Its Survival of Bodily Death*,' *Journal of Parapsychology* 68: 1 (2003) 3–43

Andreas-Salomé, Lou, *The Freud Journal* (London: Quartet Books, 1987)

Anonymous, 'Severn, Elizabetli [sic] The Discovery of the Self: A Study in Psychological Cure. Philadelphia: David McKay Company,' *Psychoanalytic Review* 25: 1 (1938) 134–136 [anonymous book review]

Anonymous, 'Nandor Fodor': http://www.survivalafterdeath.info/researchers/fodor.htm (downloaded 20/04/2020) d'Aquili, Eugene & Newberg, Andrew B., *The Mystical Mind: Probing the Biology of Religious Experience* (Minneapolis: Fortress Press, 1999)

Armstrong, Richard H., *A Compulsion to Antiquity: Freud and the Ancient World* (Ithaca: Cornell University Press, 2005)

Asprem, Egil, 'Beyond the West: Towards a New Comparativism in the Study of Esotericism,' *Correspondences* 2: 1 (2014a) 3–33

Asprem, Egil, *The Problem of Disenchantment: Scientific Naturalism and Esoteric Discourse 1900–1939* (Leiden: Brill, 2014b)

Asprem, Egil, 'Rejected Knowledge Reconsidered: Some Methodological Notes on Esotericism and Marginality,' in: Asprem, Egil & Strube, Julian (eds.), *New Approaches to the Study of Esotericism* (Leiden: Brill, 2021) 127–146

Asprem, Egil & Granholm, Kennet (eds.), *Contemporary Esotericism* (New York: Routledge, 2014a)

Asprem, Egil & Granholm, Kennet, 'Introduction,' *Contemporary Esotericism* (New York: Routledge, 2014b) 1–24

Asprem, Egil & Granholm, Kennet, 'Constructing Esotericisms: Sociological, Historical and Critical Approaches to the Invention of Tradition,' in: *Contemporary Esotericism* (New York: Routledge, 2014c) 25–48

Asprem, Egil & Strube, Julian (eds.), *New Approaches to the Study of Esotericism* (Leiden: Brill, 2021)

Atmanspacher, Harald & Fuchs, Christopher A. (eds.), *The Pauli-Jung Conjecture and Its Impact Today* (Exeter: Imprint Academic, 2014)

Atmanspacher, Harald & Rickles, Dean, *Dual-Aspect Monism and the Deep Structure of Meaning* (New York: Routledge, 2022)

Atzert, Stephan, 'Schopenhauer and Freud,' in: Vandenabeele, Bart (ed.), *A Companion to Schopenhauer* (Chichester: Blackwell, 2012) 317–332

Atzert, Stephan, 'Schopenhauer and the Unconscious,' in: Wicks, Robert L. (ed.), *The Oxford Handbook of Schopenhauer* (New York: Oxford University Press, 2020) 497–516

Auchincloss, Elizabeth L., *The Psychoanalytic Model of the Mind* (Washington: American Psychiatric Publishing, 2015)

Bair, Deirdre, *Jung: A Biography* (London: Little, Brown, 2004)

Bakan, David, *Sigmund Freud and the Jewish Mystical Tradition* [2nd ed.] (New York: Dover Publications, 2004 [1958])

Balint, Enid & Michael Papers (box 30), Special Collections, The Albert Sloman Library, University of Essex

Balint, Michael, 'Sandor Ferenczi, Obit 1933,' *The International Journal of Psychoanalysis* 30 (1949) 215–219

Balint, Michael, 'Notes on Parapsychology and Parapsychological Healing,' *The International Journal of Psychoanalysis* 36 (1955) 31–35

Balint, Michael, 'Sandor Ferenczi's Last Years,' *The International Journal of Psychoanalysis* 39 (1958) 68

Bandeira, Marcio Leitão, 'Unconscious Perception and Reverie: An Intersubjective Connection,' *The American Journal of Psychoanalysis* 77: 3 (2017) 265–273

Barentsen, Gord, *Romantic Metasubjectivity through Schelling and Jung: Rethinking the Romantic Subject* (New York: Routledge, 2020)

Barkhoff, Jürgen, 'Romantic Science and Psychology,' in: Saul, Nicholas (ed.), *The Cambridge Companion to German Romanticism* (New York: Cambridge University Press, 2009) 209–226

Barratt, Barnaby B., 'Notes towards the Psychoanalytic Critique of Mind-Body Dualism,' in: Mills, Jon (ed.), *Psychoanalysis and the Mind-Body Problem* (New York: Routledge, 2022) 46–68

Baruš, Imants, *Alterations of Consciousness: An Empirical Analysis for Social Scientists* [2nd ed.] (Washington: American Psychological Association, 2020)

Beard, G. M., 'The Psychology of Spiritism,' *North American Review* (1879) 65–80

Beiser, Frederick C., *The Romantic Imperative: The Concept of Early German Romanticism* (London: Harvard University Press, 2003)

Bell, Matthew, *The German Tradition of Psychology in Literature and Thought, 1700–1840* (New York: Cambridge University Press, 2005)

Beloff, John, *Parapsychology: A Concise History* (London: Athlone Press, 1993)

Bem, D., & Honorton, C., 'Does psi Exist? Replicable Evidence for an Anomalous Process of Information Transfer,' *Psychological Bulletin* 115 (1994) 4–18

Bem, Daryl, 'Feeling the Future: Experimental Evidence for Anomalous Retroactive Influences on Cognition and Affect' *Journal of Personality and Social Psychology* 100 (2011) 407–425

Benz, Ernst, *The Mystical Sources of German Romantic Philosophy* (Eugene: Pickwick Publications, 1983)

Berger, Benjamin & Whistler, Daniel (eds.), *The Schelling Reader* (London: Bloomsbury, 2021)

Berke, Joseph H., 'Psychoanalysis and Kabbalah,' *The Psychoanalytic Review* 83 (1996) 849–863

Berke, Joseph H., *The Hidden Freud: His Hassidic Roots* (London: Karnac, 2015)

Berke, Joseph H. & Schneider, Stanley, 'Repairing Worlds: An Exploration of the Psychoanalytical and Kabbalistic Concepts of Reparation and *Tikkun*,' *The Psychoanalytic Review* 90 (2003) 723–749

Berke, Joseph H. & Schneider, Stanley, 'The Self and the Soul,' *Mental Health, Religion and Culture* 9: 4 (2006) 333–354

Berke, Joseph H. & Schneider, Stanley, *Centers of Power: The Convergence of Psychoanalysis and Kabbalah* (Northvale: Jason Aronson, 2008)

Bettelheim, Bruno, *Freud and Man's Soul* (New York: Vintage Books, 1984)

Bishop, Paul, *Analytical Psychology and German Classical Aesthetics: Goethe, Schiller, and Jung Vol. 2 The Constellation of the Self* (New York: Routledge, 2009)

Bishop, Paul, 'Schopenhauer's *Fin de Siècle* Reception in Austria,' in: Wicks, Robert L. (ed.), *The Oxford Handbook of Schopenhauer* (New York: Oxford University Press, 2020) 535–555

Bishop, Paul, '*Katabasis* in Reverse: Heraclitus, the Archaic, and the Abyss,' in: Bishop, Paul et al. (eds.), *The Descent of the Soul and the Archaic: Katábasis and Depth Psychology* (New York: Routledge, 2023) 31–51

Black, David M., 'Introduction,' in: Black, David M. (ed.), *Psychoanalysis and Religion in the 21st Century: Competitors or Collaborators?* (New York: Routledge, 2006) 1–20

Blanco, María del Pilar & Peeren, Esther (eds.), *The Spectralities Reader: Ghosts and Hauntings in Contemporary Cultural Theory* (London: Bloomsbury, 2013)

Blass, Rachel B., 'Introduction to "on the Value of "Late Bion" to Analytic Theory and Practice",' *The International Journal of Psychoanalysis* 92: 5 (2011) 1081–1088

Bléandonu, Gérard, *Wilfred Bion: His Life and Works* [trans. Claire Pajaczkowska] (London: Free Association Books, 1994)

Boehme, Jacob, *Aurora (Morgen Röte im auffgang, 1612) and Ein gründlicher Bericht or a Fundamental Report (Mysterium Pansophicum, 1620) with a Translation, Introduction, and Commentary by Andrew Weeks and Günther Bonheim in Collaboration with Michael Spang as Editor of Grundlicher Bericht* (Leiden: Brill, 2013)

Bohak, Gideon, 'How Jewish Magic Survived the Disenchantment of the World,' *Aries* 19: 1 (2019) 7–37

Bohm, David, *Wholeness and the Implicate Order* (New York: Routledge Classics, 2002 [1980])

Bokanowski, Thierry, *The Modernity of Sandor Ferenczi* (New York: Routledge, 2018)

Bomford, Rodney, *The Symmetry of God* (London: Free Association Books, 1999)

Bomford, Rodney, 'Religious Truth in the Light of Bi-Logic,' *International Journal of Applied Psychoanalytic Studies* 1: 1 (2004) 4–17

Bonomi, Carlo, *The Cut and Building of Psychoanalysis, Volume 1: Sigmund Freud and Emma Eckstein* (New York: Routledge, 2015)

Bonomi, Carlo, *The Cut and Building of Psychoanalysis, Volume II: Sigmund Freud and Sandor Ferenczi* (New York: Routledge, 2018)

Borch-Jacobson, Mikkel, *The Emotional Tie: Psychoanalysis, Mimesis and Affect* (Stanford: Stanford University Press, 1992)

Borch-Jacobsen, Mikkel, 'Simulating the Unconscious,' *Psychoanalysis and History* 7 (2005) 5–20

Borch-Jacobson, Mikkel & Shamdasani, Sonu, *The Freud Files: An Inquiry into the History of Psychoanalysis* (New York: Cambridge University Press, 2012)

Borgogno, Franco & Merciai, Silvio Arrigo, 'Searching for Bion: *Cogitations,* a New "Clinical Diary"?' in: Bion Talamo, Parthenope et al. (eds.), *W. R. Bion: Between Past and Future* (London: Karnac, 2000) 56–78

Bowie, Andrew, 'Romantic Philosophy and Religion,' in: Saul, Nicholas (ed.), *The Cambridge Companion to German Romanticism* (New York: Cambridge University Press, 2009) 175–190

Bowie, Andrew, 'The Philosophical Significance of Schelling's Conception of the Unconscious,' in: Nicholls, Angus & Liebscher, Martin (eds.), *Thinking the Unconscious: Nineteenth-Century German Thought* (New York: Cambridge University Press, 2010) 57–86

Boyle, John, 'Esoteric Traces in Contemporary Psychoanalysis,' *American Imago* 73: 1 (2016) 95–119

Boyle, John, 'Before and after Science: Esoteric Traces in the Formation of the Freudian Psychoanalytic Subject,' *Journal of the Irish Society for the Academic Study of Religions* 7 (2019) 59–103

Boyle, John, 'From Metapsychology to Magnetic Gnosis: An Esoteric Context for Interpreting Traumatic Modes of Transcendence in Sándor Ferenczi's *Clinical Diary* and Elizabeth Severn's *The Discovery of the Self,*' *Psychoanalysis and History* 23: 3 (2021) 297–323

Boyle, John, 'Mystical *Gnosis* and Esoteric *Technē* in the Writings of W.R. Bion,' *American Imago* 80: 2 (2023) 321–347

Brabant, Eva, Falzeder, Ernst & Giampieri-Deutch, Patrizia (eds.), *The Correspondence of Sigmund Freud and Sandor Ferenczi Vol. 1, 1908–1914* (Cambridge MA: Harvard University Press, 1993)

Brach, Jean-Pierre & Hanegraaff, Wouter J., 'Correspondences,' in: Hanegraaff, Wouter J. et al. (eds.), *Dictionary of Gnosis and Western Esotericism* (Leiden: Brill, 2006) 275–279

Brennan, William B., 'Decoding Ferenczi's Clinical Diary: Biographical Notes,' *The American Journal of Psychoanalysis* 75: 1 (2015) 5–18

Britton, Ronald, *Between Mind and Brain: Models of the Mind and Models in the Mind* (London: Karnac, 2015)

Broek, Roelof van den, 'Gnosticism I: Gnostic Religion,' in: Hanegraaff, Wouter J. et al. (eds.), *Dictionary of Gnosis and Western Esotericism* (Leiden: Brill, 2006) 403–416

Bromberg, Philip M., *The Shadow of the Tsunami and the Growth of the Relational Mind* (New York: Routledge, 2011)

Bromberg, Philip M., 'Stumbling along and Hanging in: If This Be Technique, Make the Most of It!' *Psychoanalytic Inquiry* 32 (2012) 3–17

Brottman, Mikita, *Phantoms of the Clinic: From Thought-Transference to Projective Identification* (London: Karnac, 2011)

Brower, Brady M., *Unruly Spirits: The Science of Psychic Phenomena in Modern France* (Chicago: University of Illinois Press, 2010)

Brown, Robert F., *The Later Philosophy of Schelling 1809–1815* (Lewisburg: Bucknell University Press, 1977)

Brown, Robin S. (ed.), *Re-Encountering Jung: Analytical Psychology and Contemporary Psychoanalysis* (New York: Routledge, 2018)

Brown, Robin S., *Groundwork for a Transpersonal Psychoanalysis: Spirituality, Relationship, and Participation* (New York: Routledge, 2020)

Burdett, Carolyn, 'Modernity, the Occult, and Psychoanalysis,' in: Marcus, Laura & Mukherjee, Ankhi (eds.), *A Concise Companion to Psychoanalysis, Literature and Culture* (Chichester: Wiley Blackwell, 2014) pp. 49–65

Burns, Dylan M., 'Ancient Esoteric Traditions: Mystery, Revelation, Gnosis,' in: Partridge, Christopher (ed.), *The Occult World* (New York: Routledge, 2015) 15–33

Calvesi, Alessandro, 'The Analytic Relationship and its Therapeutic Factors from A Parapsychological Viewpoint,' *The Psychoanalytic Review* 70 (1983) 387–402

Caper, Robert, 'Review of: *The Clinical Thinking of Wilfred Bion,* Symington, J., Symington, N., *The International Journal of Psychoanalysis* 79 (1998) 417–420

Carabine, Deidre, *The Unknown God-Negative Theology in the Platonic Tradition: Plato to Eriugena* (Eugene: Wipf Publishers, 2015)

Cardina, Etzel, Lynn, Stephen J. & Krippner, Stanley (eds.), *Varieties of Anomalous Experience: Examining the Scientific Evidence* [2nd ed.] (Washington: American Psychological Association, 2014)

Carrette, Jeremy R., 'Post-structuralism and the Psychology of Religion: The Challenge of Critical Psychology,' in: Jonte-Pace, Diane & Parsons, William B. (eds.), *Religion and Psychology: Mapping the Terrain* (London: Routledge, 2001) 110–126.

Carter, David (ed.), *Sigmund Freud on Cocaine* (London: Hesperus Press, 2011)

Cartwright, David. E., *Schopenhauer: A Biography* (New York: Oxford University Press, 2010)

Cartwright, David E., 'Schopenhauer's Haunted World: The Use of Weird and Paranormal Phenomena to Corroborate His Metaphysics,' in: Wicks, Robert L. (ed.), *The Oxford Handbook of Schopenhauer* (New York: Oxford University Press, 2020) 175–192

Carvalho, Richard, 'Matte Blanco and the Multidimensional Realm of the Unconscious,' *British Journal of Psychotherapy* 26 (2010) 324–334

Carvalho, Richard, 'Synchronicity, the Infinite Unrepressed, Dissociation and the Interpersonal,' *The Journal of Analytical Psychology* 59 (2014) 366–384

Casement, Ann (ed.), *Who Owns Psychoanalysis?* (London: Karnac, 2004)

Castle, Terry, *The Female Thermometer: Eighteenth-Century Culture and the Invention of the Uncanny* (New York: Oxford University Press, 1995)

Cavalli, Alessandra, 'Transgenerational Transmission of Indigestible Facts: From Trauma, Deadly Ghosts and Mental Voids to Meaning-making Interpretations,' *The Journal of Analytical Psychology* 57: 5 (2012) 597–614

Chan, Yiukee, *Experience into Psychoanalytic Ideas: A Psychobiographical Study of Ferenczi's Introjection* (PhD thesis, Centre for Psychoanalytic Studies, University of Essex, 2015)

Charet, F. X., *Spiritualism and the Foundations of C. G. Jung's Psychology* (Albany: State University of New York Press, 1993)

Chertok, Léon & Stengers, Isabelle, *A Critique of Psychoanalytic Reason: Hypnosis as a Scientific Problem from Lavoisier to Lacan* (Stanford: Stanford University Press, 1992)

Civitarese, Giuseppe, *Psychoanalytic Field Theory: A Contemporary Introduction* (New York: Routledge, 2022)

Civitarese, Giuseppe, 'Intuition and We-Ness in Bion and Post-Bionian Field Theory,' *International Journal of Psychoanalysis* 125 (2024) 13–39

Cooper, Paul, 'Zen Meditation, Reverie, and Psychoanalytic Listening,' *The Psychoanalytic Review* 101: 6 (2014) 795–813

Copleston, Frederick, *A History of Philosophy Volume 7 Part I: Fiche to Hegel* (New York: Image Books, 1965a)

Copleston, Frederick, *A History of Philosophy Volume 7 Part II: Schopenhauer to Nietzsche* (New York: Image Books, 1965b)

Corbett, Lionel, 'Is the Self Other to the Self? Why Does the Numinosum Feel Like another? The Relevance of Matte Blanco to Our Understanding of the Unconscious,' *Journal of Analytical Psychology* 65: 4 (2020) 672–684

Corbin, Henry, *The Man of Light in Iranian Sufism* [trans. Nancy Pearson] (Lebanon, NY: Omega Publications, 1994)

Couliano, Ioan P., *The Tree of Gnosis: Gnostic Mythology from Early Christianity to Modern Nihilism* (San Francisco: Harper Collins, 1992)

Counet, J. M., 'Cusa, Nicholas of (Niklaus Krebs), 1401–1464,' in Hanegraaff, Wouter J. et al. (eds.), *Dictionary of Gnosis and Western Esotericism* (Leiden: Brill, 2006) 293–296

Coverley, Merlin *Hauntology: Ghosts of Futures Past* (Harpenden: Oldcastle Books Ltd, 2020)

Cox, Stephen D., *The Stranger Within Thee: Concepts of the Self in Late Eighteenth Century Literature* (Pittsburgh, PA: University of Pittsburgh Press, 1980)

Crabtree, Adam, *From Mesmer to Freud: Magnetic Sleep and the Roots of Psychological Healing* (New Haven: Yale University Press, 1993)

Crabtree, Adam, 'The Transition to Secular Psychotherapy: Hypnosis and the Alternate Consciousness Paradigm,' in: Wallace, Edwin R. & Gach, John (eds.), *History of Psychiatry and Medical Psychology* (New York: Springer, 2008) 555–586

Crabtree, Adam, 'Hypnosis Reconsidered, Resituated, and Redefined,' *Journal of Scientific Exploration* 26: 2 (2012) 297–327

Crabtree, Adam, 'Mesmer and Animal Magnetism,' in: Magee, Glenn Alexander (ed.), *The Cambridge Handbook of Western Mysticism and Esotericism* (New York: Cambridge University Press, 2016) 223–234

Crabtree, Adam & Osei-Bonsu, Sarah (ed. & trans.), *The Marquis de Puységur, Artificial Somnambulism, and the Discovery of the Unconscious Mind: Memoirs to Serve the History and Establishment of Animal Magnetism* (New York: Routledge, 2025)

Critchley, Simon, *On Mysticism: The Experience of Ecstasy* (London: Profile Books, 2024)

Culbert-Koehn, Joann, 'Between Bion and Jung: A Talk with James Grotstein,' *The San Francisco Jung Institute Library Journal* 15: 4 (1997) 15–32

Culbert-Koehn, Joann, 'Where Is James Grotstein? Response to James Grotstein,' *Journal of Analytical Psychology* 46 (1998) 369–375

Culbert-Koehn, Joann et al., 'James Grotstein (8 November 1925–30 May 2015),' *The Journal of Analytical Psychology* 60: 5 (2015) 752–755

Dan, Joseph, 'Foreword,' in: Scholem, Gershom (ed.), *On the Mystical Shape of the Godhead: Basic Concepts in the Kabbalah* (New York: Schocken Books, 1991 [1962]) 3–14

Danziger, Kurt, *Constructing the Subject: Historical Origins of Psychological Research* (New York: Cambridge University Press, 1990)

Davies, J. Keith & Fichtner, Gerhard (eds.), *Freud's Library: A Comprehensive Catalogue/ Freuds Bibliothek: Vollständiger Katalog* (Introductory volume and CD-ROM: The Freud Museum London and Tübingen: edition diskord, 2006)

Davies, James, *The Making of Psychotherapists: An Anthropological Analysis* (London: Karnac, 2009)

Davis, Colin, *Haunted Subjects: Deconstruction, Psychoanalysis and the Return of the Dead* (Basingstoke: Palgrave Macmillan, 2007)

Dean, Jason, 'Psychoanalysis as a Philosophical Revolution: Freud's Divergence from the Philosophy of Kant, Schopenhauer, and Nietzsche,' *The Psychoanalytic Review* 103: 4 (2016) 455–482

DeConick, April D., *The Gnostic New Age* (New York: Columbia Press, 2016)

Deghaye, Pierre, 'Jacob Boehme and His Followers,' in: Faivre, Antoine & Needleman, Jacob (eds.), *Modern Esoteric Spirituality* (London: SCM Press, 1993) 210–247

Deleuze, Gilles *Difference and Repetition* [trans. Paul Patton] (London: Bloomsbury, 2014)

Derrida, Jacques, 'Telepathy' [trans. Nicolas Royle], *Oxford Literary Review* 10 (1988) 3–43

Derrida, Jacques, *Archive Fever: A Freudian Impression* (Chicago: Chicago University Press, 1998)

Derrida, Jacques, *Writing and Difference* (New York: Routledge, 2001)

De Saussure, Raymond, 'Transference and Animal Magnetism,' *The Psychoanalytic Quarterly* 12 (1943) 194–201

Desmet, Mattias, *Lacan's Logic of Subjectivity: A Walk on the Graph of Desire* (Ghent: Owl Press, 2019)

Devereux, George (ed.), *Psychoanalysis and the Occult* (London: Souvenir Press, 1974 [1953])

Dingwall, E. (ed.), *Abnormal Hypnotic Phenomena* (New York: Barnes & Noble, 1968)

Dongen, Hein van, Gerding, Hans & Sneller, Rico, *Wild Beasts of the Philosophical Desert: Philosophers on Telepathy and Other Exceptional Experiences* (Newcastle upon Tyne: Cambridge Scholars Publishing, 2014)

Drob, Sanford L., *Symbols of the Kabbalah* (Northvale: Jason Aronson, 2000a)

Drob, Sanford L., *Kabbalistic Metaphors: Jewish Mystical Themes in Ancient and Modern Thought* (Northvale: Jason Aronson, 2000b)

Drob, Sanford L., *Kabbalistic Visions: C. G. Jung and Jewish Mysticism* (New Orleans: Spring Journal Books, 2010)

Duffy, Kathleen, *Freud's Early Psychoanalysis, Witch Trials and the Inquisitorial Method: The Harsh Therapy* (Abington: Routledge, 2020)

Dufresne, Todd, *Tales from the Freudian Crypt: The Death Drive in Text and Context* [with a foreword by Mikkel Borch-Jacobsen] (Stanford: Stanford University Press, 2000)

Dupont, Judith, 'A Multifaceted Legacy: Sandor Ferenczi's Clinical Diary,' in: Rachman, Arnold Wm. (ed.), *The Budapest School of Psychoanalysis: The Origin of a Two-Person Psychology and Emphatic Perspective* (New York: Routledge, 2016) 15–25.

Eagleton, Terry, *Culture and the Death of God* (London: Yale University Press, 2015)

Easthope, Antony, 'Freud's Spectres,' in: Banham, Gary & Blake, Charlie (eds.), *Evil Spirits: Nihilism and the Fate of Modernity* (New York: Manchester University Press, 2000) 146–164

Edel, Susanne, 'Compatibility of the "Inner Light" of Mystics and Reason: Leibniz's Engagement with Jacob Böehme,' *Aries* 18: 1 (2018) 75–95

Eigen, Michael, *The Psychoanalytic Mystic* (London: Free Association Books, 1998)

Eigen, Michael, 'Mysticism and Psychoanalysis,' *The Psychoanalytic Review* 88 (2001) 455–481

Eigen, Michael, *Kabbalah and Psychoanalysis* (London: Karnac, 2012)

Eigen, Michael, *A Felt Sense: More Explorations of Kabbalah and Psychoanalysis* (London: Karnac, 2014a)

Eigen, Michael, *The Birth of Experience* (London: Karnac, 2014b)

Eigen, Michael, *Image, Sense, Infinities, and Everyday Life* (London: Karnac, 2015)

Eigen, Michael, *Under the Totem: In Search of a Path* (London: Karnac, 2016)

Eisenbud, Jules, *Paranormal Foreknowledge: Problems and Perplexities* (New York: Human Sciences Press, 1982)

Ellenberger, Henri F., 'Mesmer and Puységur: From Magnetism to Hypnotism,' *The Psychoanalytic Review* 52B (2) (1965) 137–153

Ellenberger, Henri F., *Beyond the Unconscious: Essays of Henri F. Ellenberger in the History of Psychiatry* [intro. & ed. Mark S. Micale] (Princeton: Princeton University Press, 1993)

Ellenberger, Henri F., *The Discovery of the Unconscious: The History and Evolution of Dynamic Psychiatry* (London: Fontana Press, 1994 [1970])

Ellman, Steven J., *When Theories Touch: A Historical and Theoretical Integration of Psychoanalytic Thought* (London: Karnac, 2010)

Engler, Steven & Gardiner, Mark Q., '(Re)defining Esotericism: Fluid Definitions, Property Clusters and the Cross-Cultural Debate,' *Aries* 24 (2024a) 151–207

Engler, Steven & Gardiner, Mark Q., 'Definition as Situated Interpretational Vector: Response to Commentaries,' *Aries* 24 (2024b) 277–290

Eno, Brian, *Before and After Science* (Polydor Records, 1977)

Erös, Ferenc, 'The Ferenczi Cult: Its Historical and Political Roots,' *International Forum of Psychoanalysis* 13: 1–2 (2004) 121–128

Evrard, Renaud, Massicotte, Claudie & Rabeyron, Thomas, 'Freud as a Psychical Researcher: The Impossible Legacy,' *Imágó Budapest* 6: 4 (2017) 9–32

Faimberg, Haydee, 'The Telescoping of Generations: Genealogy of Certain Identifications,' *Contemporary Psychoanalysis* 24 (1988) 99–117

Faivre, A., '"Éloquence magique," ou descriptions des mondes de l'audelà explorés par le magnétisme animal: au carrefour de la Naturphilosophie romantique et de la théosophie chrétienne (première moitié du xixe siècle),' *Aries* 8 (2008) 191–228

Faivre, Antoine, *Access to Western Esotericism* (Albany: SUNY, 1994)

Faivre, Antoine, 'Questions of Terminology Proper to the Study of Esoteric Currents in Modern and Contemporary Europe,' in: Faivre, Antoine & Hanegraaff, Wouter J. (eds.), *Western Esotericism and the Science of Religion* (Leuven: Peeters, 1998)

Faivre, Antoine, *Theosophy, Imagination, Tradition: Studies in Western Esotericism* (Albany: SUNY, 2000)

Faivre, Antoine, 'Naturphilosophie,' in: Hanegraaff, Wouter J. et al. (eds.), *Dictionary of Gnosis and Western Esotericism* (Leiden: Brill, 2006a) 822–826.

Faivre, Antoine, 'Secrecy,' in: Hanegraaff, Wouter J. et al. (eds.), *Dictionary of Gnosis and Western Esotericism* (Leiden: Brill, 2006b) 1050–1060

Faivre, Antoine & Needleman, Jacob (eds.), *Modern Esoteric Spirituality* (New York: Crossroad, 1992)

Falzeder, Ernst (ed.), *The Complete Correspondence of Sigmund Freud and Karl Abraham 1907–1925* [trans. Caroline Schwarzacher et al.] (London: Karnac, 2002)

Falzeder, Ernst, *Psychoanalytic Filiations: Mapping the Psychoanalytic Movement* (London: Karnac, 2015)

Falzeder, Ernst & Brabant, Eva (eds.), *The Correspondence of Sigmund Freud and Sándor Ferenczi Vol. 2, 1914–1919* [trans. Peter T. Hoffer] (Cambridge MA: Harvard University Press, 1996)

Fanger, Claire, 'Introduction,' in: Fanger, Claire (ed.), *Invoking Angels: Theurgic Ideas and Practices, Thirteenth to Sixteenth Centuries* (University Park: Penn State University Press, 2012) 1–33

Farrell, Dennis, 'Freud's "Thought-Transference," Repression, and the Future of Psychoanalysis,' *International Journal of Psychoanalysis* 64 (1983) 71–81

Feldman, Bronson, 'The Haunted Mind: A Psychoanalyst Looks at the Supernatural by Nandor Fodor: A Review,' *The Psychoanalytic Review* 47B: 2 (1960) 111–113

Fenichel, Teresa, *Schelling, Freud, and the Philosophical Foundations of Psychoanalysis: Uncanny Belonging* (New York: Routledge, 2019)

Ferenczi, Sándor, 'Confusion of the Tongues between the Adults and the Child-(The Language of Tenderness and Passion),' *The International Journal of Psychoanalysis* 30 (1949 [1933]) 225–320

Ferenczi, Sándor, 'Spiritism' [trans. Nandor Fodor], *The Psychoanalytic Review* 50A: 1 (1963 [1899]) 139–144

Ferenczi, Sándor, 'My Friendship with Miksa Schachter' [trans. Borisz Szegal], *British Journal of Psychotherapy* 9: 4 (1993) 430–433

Ferenczi, Sándor, *The Clinical Diary of Sandor Ferenczi* [trans. M. Balint & N. Z. Jackson; ed. J. Dupont] (Cambridge, MA: Harvard University Press, 1995 [1932])

Ferenczi, Sándor, 'Notes and Fragments,' in: Balint, M. (ed.), *Final Contributions to the Problems and Methods of Psychoanalysis* [trans. Eric Mosbacher et al.] (New York: Routledge, 2018 [1920 and 1930–32]) 216–279

Ferenczi, Sándor, 'Child Analysis in the Analysis of Adults,' in: Balint, M. (ed.), *Final Contributions to the Problems and Methods of Psychoanalysis* [trans. Eric Mosbacher et al.] (New York: Routledge, 2018 [1931]) 126–142

Ferro, Antonino, 'Some Implications of Bion's Thought' [trans. Philip Slotkin], *The International Journal of Psychoanalysis* 83: 3 (2002) 597–607

Ferro, Antonino, 'Book Review Essay: *A Beam of Intense Darkness* by James S. Grotstein' [trans. Andrea Sabbadini], *The International Journal of Psychoanalysis* 83 (2008) 867–884

ffytche, Matt, *The Foundation of the Unconscious: Schelling, Freud and the Birth of the Modern Psyche* (New York: Cambridge University Press, 2012)

Field, Nathan, 'The Therapeutic Function of Altered States,' *The Journal of Analytical Psychology* 37 (1992) 211–234

Findlay, J. N., *Hegel: A Re-Examination* (New York: Colliers, 1962)

Fisher, Naomi, *Schelling's Mystical Platonism 1792–1802* (New York: Oxford University Press, 2024)

Fletcher, John, *Freud and the Scene of Trauma* (New York: Fordham University Press, 2013)

Fletcher, John & Ray, Nicholas (eds.), *Seductions and Enigmas: Laplanche, Theory, Culture* (London: Lawrence & Wishart, 2014)

Flournoy, Théodore, *From India to the Planet Mars: A Case of Multiple Personality with Imaginary Languages* [trans. Daniel B. Vermilye; foreword by C. G. Jung; intro. Sonu Shamdasani] (Princeton: Princeton University Press, 1994 [1899])

Flournoy, Théodore, *Spiritism and Psychology* [trans. Hereward Carrington] (New York: Cosimo Classics, 2007 [1911])

Fodor, Nandor, 'A Psychoanalytic Approach to the Problems of Occultism,' *Journal of Clinical Psychopathology and Psychotherapy* (1945) 69

Fodor, Nandor, 'The Poltergeist – Psychoanalysed,' *Psychiatric Quarterly* XXII (1948) 195–203

Fodor, Nandor, *The Search for the Beloved: A Clinical Investigation of the Trauma of Birth & Pre-Natal Condition* (New York: University Books, Inc., 1949)

Fodor, Nandor, *New Approaches to Dream Interpretation* (New York: University Books, 1951)

Fodor, Nandor, *The Haunted Mind: A Psychoanalyst Looks at the Supernatural* (New York: Garrett Publications, 1959)

Fodor, Nandor, 'Jung, Freud, and a Newly-Discovered Letter of 1909 on the Poltergeist Theme,' *The Psychoanalytic Review* 50B: 2 (1963) 119–128

Fodor, Nandor, 'Jung's Sermons to the Dead,' *The Psychoanalytic Review* 51A: 1 (1964) 74–78

Fodor, Nandor, *The Unaccountable* (New York: Award Books, 1968)

Fodor, Nandor, *Freud, Jung and Occultism* (New York: University Books Inc., 1971)

Fodor Litkei, Andrea, 'Precognition – Or Telepathy from the Past?' *The Psychoanalytic Review* 56A: 1 (1969) 138–141

Fonagy, Peter & Target, Mary, *Psychoanalytic Theories: Perspectives from Developmental Psychopathology* (London: Routledge, 2003)

Fortune, Christopher, 'Sandor Ferenczi's Analysis of "R.N.": A Critically Important Case in the History of Psychoanalysis,' *British Journal of Psychotherapy* 9: 4 (1993) 436–443

Fortune, Christopher, 'Thwarting the Psychoanalytic Detectives: Defending the Severn Legacy,' *The American Journal of Psychoanalysis* 75: 1 (2015) 19–28

Foucault, Michel, *The Order of Things: An Archaeology of the Human Sciences* (London: Routledge, 1997 [1970])

Fowden, Garth, *The Egyptian Hermes: A Historical Approach to the Late Pagan Mind* (New York: Cambridge University Press, 1986)

Franey, Maureen & Grotstein, James S., 'Conversations with Clinicians: Who Is the Writer Who Writes the Books?' *Fort Da* 14: 2 (2008) 87–116

Frank, Adam, 'Minding Matter: The Closer You Look, the More the Materialist Position in Physics Appears to rest on Shaky Ground' (2017). https://aeon.co/essays/materialism-alone-cannot-explain-the-riddle-of-consciousness

Freud, Sigmund, 'Dreams and Telepathy,' in: Devereux, G. (ed.), *Psychoanalysis and the Occult* (London: Souvenir Press, 1974 [1922]) 69–86; S.E. IV (1922 [1925]) 408–435

Freud, Sigmund, 'The Occult Significance of Dreams,' in: Devereux, G. (ed.), *Psychoanalysis and the Occult* (London: Souvenir Press, 1974 [1925]) 87–90; S.E. V (1925 [1950]) 158–162

Freud, Sigmund, 'Dreams and Occultism,' in: Devereux, G. (ed.), *Psychoanalysis and the Occult* (London: Souvenir Press, 1974 [1933]) 91–112; S.E. XXII (1932–1936) 1–182

Freud, Sigmund, *Jokes and Their Relation to the Unconscious* (New York: Pelican, 1976); S.E. VIII (1960 [1916])

Freud, Sigmund, *The Interpretation of Dreams* (London: Penguin, 1991); S.E. IV (1900 [1953])

Freud, Sigmund, 'A Note on the Unconscious in Psychoanalysis,' in: *On Metapsychology* (London: Penguin, 1991); S.E. XII (1958 [1912]) 45–57

Freud, Sigmund, 'A Note Upon the "Mystic Writing-Pad",' in: *On Metapsychology* (London: Penguin, 1991 [1925]) 427–434; S.E. XIX (1923–1925) 225–232

Freud, Sigmund, *New Introductory Lectures* [trans. James Strachey] (London: Penguin, 1991) S.E. XXII (1933 [1964])

Freud, Sigmund, 'A Short Account of Psychoanalysis,' in: *Sigmund Freud: Historical and Expository Works on Psychoanalysis* (London: Penguin, 1993) S.E. XVIIII (1923 [1924]) 189–209

Frieden, Ken, *Freud's Dream of Interpretation* [Foreword by Harold Bloom] (Albany: SUNY, 1990)

Frosh, Stephen, 'Psychoanalysis and Judaism,' in: David M. Black (ed.), *Psychoanalysis and Religion in the 21st Century: Competitors or Collaborators?* (New York: Routledge, 2006) 205–222

Frosh, Stephen, *Hauntings: Psychoanalysis and Ghostly Transmissions* (Basingstoke: Palgrave Macmillan, 2013)

Frosh, Stephen, 'The Freudian Century,' in: Marcus, Laura & Mukherjee, Ankhi (eds.), *A Concise Companion to Psychoanalysis, Literature and Culture* (Chichester: Wiley Blackwell, 2014) 15–33

Fulgencio, Leopoldo, 'Freud's Metapsychological Speculations,' *The International Journal of Psychoanalysis* 86: 1 (2005) 99–123

Garb, Jonathan, *Yearnings of the Soul: Psychological Thought in Modern Kabbalah* (London: University of Chicago Press, 2015)

Garcia-Alandete, Joaquin, 'Metaphysics and Physiology in Animal Magnetism According to Schopenhauer,' *Limite (Arica)* (2025) 1–14

Gardner, Sebastian, 'Schopenhauer, Will and the Unconscious,' in: Janaway, Christopher (ed.), *The Cambridge Companion to Schopenhauer* (New York: Cambridge University Press, 1999) 375–421

Gargiulo, Gerald J., 'Who is the Dreamer Who Dreams the Dream? A Review Essay,' *The Psychoanalytic Review* 88 (2001) 483–488

Gauld, Alan, *A History of Hypnotism* (New York: Cambridge University Press, 1992)

Gay, Peter, *Freud: A Life for Our Time* (London: Papermac, 1989)

Gerson, Sam, 'Afterword,' in: Harris, Adrienne, Kalb, Margery & Klebanoff, Susan (eds.), *Ghosts in the Consulting Room: Echoes of Trauma in Psychoanalysis* (New York: Routledge, 2016) 199–203

Gleig, Ann, 'The Return of the Repressed? Psychoanalysis as Spirituality,' *Implicit Religion* 15: 2 (2012) 209–224

Godwin, Robert W., 'Wilfred Bion and David Bohm: Towards a Quantum Metapsychology,' *Psychoanalysis and Contemporary Thought* 14: 4 (1991) 625–654

Goodrick-Clarke, Nicholas, *The Western Esoteric Traditions: A Historical Introduction* (New York: Oxford University Press, 2008)

Gordon, Kerry, 'The Tiger's Stripe: Some Thoughts on Psychoanalysis, Gnosis, and the Experience of Wonderment,' *Contemporary Psychoanalysis* 40 (2004) 5–45

Govrin, Aner, *Conservative and Radical Perspectives on Psychoanalytic Knowledge: The Fascinated and the Disenchanted* (New York: Routledge, 2016)

Granholm, Kennet, 'Esoteric Currents as Discursive Complexes,' *Religion* 43: 1 (2013) 46–69

Green, Andre, 'The Illusion of Common Ground and Mythical Pluralism,' *The International Journal of Psychoanalysis* 86 (2005) 627–632

Greenberg, Jay R. & Mitchell, Stephen A., *Object Relations in Psychoanalytic Theory* (Cambridge: Harvard University Press, 1983)

Greene, Liz, *Magi and Maggidim: The Kabbalah in British Occultism 1860–1940* (Trinity Saint David Ceredigon: Sophia Centre Press, 2012)

Grimwade, Robert, 'Freud's Philosophical Inheritance: Schopenhauer and Nietzsche in *Beyond the Pleasure Principle*,' *Psychoanalytic Review* 99: 3 (2012) 359–395

Grotstein, James S., 'Wilfred. R. Bion: The Man, The Psychoanalyst, the Mystic-a Perspective on his Life and Work,' in: Grotstein, James S. (ed.), *Do I Dare Disturb the Universe? A Memorial to W. R. Bion* (London: Karnac, 1981) 1–36

Grotstein, James S., 'Reflections on a Century of Freud: Some Paths Not Chosen,' *British Journal of Psychotherapy* 9 (1992) 181–187

Grotstein, James S., 'Foreword,' in: Gargiulo, Gerald J. (ed.), *Psyche, Self and Soul* (London: Whurr Pub., 1994)

Grotstein, James S., 'Thinking, Feeling, and Being: Clinical Reflections on the Fundamental Antinomy of Human Beings and World.: By Ignacio Matte Blanco. New York: Routledge, 1988. Pp. 347' [Review], *The International Journal of Psychoanalysis* 77 (1996) 1053–1058

Grotstein, James S., 'Bion, the Pariah of O,' *British Journal of Psychotherapy* 14: 1 (1997) 77–89

Grotstein, James S., 'The Numinous and Immanent Nature of the Psychoanalytic Subject,' *Journal of Analytical Psychology* 43 (1998) 41–68

Grotstein, James S., *Who is the Dreamer Who Dreams the Dream? A Study of Psychic Presences* (New York: Routledge, 2000a)

Grotstein, James S., 'Notes on Bion's "Memory and Desire",' *Journal of the American Academy of Psychoanalysis and Dynamic Psychiatry* 28 (2000b) 687–694

Grotstein, James S., 'The Unconscious, the Infinite and God: A Discussion of Rodney Bomford's "Religious Truth in the Light of Bi-Logic,' *Fort Da* 7A (2001) 56–69

Grotstein, James S., 'Foreword,' in: Casement, Ann & Tacey, David (eds.), *The Idea of the Numinous: Contemporary Jungian and Psychoanalytic Perspectives* (New York: Routledge, 2006) xi–xv.

Grotstein, James S., *A Beam of Intense Darkness: Wilfred Bion's Legacy to Psychoanalysis* (London: Karnac, 2007)

Grotstein, James S. & Franey, Maureen, 'Conversations with Clinicians: Who Is the Writer Who Writes the Books?' *Fort Da* 14B (2008) 87–116

Grotstein, James S., ". . . *But at the Same Time and on Another Level* . . ." *Psychoanalytic Theory and Technique in the Kleinian/Bionian Mode Vol. 1* (London: Karnac, 2009a)

Grotstein, James S., ". . . *But at the Same Time and on Another Level* . . ." *Psychoanalytic Theory and Technique in the Kleinian/Bionian Mode Vol. 2* (London: Karnac, 2009b)

Grubrich-Simitis, Ilse, 'How Freud Wrote and Revised His *Interpretation of Dreams:* Conflicts around the Subjective Origins of the Book of the Century,' in: Pick, Daniel & Roper Lyndal (eds.), *Dreams and History: The Interpretation of Dreams from Ancient Greece to Modern Psychoanalysis* (New York: Routledge, 2004) 23–36

Guest, Hazel, 'The Origins of Transpersonal Psychology,' *British Journal of Psychotherapy* 6 (1989) 62–69

Gurevich, Hayuta, 'Orpha, Orphic Functions, and the Orphic Analyst: Winnicott's "regression to Dependence" in the Language of Ferenczi,' *The American Journal of Psychoanalysis* 76 (2016) 322–340

Gutierrez, Cathy, 'Spiritualism,' in: Magee, Glenn Alexander (ed.), *The Cambridge Handbook of Western Mysticism and Esotericism* (New York: Cambridge University Press, 2016) 237–247

Gutiérrez-Peláez, Miguel, 'Trauma Theory in Sándor Ferenczi's Writings of 1931 and 1932,' *The International Journal of Psychoanalysis* 90: 6 (2009) 1217–1233

Gyimesi, Julia, 'The Problem of Demarcation: Psychoanalysis and the Occult,' *American Imago* 66: 4 (2009) 457–470

Gyimesi, Julia, 'Sandor Ferenczi and the Problem of Telepathy,' *History of the Human Sciences* 25: 2 (2012) 131–148

Gyimesi, Julia, 'Between Religion and Science: Spiritualism, Science and Early Psychology in Hungary,' *International Psychology, Practice and Research* 5 (2014) 1–23

Gyimesi, Julia, 'From Spooks to Symbol Formation: Early Viennese Psychoanalysis and the Occult,' in: Hödl, Hans Gerald & Pokorny, Lukas (eds.), *Religion in Austria Vol. 3* (Wein: Praesens Verlag, 2016a) 41–60

Gyimesi, Julia, 'Why "Spiritism"?' *The International Journal of Psychoanalysis* 97 (2016b) 357–383

Gyimesi, Julia, 'Introduction' *Imago Budapest* 6: 4 (2017a) 3–8

Gyimesi, Julia, 'The Unorthodox Silberer,' *Imago Budapest* 6: 4 (2017b) 33–58

Hamilton, Victoria, *The Analyst's Preconscious* (Hillsdale: The Analytic Press, 1996)

Hamilton, Trevor, *Immortal Longings: F. W. H. Myers and the Victorian Search for Life after Death* (Exeter: Imprint Academic, 2009)

Hanegraaff, Wouter J., *New Age Religion and Western Culture: Esotericism in the Mirror of Secular Thought* (New York: SUNY, 1998)

Hanegraaff, Wouter J., 'A Woman Alone: The Beatification of Friederike Hauffe née Wanner,' in: Korte, Anne-Marie (ed.), *Women and Miracle Stories: A Multidisciplinary Exploration* (Leiden: Brill, 2001) 211–247

Hanegraaff, Wouter J., 'Forbidden Knowledge: Anti-Esoteric Polemics and Academic Research,' *Aries* 5: 2 (2005) 225–254

Hanegraaff, Wouter J., 'Esotericism,' in: Hanegraaff, Wouter J. et al. (eds.), *Dictionary of Gnosis and Western Esotericism* (Leiden: Brill, 2006a) 336–340

Hanegraaff, Wouter J., 'Occult/Occultism,' in: Hanegraaff, Wouter J. et al. (eds.), *Dictionary of Gnosis and Western Esotericism* (Leiden: Brill, 2006b) 884–889

Hanegraaff, Wouter J., 'Kerner, Justinus Andreas Christian,' in: Hanegraaff, Wouter J. et al. (eds.), *Dictionary of Gnosis and Western Esotericism* (Leiden: Brill, 2006c) 660–662

Hanegraaff, Wouter J., 'Leaving the Garden (in Search of Religion): Jeffrey J. Kripal's Vision of a Gnostic Study of Religion,' *Religion* 38 (2008) 259–276

Hanegraaff, Wouter J., 'Magnetic Gnosis: Somnambulism and the Quest for Absolute Knowledge,' in: Kilcher, Andreas B. & Theisohn, Philipp (eds.), *Die Encyklopädik der Esoterik: Allwissenheitsmythen und universalwissenschaftliche Modelle in der esoteric der Neuzeit* (Wilhelm Fink: Paderborn, 2010) 118–134

Hanegraaff, Wouter J., *Esotericism and the Academy: Rejected Knowledge in Western Culture* (Cambridge: Cambridge University Press, 2012a)

Hanegraaff, Wouter J., 'Foreword: Bringing Light to the Underground,' in: Bogdan, Henrik & Starr, Martin P. (eds.), *Aleister Crowley and Western Esotericism* (Oxford: Oxford University Press, 2012b)

Hanegraaff, Wouter J., *Western Esotericism: A Guide for the Perplexed* (London: Bloomsbury, 2013a)

Hanegraaff, Wouter J., 'The Power of Ideas: Esotericism, Historicism, and the Limits of Discourse,' *Religion* 43: 2 (2013b) 252–273

Hanegraaff, Wouter J., 'The Globalization of Esotericism,' *Correspondences* 3 (2015a) 55–91

Hanegraaff, Wouter J., 'Jacob Boehme and Christian Theosophy,' in: Partridge, Christopher (ed.), *The Occult World* (New York: Routledge, 2015b) 119–127

Hanegraaff, Wouter J., 'Trance,' in: Segal, Robert A. & von Stuckrad, Kocku (eds.), *Vocabulary for the Study of Religion: Volume 3* (Leiden: Brill, 2015c) 511–513

Hanegraaff, Wouter, J., 'Gnosis,' in: Magee, Glenn Alexander (ed.), *The Cambridge Handbook of Western Mysticism and Esotericism* (New York: Cambridge University Press, 2016) 381–392.

Hanegraaff, Wouter J., *Hermetic Spirituality and the Historical Imagination: Altered States of Knowledge in Late Antiquity* (New York: Cambridge University Press, 2022)

Hanegraaff, Wouter J., 'The Unnecessity of Definition,' *Aries* 24 (2024) 227–230

Hanegraaff, Wouter J., *Esotericism in Western Culture: Counter-Normativity and Rejected Knowledge* (London: Bloomsbury, 2025)

Hannak, Kristine, 'Boehme and German Romanticism,' in: Hessayon, Ariel & Apetrei, Sarah (eds.), *An Introduction to Jacob Boehme: Four Centuries of Thought and Reception* (New York: Routledge, 2014) 162–179

Harrington, Anne, 'Hysteria, Hypnosis, and the Lure of the Invisible: The Rise of Neo-mesmerism in fin de siècle French Psychiatry,' in: Bynum, William F., Porter, Roy & Shepherd, Michael (eds.), *The Anatomy of Madness: Essays in the History of Psychiatry, Vol. 3* (New York: Routledge, 2004) 226–246

Harris, Adrienne, 'The Relational Unconscious: Commentary on Papers by Michael Eigen and James Grotstein,' *Psychoanalytic Dialogues* 14: 1 (2004) 131–137

Harris, Adrienne & Aron, Lewis, 'The Work of Elizabeth Severn: An Appreciation,' in: Severn, Elizabeth, *The Discovery of the Self: A Study in Psychological Cure* [ed. with an introduction by Peter L. Rudnytsky & an essay by Adrienne Harris & Lewis Aron] (Abingdon: Routledge, 2017 [1933]) x–xviii.

Harris, Adrienne, Kalb, Margery & Klebanoff, Susan (eds.), *Ghosts in the Consulting Room: Echoes of Trauma in Psychoanalysis* (New York: Routledge, 2016a)

Harris, Adrienne, Kalb, Margery & Klebanoff, Susan (eds.), 'Introduction,' in: *Ghosts in the Consulting Room: Echoes of Trauma in Psychoanalysis* (New York: Routledge, 2016b) 1–15

Harris, Adrienne, Kalb, Margery & Klebanoff, Susan (eds.), *Demons in the Consulting Room: Echoes of Genocide, Slavery and Extreme Trauma in Psychoanalytic Practice* (New York: Routledge, 2017)

Harrison, Peter, *The Territories of Science and Religion* (London: University of Chicago Press, 2015)

Harrison, Peter, *Some New World: Myths of Supernatural Belief in a Secular Age* (New York: Cambridge University Press, 2024)

Hart, David Bentley, *All Things Are Full of Gods: The Mysteries of Mind and Life* (London: Yale University Press, 2024)

Hartmann, Eduard von, *Philosophy of the Unconscious* (New York: Routledge, 2010 [1868])

Haule, John R., 'From Somnambulism to the Archetypes: The French Roots of Jung's Split with Freud,' *The Psychoanalytic Review* 71: 4 (1984) 635–660

Haynal, André, 'A "Wise Baby"? Ferenczi's Presence,' in: Rachman, Arnold Wm. (ed.), *The Budapest School of Psychoanalysis: The Origin of a Two-Person Psychology and Emphatic Perspective* (New York: Routledge, 2017) 83–103

Hayward, Rhodri, 'Policing Dreams: History and the Moral Uses of the Unconscious,' in: Pick, Daniel & Roper, Lyndal (eds.), *Dreams and History: The Interpretation of Dreams from Ancient Greece to Modern Psychoanalysis* (New York: Routledge, 2004) 159–178

Hayward, Rhodri, *Resisting History: Religious Transcendence and the Invention of the Unconscious* (New York: Manchester University Press, 2007)

Henderson, David, *Apophatic Elements in the Theory and Practice of Psychoanalysis: Pseudo-Dionysius and C.G. Jung* (Abington: Routledge, 2014)

Henderson, David, 'Freud and Jung: The Creation of the Psychoanalytic Universe,' *Psychodynamic Practice: Individuals, Groups and Organizations* (2015) 1–6

Henderson, David, '*Apophasis* and Psychoanalysis,' in: Cattoi, Thomas & Odorisio, David M. (eds.), *Depth Psychology and Mysticism* (London: Palgrave Macmillan, 2018) 199–212

Hernandez-Halton, Isabel, 'Klein, Ferenczi and the Clinical Diary,' *The American Journal of Psychoanalysis* 75: 1 (2015) 76–85

Hessayon, Ariel, 'Boehme's Life and Times,' in: Hessayon, Ariel & Apetrei, Sarah (eds.), *An Introduction to Jacob Boehme: Four Centuries of Thought and Reception* (New York: Routledge, 2014) 13–38

Hessayon, Ariel & Apetrei, Sarah, 'Introduction: Boehme's Legacy in Perspective,' in: Hessayon, Ariel & Apetrei, Sarah (eds.), *An Introduction to Jacob Boehme: Four Centuries of Thought and Reception* (New York: Routledge, 2014) 1–12

Hewitt, Marsha Aileen, *Freud on Religion* (New York: Routledge, 2014)

Hewitt, Marsha Aileen, *Legacies of the Occult: Psychoanalysis, Religion, and Unconscious Communication* (Sheffield: Equinox, 2020)

Hiller, Susan, *The Provisional Texture of Reality: Selected Talks and Texts 1977–2007* [ed. Alexandra M. Kikoli] (Dijon: JRP/Ringier, Zurich, & Les Presses du réel, 2008)

Hinshelwood, R. D., *W.R. Bion as Clinician: Steering Between Concept and Practice* (New York: Routledge, 2023)

Hinshelwood, Robert D., 'Psychoanalysis in Britain: Points of Cultural Access,' *International Journal of Psychoanalysis* 76 (1995) 135–151

Hinshelwood, Robert D., 'The Tavistock Years,' in: Torres, Nuno & Hinshelwood, R. D. (eds.), *Bion's Sources: The Shaping of a Paradigm* (New York: Routledge, 2013) 44–55

Hinshelwood, Robert D. & Torres, Nuno, 'Preface,' in: Torres, Nuno & Hinshelwood, R. D. (eds.), *Bion's Sources: The Shaping of a Paradigm* (New York: Routledge, 2013) xiv–xvii

Hinton, Ladson, 'The Enigmatic Signifier and the Decentred Subject,' *The Journal of Analytical Psychology* 54 (2009) 637–657

Horn, Friedemann, *Schelling and Swedenborg: Mysticism and German Idealism* (West Chester: Swedenborg Foundation, 1997)

Hristeva, Galina, '"Uterus Loquitur": Trauma and the Human Organism in Ferenczi's "Physiology of Pleasure",' *The American Journal of Psychoanalysis* 73: 4 (2013) 339–352

Hristeva, Galina, '"Primordial Chant". Sándor Ferenczi as an Orphic Poet,' *The American Journal of Psychoanalysis* 79 (2019) 517–539

Hutton, Ronald, *The Witch: A History of Fear, from Ancient Times to the Present* (New Haven: Yale University Press, 2017)

Ivan, Anca, 'Book Review: *Extraordinary Knowing: Science, Skepticism and the Inexplicable Powers of the Human Mind* by Elizabeth Lloyd Mayer, Ph.D. New York: Bantam Dell, 2007, 302 pp.,' *Fort Da* 15: 1 (2009) 105–111

Jacoby, Mario, 'The Growing Convergence of Psychoanalysis and Jungian Analysis,' *Psychoanalytic Dialogues* 10 (2000) 489–503

James, William, *The Principles of Psychology*, Vols. 1 & 2 (New York: Dover Publications, 1950 [1890])

James, William, 'Human Immortality: Two Supposed Objections to the Doctrine,' in: Murphy, Gardner & Ballou, Robert O. (eds.), *William James on Psychical Research* (London: Chatto & Windus, 1960 [1897]) 279–308

James, William, 'Frederick Myers's Service to Psychology,' in: Murphy, Gardner & Ballou, Robert O. (eds.), *William James on Psychical Research* (London: Chatto & Windus, 1960 [1901]) 213–225

Janaway, Christopher, 'The Real Essence of Human Beings: Schopenhauer and the Unconscious Will,' in: Nicholls, Angus & Liebscher, Martin (eds.), *Thinking the Unconscious; Nineteenth Century German Thought* (Cambridge University Press, 2010) 140–155

Janz, Bruce B., 'Conclusion: Why Boehme Matters Today,' in: Hessayon, Ariel & Apetrei, Sarah (eds.), *An Introduction to Jacob Boehme: Four Centuries of Thought and Reception* (New York: Routledge, 2014) 279–294

St John of the Cross, *The Ascent of Mount Carmel* [trans. David Lewis] (London: Thomas Baker, 1922)

Johnson, Jay, 'The Body in Occult Thought,' in: Partridge, Christopher (ed.), *The Occult World* (New York: Routledge, 2015) 659–671

Johnson, Sarah Iles, *Hekate Soteria* (Atlanta: Scholars Press, 1990)

Johnson, Sarah Iles, 'Magic and Theurgy,' in: Frankfurter, David (ed.), *Guide to the Study of Ancient Magic* (Leiden; Brill, 2019) 694–719

Jones, Ernest, *Sigmund Freud: The Last Phase 1919–1939* (London: Hogarth Press, 1957)

Jonte-Pace, Diane & Parsons, William B. (eds.), *Religion and Psychology: Mapping the Terrain* (London: Routledge, 2001)

Jordan-Moore, Juan Francisco, 'Obituary: Ignacio Matte Blanco 1908–1995,' *The International Journal of Psychoanalysis* 76 (1995) 1035–1041

Josephson-Storm, Jason Ā., *The Myth of Disenchantment: Magic, Modernity, and the Birth of the Human Sciences* (London: University of Chicago Press, 2017)

Jung, C. G., 'Synchronicity: An Acausal Connecting Principle,' in: Read, H. et al. (eds.), *The Collected Works of C.G. Jung: Vol. 8. The Structure and Dynamics of the Psyche* (New York: Routledge & Kegan Paul, 1960) 419–519

Jung, C. G., 'On the Nature of the Psyche,' in: Read, H. et al. (eds.), *The Collected Works of C. G. Jung: Vol. 8. The Structure and Dynamics of the Psyche* [2nd ed.] (New York: Routledge & Kegan Paul, 1969 [1947; rev. 1954]) 237–279

Jung, C. G., 'On the Psychology and Pathology of So-Called Occult Phenomena,' in: Read, H. et al. (eds.), *The Collected Works of C. G. Jung: Vol. 1. Psychiatric Studies* [2nd ed.] (Oxford: Princeton University Press, 1970 [1902]) 3–88.

Jung, C. G., *C.G. Jung Letters*, 2 vols. [ed. Gerhard Adler; trans. R. F. C. Hull] (New York: Routledge & Kegan Paul, 1976)

Jung, C. G., *Memories, Dreams, Reflections* [ed. Aniela Jaffé; trans. Richard & Clara Winston] (London: Fontana, 1995 [1963])

Jung, C. G., *The Red Book: A Reader's Edition* [ed. with an introduction by Sonu Shamdasani] (London: Norton, 2009)

Jung, C. G., *Analytical Psychology* (New York: Routledge Classics, 2014 [1935])

Jung, C. G., 'Psychotherapy Today,' in: *The Collected Works of C.G. Jung: Vol. 16. The Practice of Psychotherapy* [2nd ed.] [trans. R. F. C. Hull] (New York: Routledge, 2014 [1954]) 94–110

Kakar, Sudhir, 'Psychoanalysis and Eastern Spiritual Healing Traditions,' *The Journal of Analytical Psychology* 48: 5 (2003) 659–678

Kalsched, Donald, 'Trauma and Daimonic Reality in Ferenczi's Later Work,' *The Journal of Analytical Psychology* 48: 4 (2003) 479–489

Kalsched, Donald, *Trauma and the Soul: A Psycho-spiritual Approach to Human Development and Its Interruption* (New York: Routledge, 2013)

Kastrup, Bernardo, *Decoding Schopenhauer's Metaphysics* (Washington: IFF Books, 2020)

Kastrup, Bernardo, *Decoding Jung's Metaphysics* (Washington: IFF Books, 2021)

Katz, S. Montana, *Contemporary Psychoanalytic Field Theory: Stories, Dreams and Metaphor* (New York: Routledge, 2017)

Keeley, James P., 'Subliminal Promptings: Psychoanalytic Theory and the Society for Psychical Research,' *American Imago* 58 (2001) 767–791

Keller, Catherine & Rubenstein, Mary-Jane (eds.), *Entangled Worlds: Religion, Science, and the New Materialism* (New York: Fordham University Press, 2017)

Kelly, Edward F., Crabtree, Adam & Marshall, Paul (eds.), *Beyond Physicalism; Towards Reconciliation of Science And Spirituality* (New York: Rowman & Littlefield, 2015)

Kelly, Edward F., Kelly, Williams, Crabtree, Adam, Gauld, Adam, Grosso, Michael & Greyson, Bruce (eds.), *Irreducible Mind: Towards a Psychology for the 21st Century* (New York: Rowman & Littlefield, 2007)

Kelly, Edward F. & Marshall, Paul (eds.), *Consciousness Unbound: Liberating Mind from the Tyranny of Materialism* (New York: Rowman & Littlefield, 2021)

Kerner, Justinus, *The Seeress of Prevorst* (New York: Cambridge University Press, 2011 [1829])

Kerr, John, *A Dangerous Method* (London: Atlantic Books, 2012)

Kerslake, Christian, *Deleuze and the Unconscious* (London: Continuum, 2007)

Keve, Tom, *Triad: The Physicists, the Analysts, the Kabbalists* (London: Rosenberger & Krausz, 2000)

Keve, Tom, 'The Jung-Ferenczi Dossier,' *The American Journal of Psychoanalysis* 75 (2015) 94–109

Kielholz, A., 'On the Genesis and Dynamics of Inventor's Delusion,' *The International Journal of Psychoanalysis* 5 (1924) 451–461

Kingsley, Peter, *Catafalque: Carl Jung and the End of Humanity*, Vols. 1 & 2 (London: Catafalque Press, 2018)

Kirschner, Suzanne R., *The Religious and Romantic Origins of Psychoanalysis: Individuation and Integration in Post-Freudian Theory* (Cambridge: Cambridge University Press, 1996)

Kittler, Friedrich A., *Discourse Networks 1800/1900* (Stanford: Stanford University Press, 1990)

Kleinberg, Ethan, *Haunting History: For a Deconstructive Approach to the Past* (Stanford: Stanford University Press, 2017)

Knapp, Krister Dylan, *William James: Psychical Research and the Challenge of Modernity* (Chapel Hill: University of North Carolina Press, 2017)

Knight, Gareth, *Dion Fortune and the Inner Light* (Loughborough: Thoth Publications, 2000)

Knowlson, James, *Damned to Fame: The Life of Samuel Beckett* (London: Bloomsbury, 1996)

Kokoli, Alexandra M., 'Moving Sideways and Other "Sleeping Metaphors": Susan Hiller's Paraconceptualism,' in: Gallagher, Ann (ed.), *Susan Hiller* (London: Tate Publishing, 2011) 143–154

Kradin, Richard, *The Parting of the Ways: How Esoteric Judaism and Christianity Influenced the Psychoanalytic Theories of Sigmund Freud and Carl Jung* (Boston: Academic Studies Press, 2016)

Krell, David Farrell, *The Tragic Absolute: German Idealism and the Languishing of God* (Bloomington: University of Indiana Press, 2005)

Kripal, Jeffrey J., *Roads of Excess, Palaces of Wisdom: Eroticism and Reflexivity in the Study of Mysticism* (Chicago: University of Chicago Press, 2001)

Kripal, Jeffrey J., *The Serpent's Gift: Gnostic Reflections on the Study of Religion* (Chicago: University of Chicago Press, 2007)

Kripal, Jeffrey J., 'Gnosissss-A Response to Wouter Hanegraaff,' *Religion* 38 (2008a) 277–279

Kripal, Jeffrey J., 'Mysticism,' in: Segal, Robert A. (ed.), *The Blackwell Companion to the Study of Religion* (Oxford: Blackwell Pub., 2008b) 321–335

Kripal, Jeffrey J., *Authors of the Impossible: The Paranormal and the Sacred* (London: University of Chicago Press, 2010)

Kripal, Jeffrey J., *Comparing Religions* (Chichester: Wiley Blackwell, 2014)

Kripal, Jeffrey J., *Secret Body: Erotic and Esoteric Currents in the History of Religions* (London: University of Chicago Press, 2017)

Kripal, Jeffrey J., *The Flip: Epiphanies of Mind and the Future of Knowledge* (New York: Bellevue Press, 2019)

Kripal, Jeffrey J., 'The Future of the Human(ities): Mystical Literature, Paranormal Phenomena, and the Contemporary Politics of Knowledge,' in: Kelly, Edward F. & Marshall, Paul (eds.), *Consciousness Unbound: Liberating Mind from the Tyranny of Materialism* (New York: Rowman & Littlefield, 2021) 359–405

Kripal, Jeffrey J., *How To Think Impossibly: About Souls, UFOs, Time, Belief, and Everything Else* (London: University of Chicago Press, 2024)

Kripal, Jeffrey J. et al., *Comparing Religions: The Study of Us That Changes Us* [2nd ed.] (Chichester: Wiley Blackwell, 2024)

Kuhn, Philip, *Psychoanalysis in Britain, 1893–1913: Histories and Historiography* (London: Lexington Books, 2017)

Kutzky, Harriet, 'Reparation and Tikkun: A Comparison of the Kleinian and Kabbalistic Concepts,' *The International Review of Psychoanalysis* 16 (1989) 449–458

Lachapelle, Sofie, *Investigating the Supernatural: From Spiritism and Occultism to Psychical Research and Metapsychics in France, 1853–1931* (Baltimore: Johns Hopkins University Press, 2011)

Laplanche, Jean, 'The Theory of Seduction and the Problem of the Other,' *The International Journal of Psychoanalysis* 78 (1997) 653–666

Laplanche, Jean, 'The Unfinished Copernican Revolution' [trans. Luke Thurston], in: *Essays on Otherness* [intro. by John Fletcher] (New York: Routledge, 1999) 52–83

Laplanche, Jean, 'Sublimation and/or Inspiration' [trans. John Fletcher & Luke Thurston], in: Fletcher, John & Ray, Nicholas (eds.), *Seductions and Enigmas: Laplanche, Theory, Culture* (London: Lawrence & Wishart, 2014) 77–104

Laplanche, Jean & Pontalis, Jean-Bertrand, *The Language of Psychoanalysis* (London: Karnac, 1988 [1973])

Lazar, Susan G., 'Knowing, Influencing, and Healing: Paranormal Phenomena and Implications for Psychoanalysis and Psychotherapy,' *Psychoanalytic Inquiry* 21 (2001) 113–131

Leahey, Thomas Hardy & Leahey, Grace Evans, *Psychology's Occult Doubles: Psychology and the Problem of Pseudoscience* (Chicago: Nelson-Hall Inc., 1983)

Le Clair, Robert C. (ed.), *The Letters of William James and Théodore Flournoy* (London: University of Wisconsin Press, 1966)

Loewald, Hans, 'On the Therapeutic Action of Psychoanalysis,' *The International Journal of Psychoanalysis* 41 (1960) 16–33

Lombardi, Karen, 'Whole and/or in Bits: Bohm, Matte Blanco, and (Un)consciousness,' *The International Journal of Psychoanalysis* 100: 3 (2019) 438–446

Lombardi, Riccardo, *Formless Infinity: Clinical Explorations of Matte Blanco and Bion* [Preface by Owen Renik; trans. Karen Christenfeld et al.] (New York: Routledge, 2016)

Lopez-Corvo, Rafael E., *The Dictionary of the Work of W. R. Bion* (New York: Routledge, 2018 [2003])

Luckhurst, Roger, '"Something Tremendous, Something Elemental": On the Ghostly Origins of Psychoanalysis,' in: Peter Buse & Andrew Stott (eds.), *Ghosts: Deconstruction, Psychoanalysis, History* (London: Macmillan Press, 1999) 50–71

Luckhurst, Roger, *The Invention of Telepathy: 1870–1901* (Oxford: Oxford University Press, 2002)

Macdonald, Molly, *Hegel and Psychoanalysis: A New Interpretation of Phenomenology of Spirit* (New York: Routledge, 2014)

MacDonald, Paul S., *History of the Concept of Mind: Speculations about Soul, Mind and Spirit from Homer to Hume (Volume 1)* (Aldershot: Ashgate, 2003)

MacDonald, Paul S., *History of the Concept of Mind: The Heterodox and Occult Tradition (Volume 2)* (Aldershot: Ashgate, 2007)

Magee, Glen Alexander, *Hegel and the Hermetic Tradition* (London: Cornell University Press, 2001)

Magee, Glenn Alexander, 'Hegel on the Paranormal: Altered States of Consciousness in the Philosophy of Subjective Spirit,' *Aries* 8 (2008) 21–36

Magee, Glenn Alexander, 'Hegel's Reception of Jacob Boehme,' in: *An Introduction to Jacob Boehme* (New York: Routledge, 2014) 224–243

Magee, Glenn Alexander (ed.), 'Editor's Introduction,' in: *The Cambridge Handbook of Western Mysticism and Esotericism* (New York: Cambridge University Press, 2016a) xiii–xxxv

Magee, Glenn Alexander (ed.), 'Jacob Boehme and Christian Theosophy,' in: *The Cambridge Handbook of Western Mysticism and Esotericism* (New York: Cambridge University Press, 2016b) 184–199

Magee, Glenn Alexander, 'A Neo-Hegelian Theory of Mystical Experience and Other Extraordinary Phenomena,' in: Kelly, Edward F. & Marshall, Paul (eds.), *Consciousness Unbound: Liberating Mind from the Tyranny of Materialism* (New York: Rowman & Littlefield, 2021) 229–255

Maier, Christian, 'Bion and C. G. Jung. How Did the Container-contained Model Find Its Thinker? The Fate of a Cryptomnesia,' *The Journal of Analytical Psychology* 61: 2 (2016) 134–154

Maillard, Christine, 'Jung, Carl Gustav, 1875–1961,' in: Hanegraaff, Wouter et al. (eds.), *Dictionary of Gnosis and Western Esotericism* (Leiden: Brill, 2006) 648–653

Main, Roderick, 'Ruptured Time and the Re-enchantment of Modernity,' in: Casement, Ann (ed.), *Who Owns Jung* (London: Karnac, 2007) 19–38

Main, Roderick, *The Rupture of Time: Synchronicity and Jung's Critique of Modern Western Culture* (New York: Routledge, 2013a [2004])

Main, Roderick, 'Secular *and* Religious: The Intrinsic Doubleness of Analytical Psychology and the Hegemony of Naturalism in the Social Sciences,' *Journal of Analytical Psychology* 58: 3 (2013b) 366–386

Main, Roderick, 'Psychology and the Occult: Dialectics of Disenchantment and Re-Enchantment in the Modern Self,' in: Partridge, Christopher (ed.), *The Occult World* (New York: Routledge, 2015) 732–743

Majercik, Ruth, *The Chaldean Oracles: Text, Translation and Commentary* (Leiden: Brill, 1989)

Makari, George, *Soul Machine: The Invention of the Modern Mind* (New York: Norton & Co., 2015).

Malin, Barnet D., 'Who is the Dreamer Who Dreams the Dream? A Study of Psychic Presences: James S. Grotstein: Hillsdale, NJ: The Analytic Press. 2000. Pp. 304,' *The International Journal of Psychoanalysis* 83 (2002) 982–986

Mancia, Maura, 'Memoir of the Future and Memoir of the Numinous,' in: Giuseppe Civitarese (ed.), *Bion and Contemporary Psychoanalysis: Reading a Memoir of the Future* (New York: Routledge, 2018) 65–78

Mansfield, Nick, *Subjectivity: Theories of the Self from Freud to Haraway* (St Leonards NSW: Allen & Unwin, 2000)

Marinelli, Lydia & Mayer, Andreas, *Dreaming by the Book: Freud's The Interpretation of Dreams and the History of the Psychoanalytic Movement* (New York: Other Press, 2003)

Massicotte, Claudie, *Hélène Smith: Occultism and the Discovery of the Unconscious* (New York: Oxford University Press, 2023)

Masson, Jeffrey Moussaieff (trans. & ed.), *The Complete Letters of Sigmund Freud to Wilhelm Fliess 1887–1904* (Cambridge MA: Harvard University Press, 1985)

Matte-Blanco, Ignacio, 'Comentarios sobre la obra "La sincronidad como un principio de relaciones no casuals" de C.G. Jung,' *Actas Lusas-Españolas de Neurologia y Psiquiatría* 21 (1962) 283–292

Matte-Blanco, Ignacio, 'Reflecting with Bion,' in: Grotstein, James S. (ed.), *Do I Dare Disturb the Universe? A Memorial to W.R. Bion* (London: Karnac, 1983)

Matte-Blanco, Ignacio, *The Unconscious as Infinite Sets: An Essay in Bi-Logic* [with a Foreword by Eric Rayner] (London: Karnac, 1998a [1975])

Matte-Blanco, Ignacio, *Thinking, Feeling and Being: Clinical Reflections on the Fundamental Antinomy of Human Beings and World* [intro. Eric Rayner and David Tuckett] (New York: Routledge, 1998b)

Matte-Blanco, Ignacio, 'The Four Antinomies of the Death Instinct' [trans. Richard Carvalho], *The International Journal of Psychoanalysis* 86: 5 (2005) 1463–1476

Mavromatis, Andreas, *Hypnagogia* (London: Thyrsos Press, 1987)

Mawson, Chris (ed.) & Bion, Francesca (consultant ed.), *The Complete Works of W.R. Bion*, Vols. I–XVI (London: Karnac, 2014)

Mayer, Andreas, *Sites of the Unconscious: Hypnosis and the Emergence of the Psychoanalytic Setting* (London: University of Chicago Press, 2013)

Mayer, Elizabeth L., 'Changes in Science and Changing Ideas about Knowledge and Authority in Psychoanalysis,' *The Psychoanalytic Quarterly* 65 (1996a) 158–200

Mayer, Elizabeth L., 'Subjectivity and Intersubjectivity of Clinical Facts,' *International Journal of Psychoanalysis* 77 (1996b) 709–737

Mayer, Elizabeth L., 'On "Telepathic Dreams?": An Unpublished Paper by Robert J. Stoller,' *Journal of the American Psychoanalytic Association* 49 (2001) 629–657

Mayer, Elizabeth L., 'Freud and Jung: The Boundaried Mind and the Radically Connected Mind,' *The Journal of Analytical Psychology* 47 (2002) 91–99

Mayer, Elizabeth L., *Extraordinary Knowing: Science, Skepticism, and the Inexplicable Powers of the Human Mind* (New York: Bantam Books, 2007)

Mayer, Paola, *Jena Romanticism and Its Appropriation of Jacob Boehme* (Montreal: McGill-Queen's University Press, 1999)

Mazur, Zeke, '*Unio Magica*: Part II: Plotinus, Theurgy, and the Question of Ritual,' *Dionysius* 22 (2004), 29–56.

McCalla, Arthur, 'Romanticism,' in: Hanegraaff, Wouter J. et al. (eds.), *Dictionary of Gnosis and Western Esotericism* (Leiden: Brill, 2006) 1000–1007

McCullough, Glenn J., *Jacob Boehme and the Spiritual Roots of Psychodynamic Psychotherapy: Dreams, Ecstasy, and Wisdom* (Unpublished PhD, University of St. Michael's College, 2019)

McGilchrist, Iain, *The Master And His Emissary: The Divided Brain and the Making of the Western World* [expanded ed.] (London: Yale University Press, 2019)

McGilchrist, Iain, *The Matter with Things: Our Brains, Our Delusions, and the Unmaking of the World*, Vols. 1+2 (London: Perspectiva Press, 2021)

McGrath, Sean J., *The Dark Ground of Spirit: Schelling and the Unconscious* (New York: Routledge, 2012)

McGrath, Sean J., 'The Question Concerning Metaphysics: A Schellingian Intervention in Analytical Psychology,' *International Journal of Jungian Studies* 6: 1 (2014a) 23–51

McGrath, Sean J., 'The Psychology of Productive Dissociation, or What Would Schellingian Psychotherapy Look Like? *Comparative and Continental Philosophy* 6: 1 (2014b) 35–48

McGrath, Sean J., 'Schelling and the History of the Dissociative Self,' *Symposium* 19: 1 (2015) 52–66

McGrath, Sean J., *The Philosophical Foundations of the Late Schelling: The Turn to the Positive* (Edinburgh: Edinburgh University Press, 2021)

McGuire, William (ed.), *The Freud/Jung Letters* (London: Penguin, 1991)

Méheust, Bertrand, 'Animal Magnetism/Mesmerism,' in: Hanegraaff, Wouter J. et al. (eds.), *Dictionary of Gnosis and Western Esotericism* (Leiden: Brill, 2006) 75–82

Melzer, Arthur M., *Philosophy between the Lines: The Lost History of Esoteric Writing* (London: University of Chicago Press, 2014)

Mercer, Michael, 'Bearable or Unbearable? Unconscious Communication in Management,' in: Gordon, J. & Kirtchuk, G. (eds.), *Psychic Assaults and Frightened Clinicians: Countertransference in Forensic Settings* (London: Karnac, 2008)

Merkur, Dan, *Explorations of the Psychoanalytic Mystics* (New York: Contemporary Psychoanalytic Studies, 2010)

Merkur, Dan, 'Drugs and the Occult,' in: Partridge, Christopher (ed.), *The Occult World* (New York: Routledge, 2015) 672–680

Meszaros, Judit, 'Sandor Ferenczi and the Budapest School of Psychoanalysis,' *Psychoanalytic Perspectives* 7: 1 (2010) 69–89

Meszaros, Judit, *Ferenczi and beyond: Exile of the Budapest School and Solidarity in the Psychoanalytic Movement during the Nazi Years* (London: Karnac, 2014)

Meyer, Andreas, *Sites of the Unconscious: Hypnosis and the Emergence of the Psychoanalytic Setting* (London: University of Chicago Press, 2013)

Mills, Jon, *The Unconscious Abyss: Hegel's Anticipation of Psychoanalysis* (Albany: SUNY, 2002)

Mills, Jon, *Underworlds: Philosophies of the Unconscious from Psychoanalysis to Metaphysics* (New York: Routledge, 2014)

Mills, Jon, 'A Critique of Materialism,' in: Mills, Jon (ed.,) *Psychoanalysis and the Mind-Body Problem* (New York: Routledge, 2022)

Mitchell, Stephen A. & Black, Margaret J., *Freud and Beyond: A History of Modern Psychoanalytic Thought* (New York: Basic Books, 1995)

Mondrzak, Viviane Sprinz, 'Psychoanalytic Process and Thought: Convergence of Bion and Matte-Blanco,' *The International Journal of Psychoanalysis* 85 (2004) 597–614

Monk, Alex, *Trauma and the Supernatural in Psychotherapy: Working with the Curse Position in Clinical Practice* (New York: Routledge, 2023)

Moreau-Ricaud, Michelle 'Healing Boredom: Ferenczi and his circle of literary friends' in: Judit Szekacs-Weisz & Tom Keve (eds.) *Ferenczi and his World: Rekindling the Spirit of the Budapest School* (New York; Routledge, 2012), 87–96.

Muratori, Cecilia, *The First German Philosopher: The Mysticism of Jakob Böhme as Interpreted by Hegel* (New York: Springer, 2016)

Myers, F. W. H., *Human Personality and Its Survival of Bodily Death* (Charlottesville: Hampton Roads Publishing, 2001 [1903–1904])

Nelson, Marie Coleman, 'Nandor Fodor: 1895–1964,' *The Psychoanalytic Review* 51B: 2 (1964) 155–157

Nelson, Marie Coleman, 'Contributions of Parapsychology: Introduction,' *The Psychoanalytic Review* 56A: 1 (1969) 3–8

Nelson, Victoria, *The Secret Life of Puppets* (Cambridge, MA.: Harvard University Press, 2001)

Newberg, Andrew B., *Principles of Neurotheology* (New York: Routledge, 2016)

Newman, Barbara, *The Permeable Self: Five Medieval Relationships* (Philadelphia: Penn University Press, 2021)

Nicholls, Angus & Liebscher, Martin (eds.), *Thinking the Unconscious; Nineteenth Century German Thought* (Cambridge University Press, 2010)

Nicholls, Moira, 'The Influences of Eastern Thought on Schopenhauer's Doctrine of the Thing-in-Itself,' in: Janaway, Christopher (ed.), *The Cambridge Companion to Schopenhauer* (New York: Cambridge University Press, 1999) 171–212

Nicolescu, Basarab, *Science, Meaning and Evolution: The Cosmology of Jacob Boehme* (New York: Parabola Books, 1991)

Noakes, Richard, *Physics and Psychics: The Occult and the Sciences in Modern Britain* (New York: Cambridge University Press, 2019)

Norman, Judith & Welchman, Alistair, 'Schopenhauer's Understanding of Schelling,' in: Wicks, Robert L. (ed.), *The Oxford Handbook of Schopenhauer* (New York: Oxford University Press, 2020) 49–66

Northcote, Jeremy, *The Paranormal and the Politics of Truth: A Sociological Account* (Exeter: Imprint Academic, 2007)

Obeyesekere, Gananath, *The Awakened Ones: Phenomenology of Visionary Experience* (New York: Columbia University Press, 2012)

Ogden Thomas H., *Reverie and Interpretation* (London: Karnac, 1999)

Okropiridze, Dimitry, 'Interpretation Reconsidered: The Definitional Progression in the Study of Esotericism as a Case in Point for the Varifocal Theory of Interpretation,' in: Asprem, Egil & Strube, Julian (eds.), *New Approaches to the Study of Esotericism* (Leiden: Brill, 2021) 217–239

Oppenheim, Janet, *The Other World: Spiritualism and Psychical Research in England, 1850–1914* (New York: Cambridge University Press, 1985)

Orange, Donna, 'Review of *Ghosts in the Consulting Room: Echoes of Trauma in Psychoanalysis* and *Demons in the Consulting Room: Echoes of Genocide, Slavery and Extreme Trauma in Psychoanalytic Practice*,' *Psychoanalysis, Self and Context* 12: 1 (2017) 91–96

O'Regan, Cyril, *The Heterodox Hegel* (Albany: SUNY, 1994)

O'Regan, Cyril, *Gnostic Return in Modernity* (Albany: SUNY, 2001)

O'Regan, Cyril, *Gnostic Apocalypse: Jacob Boehme's Haunted Narrative* (Albany: SUNY, 2002)

Owens, Alex, *The Place of Enchantment: British Occultism and the Culture of the Modern* (London: University of Chicago Press, 2004)

Parsons, Michael, 'Ways of Transformation,' in: Black, David M. (ed.), *Psychoanalysis and Religion in the 21st Century: Competitors or Collaborators?* (New York: Routledge, 2006) 124–125.

Parsons, William B., *The Enigma of the Oceanic Feeling: Revisioning the Psychoanalytic Theory of Mysticism* (New York: Oxford University Press, 1999)

Parsons, William B., *Freud and Religion: Advancing the Dialogue* (New York: Cambridge University Press, 2021)

Pelled, Esther, 'Learning from Experience: Bion's Concept of Reverie and Buddhist Meditation: A Comparative Study,' *The International Journal of Psychoanalysis* 88 (2007) 1507–1526

Penman, Leigh T. I., 'Boehme's Intellectual Networks and the Heterodox Milieu,' in: Hessayon, Ariel & Apetrei, Sarah (eds.), *An Introduction to Jacob Boehme: Four Centuries of Thought and Reception* (New York: Routledge, 2014) 57–76

Pfeiffer, Ernst (ed.), *Sigmund Freud and Lou Andreas-Salomé: Letters* [trans. William & Elaine Robson-Scott] (London: Hogarth Press, 1972)

Phillips, Adam, *Terrors and Experts* (London: Faber, 1995)

Pickering, Judith, *The Search for Meaning in Psychotherapy: Spiritual Practice, the Apophatic Way and Bion* (New York: Routledge, 2019)

Pierri, Maria, *Occultism and the Origins of Psychoanalysis: Freud, Ferenczi and the Challenge of Thought Transference* [trans. Adam Elgar] (New York: Routledge, 2022a)

Pierri, Maria, *Sigmund Freud and the Forsythe Case: Coincidences and Thought Transmission in Psychoanalysis* [trans. Adam Elgar] (New York: Routledge, 2022b)

Pietrantonio, Violet, 'Why Bion Field Theory?' *Romanian Journal of Psychoanalysis* 11: 2 (2018) 97–120

Pilard, Nathalie, 'C. G. Jung and Intuition: From the Mindscape of the Paranormal to the Heart of Psychology,' *The Journal of Analytical Psychology* 63: 1 (2018) 65–84

Pine, Fred, *Drive, Ego, Object and Self: A Synthesis for Clinical Work* (New York: Basic Books, 1990)

Prel, Carl du, *The Philosophy of Mysticism Vol. 1* [intro. Rico Sneller: trans. C. C. Massey] (Hermitix Pub. Re-edition, 2022 [1885])

Prokhoris, Sabine, *The Witch's Kitchen: Freud, Faust, and the Transference* (London: Cornell University Press, 1995)

Pruett, Gordon E., 'Will and Freedom: Psychoanalytic Themes in the Work of Jacob Boehme,' *Studies in Religion* 6: 3 (1976–77) 241–251

Rabeyron, Thomas, 'Why Most Research Findings about Psi are False: The Replicability Crisis, the Psi Paradox and the Myth of Sisyphus,' *Frontiers in Psychology* 11 (2020) 1–11

Rabeyron, Thomas & Evrard, Renaud, 'Historical and Contemporary Perspectives on Occultism in the Freud-Ferenczi Correspondence,' *Recherches en psychoanalyse* 13: 1 (2012) 98–111

Rabeyron, Thomas, Evrard, Renaud & Massicote, Claude, 'Psychoanalysis and the Sour Apple: Thought-transference in Historical and Contemporary Psychoanalysis,' *Contemporary Psychoanalysis* 56: 4 (2020) 612–652

Rabeyron, Thomas, Evrard, Renaud & Massicote, Claude, 'Psychoanalysis and Telepathic Processes,' *Journal of the American Psychoanalytical Association* 69: 3 (2021) 535–571

Rabeyron, Thomas & Loose, Tianna, 'Anomalous Experiences, Trauma, and Symbolization Processes at the Frontiers between Psychoanalysis and Cognitive Neurosciences,' *Frontiers in Psychology* 6: Art. 1926 (2015) 1–17

Rachman, Arnold William, 'The Origins of a Relational School in the Ideas of Sandor Ferenczi and the Budapest School of Psychoanalysis,' *Psychoanalytic Perspectives* 7: 1 (2010) 43–60

Rachman, Arnold William (ed.), *The Budapest School of Psychoanalysis: The Origin of a Two-Person Psychology and Emphatic Perspective* (New York: Routledge, 2017)

Rachman, Arnold William, *Elizabeth Severn: The 'Evil Genius' of Psychoanalysis* (Abingdon: Routledge, 2018)

Rachman, Arnold William, 'The Psychoanalysis between Sandor Ferenczi and Elizabeth Severn: Mutuality, Unconscious Communication, and the Development of Countertransference Analysis,' *Psychoanalytic Inquiry* 39: 3–4 (2019) 276–281

Raia, Courtenay, *The New Prometheans: Faith, Science, and the Supernatural Mind in the Victorian Fin de Siècle* (London: University of Chicago Press, 2019)

Rand, Nicolas T., 'Introduction,' in: Nicolas Abraham & Maria Torok (eds.), *The Shell and The Kernel* (London: University of Chicago Press, 1994) 1–22

Rand, Nicolas T., 'The Hidden Soul: The Growth of the Unconscious, 1750–1900,' *American Imago* 61: 3 (2004) 257–289

Rayner, Eric, *Unconscious Logic: An Introduction to Matte Blanco's Bi-Logic and Its Uses* (New York: Routledge, 1995)

Reghintovschi, Simona, 'The Unconscious Sibling Rivalry in Psychoanalytic Institutions,' *Frontiers in Psychology* (2025), 1–13

Reichbart, Richard, *The Paranormal Surrounds Us: Psychic Phenomena in Literature, Culture and Psychoanalysis* [foreword by Mikita Brottman; afterword by Michael Prescott] (Jefferson: McFarland & Company, Inc., Publishers, 2019)

Reiner, Annie, 'Ferenczi's "Astra" and Bion's "O": A Clinical Perspective,' in: Reiner, Annie (ed.), *Of Things Invisible to Mortal Sight: Celebrating the Work of James S. Grotstein* (London: Karnac, 2017) 131–148

Resnik, Salomon, *The Theatre of the Dream* (New York: Routledge, 2000)

Ricaud, Michelle Moreau, 'Michael Balint: An Introduction,' *The American Journal of Psychoanalysis* 62: 1 (2002) 17–24

Richardson, Robert D., *William James: In the Maelstrom of American Modernism* (New York: Houghton Mifflin, 2006)

Rickman, John, 'Obituary: Sandor Ferenczi,' *Journal of the Society for Psychical Research* XXVIII (1933–1934) 124–125

Roazen, Paul, *Freud and His Followers* (New York: Alfred A. Knopf, 1975)

Robbins, Michael, *The Primordial Mind in Health and Illness: A Cross-Cultural Perspective* (New York: Routledge, 2011)

Roseneil, Sasha, 'Haunting in an Age of Individualization,' *European Societies* 11: 3 (2009) 411–430

Roudinesco, Élizabeth *Freud in His Time and Ours* (London: Harvard University Press, 2016)

Rousse-Lacordaire, Jérôme, 'Mysticism,' in: Hanegraaff, Wouter J. et al. (eds.), *Dictionary of Gnosis and Western Esotericism* (Leiden: Brill, 2006) 818–820

Rowland, Susan, *Remembering Dionysus: Revisioning Psychology and Literature in C. G. Jung and James Hillman* (New York: Routledge, 2017)

Rudbøg, Tim, *The Academic Study of Western Esotericism: Early Developments and Related Fields* (Copenhagen: Hermes Academic Press, 2013)

Rudnytsky, Peter L., 'Series Editor's Foreword,' in: Szekacs-Weisz, Judit & Keve, Tom (eds.), *Ferenczi and His World: Rekindling the Spirit of the Budapest School* (New York: Routledge, 2018) xiii–xix

Rudnytsky, Peter L., *Mutual Analysis: Ferenczi, Severn, and the Origins of Trauma Theory* (Abington: Routledge, 2022)

Samuels, Andrew, Shorter, Bani & Plaut, Fred, *A Critical Dictionary of Jungian Analysis* (Abington: Routledge, 1986)

Sandler, Joseph, 'Reflections on Some Relations between Psychoanalytic Concepts and Psychoanalytic Practice,' *The International Journal of Psychoanalysis* 64 (1983) 35–45

Sandler, Joseph et al., *Freud's Models of the Mind: An Introduction* (London: Karnac, 1997)

Sandler, Paulo Cesar, *The Language of Bion: A Dictionary of Concepts* (London: Karnac, 2005)

Sandler, Paulo Cesar, 'The Origins of Bion's Work,' *International Journal of Psychoanalysis* 87: 1 (2006) 179–201

Saul, Nicholas (ed.), *The Cambridge Companion to German Romanticism* (New York: Cambridge University Press, 2009)

Schelling, F. W. J., *Clara: Or, On Nature's Connection to the Spirit World* [trans. with an intro. by Fiona Steinkamp] (Albany: SUNY, 2002)

Schilbrack, Kevin, 'Religions: Are There Any?' *Journal of the American Academy of Religion* 78: 4 (2010) 1112–1138

Schneider, Stanley & Berke, Joseph H., 'Sigmund Freud and the Lubavitcher Rebbe,' *The Psychoanalytic Review* 87 (2000) 39–59

Schneider, Stanley & Berke, Joseph H., 'The Oceanic Feeling, Mysticism and Kabbalah: Freud's Historical Roots,' *The Psychoanalytic Review* 95 (2008) 131–156

Schneider, Stanley & Berke, Joseph H., 'Freud's Meeting with Rabbi Alexandre Safran,' *Psychoanalysis and History* 12 (2010) 15–28

Scholem, Gershom, *Kabbalah* (New York: Meridian, 1978)

Scholem, Gershom, *On the Mystical Shape of the Godhead: Basic Concepts in the Kabbalah* [Foreword by Joseph Dan] (New York: Schocken Books, 1991 [1962])

Scholem, Gershom, *Major Trends in Jewish Mysticism* (New York: Schocken Books, 1995 [1946])

Scholem, Gershom, *On the Kabbalah and its Symbolism* (New York: Schocken Books, 1996 [1965])

Schopenhauer, Arthur, *The World as Will and Representation*, Vols. 1 & 2 [trans. E. F. J. Payne] (New York: Dover, 1969)

Schopenhauer, Arthur, 'Essay on Spirit Seeing and Related Issues,' in: *Parerga and Paralipomena: Short Philosophical Essays, Vol. 1* [trans./ed. Sabine Roehr, Christopher Janaway with an intro. Christopher Janaway] (Cambridge: Cambridge University Press, 2014a [1851]) 198–272

Schopenhauer, Arthur, *The World as Will and Representation, Vol. 1* [trans./ed. Judith Norman, Alistair Welchman & Christopher Janaway; intro. Christopher Janaway] (Cambridge: Cambridge University Press, 2014b)

Schreber, Daniel Paul, *Memoirs Of My Nervous Illness* (New York: NYRB, 2000)

Schwarz, Berthold Eric, 'Freud, Jung and Occultism by Nandor Fodor: A Review,' *The Psychoanalytic Review* 60: 4 (1973–1974) 636–638

Segala, Marco, 'Between Science and Magic: The Case of Schopenhauer,' *Voluntas: Revista Internacional Filosofia* 11: 3 (2021) 3–16

Sells, Michael A., *Mystical Languages of Unsaying* (London: Chicago University Press, 1994)

Severn, Elizabeth, *The Discovery of the Self: A Study in Psychological Cure* [ed. with an introduction by Peter L. Rudnytsky & an essay by Adrienne Harris & Lewis Aron] (Abingdon: Routledge, 2017 [1933])

Seyhan, Azade, 'What Is Romanticism, and Where Did It Come from?' in: Saul, Nicholas (ed.), *The Cambridge Companion to German Romanticism* (New York: Cambridge University Press, 2009) 1–20

Shamdasani, Sonu, 'Automatic Writing and the Discovery of the Unconscious,' *Spring: A Journal of Archetype and Culture* 54 (1993) 100–131

Shamdasani, Sonu, *Jung and the Making of Modern Psychology: The Dream of a Science* (Cambridge: Cambridge University Press, 2003)

Shamdasani, Sonu, 'Psychologies as Ontology-making Practices: William James and the Pluralities of Psychological Experience,' in: Casement, Ann & Tacey, David (eds.), *The Idea of the Numinous; Contemporary Jungian and Psychoanalytic Perspectives* (New York: Routledge, 2006) 1–19

Shamdasani, Sonu, 'Encountering Hélène: Théodore Flournoy and the Genesis of Subliminal Psychology,' in: Shamdasani, Sonu (ed.), Théodore Flournoy, *From India to the Planet Mars* (Princeton University Press, 2015a)

Shamdasani, Sonu, '"S.W." and C.G. Jung: Mediumship, Psychiatry and Serial Exemplarity,' *History of Psychiatry* 26: 3 (2015b) 288–302

Shann, Jonathan, 'Raising Hell: Freud's Katabatic Metaphors in *The Interpretation of Dreams*,' in: Bishop, Paul et al. (eds.), *The Descent of the Soul and the Archaic: Katábasis and Depth Psychology* (New York: Routledge, 2023) 149–182

Shaw, Gregory, *Theurgy and the Soul: The Neoplatonism of Iamblichus* (Pennsylvania: Penn State Press, 1995)

Skelton, Ross M., 'Bion's Use of Modern Logic,' *The International Journal of Psychoanalysis* 76 (1995) 389–397

Skues, Richard, 'Freud and the Disenchantment of Telepathy: Thought-Transference Analysed and the History of an Unpublished Paper,' *Psychoanalysis and History* 23: 3 (2021) 267–295

Smith Nancy A., '"Orpha Reviving" Towards an Honorable Recognition of Elizabeth Severn,' *International Forum of Psychoanalysis* 7: 4 (1998) 241–246

Smith, Nancy A., 'From Oedipus to Orpha: Revisiting Ferenczi and Severn's Landmark Case,' *The American Journal of Psychoanalysis* 59: 4 (1999) 345–366

Smith, Nigel, 'Did Anyone Understand Boehme?' in: *An Introduction to Jacob Boehme* (New York: Routledge, 2014) 98–119

Snell, Robert, *Uncertainties, Mysteries, Doubts: Romanticism and the Analytic Attitude* (New York: Routledge, 2013)

Snell, Robert, *Antonino Ferro: A Contemporary Introduction* New York: Routledge, 2024)

Solms, Mark, 'A Previously Untranslated Review by Freud of a Monograph on Hypnotism,' *The International Journal of Psychoanalysis* 70 (1989) 401–403

Solms, Mark, 'A Previously-Untranslated Review by Freud of an Article Reporting an Hypnotic Experiment,' *The International Review of Psychoanalysis* 17 (1990) 365–366

Solms, Mark, *The Hidden Spring: A Journey to the Source of Consciousness* (London: Profile Books, 2021)

Solms, Mark & Turnbull, Oliver H., 'What Is Neuropsychoanalysis?' *Neuropsychoanalysis* 13: 2 (2011) 1–13

Sommer, Andreas, 'From Astronomy to Transcendental Darwinism: Carl du Prel (1839–1899),' *Journal of Scientific Exploration* 23: 1 (2009) 59–68

Sommer, Andreas, 'Are You Afraid of the Dark? Notes on the Psychology of Belief in Histories of Science and the Occult,' *European Journal of Psychotherapy & Counselling* 18: 2 (2016) 105–122

Soreanu, Raluca, 'The Psychic Life of Fragments: Splitting from Ferenczi to Klein,' *The American Journal of Psychoanalysis* 78 (2018) 421–444

Soreanu, Raluca, 'Michael Balint's Word Trail: The "Ocnophil", The "Philobat" and Creative Dyads,' *Psychoanalysis and History* 21: 1 (2019a) 53–72

Soreanu, Raluca, 'The Time of Re-Living. For an Eventful Psychoanalysis,' *Vestigia* 2: 1 (2019b) 132–153

Spielman, Ron, '"Who is the Dreamer who Dreams the Dream?": A Study of Psychic Presences,' *Journal of the American Psychoanalytic Association* 49: 3 (2001) 1051–1055

Spillius, Elizabeth, 'The Emergence of Klein's Idea of Projective Identification in Her Published and Unpublished Work,' in: Spillius, Elizabeth & O'Shaughnessy, Edna (eds.), *Projective Identification: The Fate of a Concept* (New York: Routledge, 2012) 3–18

Spraggett, Allen, 'Nandor Fodor: Analyst of the Unexplained,' *The Psychoanalytic Review* 56A: 1 (1969) 128–137

Stack Allyson, 'Culture, Cognition and Jean Laplanche's Enigmatic Signifier,' in: Fletcher, John & Ray, Nicholas (eds.), *Seductions and Enigmas: Laplanche, Theory, Culture* (London: Lawrence & Wishart, 2014) 137–158

Stang, Charles, *Our Divine Double* (Cambridge, MA: Harvard University Press, 2016)

Starr, Karen E., *Repair of the Soul: Metaphors of Transformation in Jewish Mysticism and Psychoanalysis* (New York: Routledge, 2008)

Stein, Charles, 'Ancient Mysteries,' in: Magee, Glenn Alexander (ed.), *The Cambridge Handbook of Western Mysticism and Esotericism* (New York: Cambridge University Press, 2016) 3–12

Steiner, Riccardo, 'Who Influenced Whom? And How?:-A Brief Series of Notes on E. Weiss, M. Klein (and I. Svevo) and the So-called "Origins" of "Projective and Introjective Identification",' *International Journal of Psychoanalysis* 80 (1999) 367–375

Stern, Donnel, 'Field Theory in Psychoanalysis, Part 1: Harry Stack Sullivan and Madeleine and Willy Baranger,' *Psychoanalytic Dialogues* 23: 5 (2013a) 487–501

Stern, Donnel, 'Field Theory in Psychoanalysis, Part 2: Bionian Field Theory and Contemporary Interpersonal/Relational Psychoanalysis,' *Psychoanalytic Dialogues* 23: 6 (2013b) 630–645

Stewart, Charles, 'Dreams and Desires in Ancient and Early Christian Thought,' in: Pick, Daniel & Roper, Lyndal (eds.), *Dreams and History: The Interpretation of Dreams from Ancient Greece to Modern Psychoanalysis* (Routledge: London, 2004) 37–56

Stewart, Harold, 'Michael Balint: An Overview,' *American Journal of Psychoanalysis* 62: 1 (2002) 37–52

Strawson, Galen, 'Realistic Monism: Why Physicalism Entails Panpsychism,' *Journal for Consciousness Studies* 13: 10–11 (2006) 3–31

Strube, Julian, 'Towards the Study of Esotericism without the "Western": Esotericism from the Perspective of a Global Religious History,' in: Asprem, Egil & Strube, Julian (eds.), *New Approaches to the Study of Esotericism* (Leiden: Brill, 2021) 45–66

Stuckrad, Kocku von, 'Discursive Study of Religion: Approaches, Definitions, Implications,' *Method & Theory in the Study of Religion* 25 (2013) 5–25

Stuckrad, Kocku von, 'Discursive Transfers and Reconfigurations: Tracing the Religious and the Esoteric in Secular Culture,' in: *Contemporary Esotericism* (New York: Routledge, 2014) 226–243

Stuckrad, Kocku von, *The Scientification of Religion: An Historical Study of Discursive Change 1800–2000* (Berlin: Walter de Gruyter, 2015)

Stuckrad, Kocku von, *A Cultural History of the Soul: Europe and North America from 1870 to the Present* (New York: Columbia University Press, 2022)

Sullivan, Barbara Stevens, *The Mystery of Analytical Work: Weavings from Jung and Bion* (New York: Routledge, 2010)

Summerscale, Kate, *The Haunting of Alma Fielding: A True Ghost Story* (London: Bloomsbury Circus, 2020)

Symington, Joan & Symington, Neville, *The Clinical Thinking of Wilfred Bion* (New York: Routledge, 1996)

Szekacs-Weisz, Judit & Keve, Tom (eds.), *Ferenczi and His World: Rekindling the Spirit of the Budapest School* (New York: Routledge, 2018)

Tanaseanu-Döbler, Ilinca, *Theurgy in Late Antiquity: The Invention of a Ritual Tradition* (Göttingen: Vandenhoeck & Ruprecht, 2013)

Taves, Ann, 'A Tale of Two Congresses: The Psychological Study of Psychical, Occult and Religious Phenomena, 1900–1909,' *Journal of the History of the Behavioural Sciences* 50: 4 (2015) 376–399

Taylor, Charles, *Sources of the Self: The Making of the Modern Identity* (New York: Cambridge University Press, 1992)

Taylor, Charles, *A Secular Age* (Cambridge, MA: Harvard University Press, 2007)

Taylor, Eugene, *William James on Exceptional Mental States: The 1896 Lowell Lectures* (Amherst: The University of Massachusetts Press, 1983)

Taylor, Eugene, *William James on Consciousness beyond the Margin* (Chichester: Princeton University Press, 1996)

Taylor, Mark, *After God* (Chicago: University of Chicago Press, 2007)

Thurschwell, Pamela, *Literature, Technology and Magical Thinking* (Cambridge: Cambridge University Press, 2001)

Timms, Joanna, 'Phantasm of Freud; Nandor Fodor and the Psychoanalytic Approach to the Supernatural in Interwar Britain,' *Psychoanalysis and History* 14 (2012) 5–27

Torres, Nuno, 'Intuition and Ultimate Reality in Psychoanalysis: Bion's Implicit Use of Bergson and Whitehead's Notions,' in: Torres, Nuno & Hinshelwood, R. D. (eds.), *Bion's Sources: The Shaping of His Paradigms* (New York: Routledge, 2013a) 20–34

Torres, Nuno, 'Bion's Concept of the Proto-mental and Modern Panpsychism,' in: Torres, Nuno & Hinshelwood, R. D. (eds.), *Bion's Sources: The Shaping of His Paradigms* (New York: Routledge, 2013b) 56–67

Treitel, Corinna, *A Science for the Soul: Occultism and the Genesis of the German Modern* (Baltimore: John Hopkins, 2004)

Ustinova, Yulia, *Divine Mania: Alteration of Consciousness in Ancient Greece* (Abington: Routledge, 2018)

Uždavinys, Algis, *Philosophy and Theurgy in Late Antiquity* (San Rafael: Sophia Perennis, 2010)

Uždavinys, Algis, *Orpheus and the Roots of Platonism* (London: The Matheson Trust, 2011)

Valette, Patrick, 'Schubert, Gotthilf Heinrich von,' in: Hanegraaff, Wouter J. et al. (eds.), *Dictionary of Gnosis and Western Esotericism* (Leiden: Brill, 2006) 1042–1043

Van der Hart, Onno & Friedman, Barbara, 'A Reader's Guide to Pierre Janet: A Neglected Intellectual Heritage,' in: Craparo, Giuseppe, Ortu, Francesca & van der Hart, Onno (eds.), *Rediscovering Pierre Janet: Trauma, Dissociation, and a New Context for Psychoanalysis* (New York: Routledge, 2019) 4–27

Vater, Michael, 'Schelling's Clara: Romantic Psychotherapy,' *Human Affairs* 33: 4 (2023) 439–449

Vermorel, Madeline & Vermorel, Henri, 'Was Freud a Romantic?' *The International Review of Psychoanalysis* 15 (1986) 15–37

Vermote, Rudi, *Reading Bion* (New York: Routledge, 2019)

Versluis, Arthur, *Wisdom's Children: A Christian Esoteric Tradition* (Albany: SUNY, 1999)

Versluis, Arthur, 'Western Esotericism and Consciousness,' *Journal of Consciousness Studies* 7 (6) (2000) 20–33

Versluis, Arthur, *The New Inquisitions: Heretic-Hunting and the Intellectual Origins of Modern Totalitarianism* (New York: Oxford University Press, 2006)

Versluis, Arthur, 'The Place of Jacob Boehme in Western Esotericism,' in: Hessayon, Ariel & Apetrei, Sarah (eds.), *An Introduction to Jacob Boehme: Four Centuries of Thought and Reception* (New York: Routledge, 2014) 263–278

Vida, Judith E., 'Treating The "Wise Baby",' *The American Journal of Psychoanalysis* 65: 1 (2005) 3–12

Vitz, Paul C., *Sigmund Freud's Christian Unconscious* (New York: Guilford Press, 1988)

Voegelin, Eric, *The New Science of Politics: An Introduction* [with a foreword by Dante Germino] (London: University of Chicago Press, [1952] 1987)

Vonofakos, Dimitris & Hinshelwood, R. D., 'Wilfred Bion's Letters to John Rickman (1939–1951),' *Psychoanalysis and History* 14: 1 (2012) 53–94

Walsh, David, *The Mysticism of Innerworldly Fulfillment: A Study of Jacob Boehme* (Gainesville, FL: University of Florida, 1983)

Wargo, Eric, *Time Loops: Precognition, Retrocausation, and the Unconscious* (San Antonio: Anomalist Books, 2018)

Waterfield, Robin (ed.), *Jacob Boehme* (Berkley: North Atlantic Books, 2001)

Webb, Richard E. & Sells, Michael A., 'Lacan and Bion: Psychoanalysis and the Mystical Language of "Unsaying",' *Theory and Psychology* 5: 2 (1995) 195–215

Weber, Lucila Riascos (IPA Membership Services Secretary): e-mail correspondence dated the 11/02/2020

Weeks, Andrew, *Boehme: An Intellectual Biography of the Seventeenth-Century Philosopher and Mystic* (Albany: SUNY, 1991)

Weeks, Andrew, 'Radical Reformation and the Anticipation of Modernism in Jacob Boehme,' in: Hessayon, Ariel & Apetrei, Sarah (eds.), *An Introduction to Jacob Boehme: Four Centuries of Thought & Reception* (New York: Routledge, 2014) 38–56

Wehr, Gerhard, 'C. G. Jung and Jungianism,' in: Magee, Glenn Alexander (ed.), *The Cambridge Handbook of Western Mysticism & Esotericism* (New York: Cambridge University Press, 2016) 297–307

Weiss, Frederick G. (ed.), *Hegel: The Essential Writings* [Foreword by J. N. Findlay] (London: Harper & Row Publishers, 1974)

White, Robert S., 'Bion and Mysticism,' *American Imago* 68: 2 (2011) 213–240

Whitebook, Joel, *Freud: An Intellectual Biography* (New York: Cambridge University Press, 2017)

Whyte, Lancelot Law, *The Unconscious before Freud* (New York: Basic Book, 1960)

Wieland, Christina, 'Freud's Influence on Bion's Thought: Links and Transformations,' in: Torres, Nuno & Hinshelwood, R. D. (eds.), *Bion's Sources: The Shaping of His Paradigms* (New York: Routledge, 2013) 104–123

Williams, Sherly, 'Analytic Intuition: A Meeting Place for Jung and Bion,' *British Journal of Psychotherapy* 23: 1 (2006) 83–98

Winborn, Mark, 'Bion and Jung: Intersecting Vertices,' in: Brown, Robin S. (ed.), *Re-Encountering Jung: Analytical Psychology and Contemporary Psychoanalysis* (New York: Routledge, 2018) 85–111

Witzig, James S., 'Theodore Flournoy:-A Friend Indeed,' *The Journal of Analytical Psychology* 27 (1982) 131–148

Wolffram, Heather, *The Stepchildren of Science: Psychical Research and Parapsychology in Germany, c. 1870–1939* (New York: Rodopi, 2009)

Wolfson, Elliott R., *Through A Speculum That Shines: Vision and Imagination in Medieval Jewish Mysticism* (Chichester: Princeton University Press, 1994)

Wolfson, Elliott R., 'Assaulting the Border: Kabbalistic Traces in the Margins of Derrida,' *Journal of the American Academy of Religion* 70: 3 (2002) 475–514

Wolfson, Elliott R., 'The Holy Cabbala of Changes: Jacob Böhme and Jewish Esotericism,' *Aries* 18: 1 (2018) 21–53

Young, Christopher & Brook, Andrew, 'Schopenhauer and Freud,' *The International Journal of Psychoanalysis* 75 (1994) 101–118

Young-Bruehl, Elizabeth & Schwartz, Murray M., 'Why Psychoanalysis Has No History,' *American Imago* 69: 1 (2012) 139–159

Zeavin, Hanna, 'Freud's Séance,' *American Imago* 75: 1 (2018) 53–65

Zhang, Yichi, 'Wilfred Bion's Annotations in *The Way of Zen:* An Investigation into His Practical Encounters with Buddhist Ideas,' *Psychoanalysis and History* 21: 3 (2019) 331–355

Index

For Product Safety Concerns and Information please contact our EU
representative GPSR@taylorandfrancis.com
Taylor & Francis Verlag GmbH, Kaufingerstraße 24, 80331 München, Germany

www.ingramcontent.com/pod-product-compliance
Lightning Source LLC
Chambersburg PA
CBHW070327270326
41926CB00017B/3796

9 781032 760346